100 PLACES
YOU WILL
NEVER VISIT

100 PLACES YOU WILL NEVER VISIT

THE WORLD'S MOST SECRET LOCATIONS

DANIEL SMITH

Quercus

Contents

Introduction

There are times when our world seems never to have been more open. The age of cheap air travel has allowed us the opportunity to reach almost any spot on the planet within a matter of hours. Meanwhile, the inexorable rise of social networking has blurred the boundaries between our public faces and private lives like never before. Indeed, Mark Zuckerberg – Facebook's billionaire founder – has regularly spoken of his dream of accomplishing 'a social mission – to make the world more open and connected'. Then there are the countless politicians and corporate spokesmen who constantly reassure us of their transparency and the important role that we all have in our big, open society.

Yet for all that, a great many of us feel like there is an awful lot going on in our world that we are simply not privy to. So much that affects us in our everyday lives seems to be decided behind closed doors. For most of us who live in democracies, the idea of secrecy is a perturbing one. We associate it with oppressive regimes, such as those of Hitler and Stalin that resulted in the deaths of millions in the 20th century.

We think of wars that have been fought on our behalf for reasons never fully explained to us, of business decisions that we knew nothing of until they cost us our jobs, of public figures who tell us to do one thing in public and do quite another themselves when away from the public gaze.

Samuel Johnson, arguably England's greatest man of letters and responsible for the landmark Dictionary of the English Language published in 1755, had his own thoughts on secrets. A renowned social commentator in his day, he once noted that: 'Where secrecy or mystery begins, vice or roguery is not far off.' But was Dr Johnson's conclusion overly simplistic? There has always been a tension that exists between what we need to know, what we would like to know and what others think it is best for us to know – a tug-of-war where it is

not always clear in which direction it is best to pull.

In contrast to Johnson, Cardinal Richelieu was notably less concerned with moral navel-gazing. As the French King Louis XIII's Chief Minister from 1624 to 1642, he was the arch exponent of *realpolitik* long before the phrase had even been coined. Where Niccolò Machiavelli laid out his principles of statecraft in such notable works as The Prince (his philosophy often broadly summarized as 'the end justifies the means'), Richelieu put it into vivid practice, forging for himself a role as the ultimate 'power behind the throne'. He laid the groundwork for an absolutist monarchy that met its fullest realization in the rule of Louis XIV and governed under the premise that sometimes what needed to be done could not be executed in the cold light of public scrutiny. For Richelieu there was but one natural conclusion: 'Secrecy is the first essential in affairs of the State.'

We may initially baulk at the notion, but in many spheres of life we are quite accepting of the need for secrecy. If your football team were about to contest a cup final, for instance, you might be appalled if the manager revealed to the world his line-up and proposed tactics ahead of kick-off. Nor would you reasonably expect the opposition to do anything other than play their

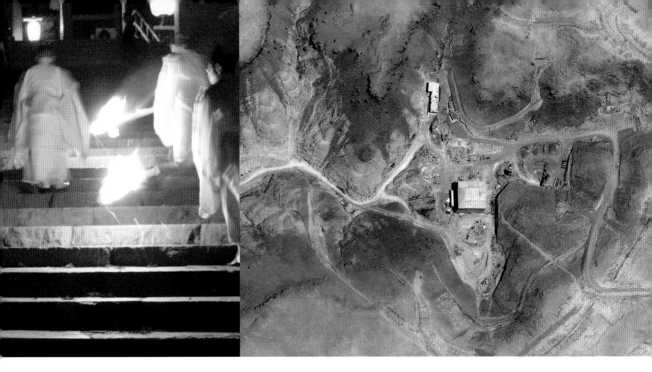

cards close to their chest too. In this context, it is all part of the game. At some level, we understand that secrecy is on occasions essential to achieving long-term goals. It is often so in public life too, with many a war ended by 'secret peace talks' and countless jobs saved or created by 'secret business deals'.

Ultimately, there will always be a conflict between the need for secrecy and our distrust of it. Indeed, very often it is the same people demanding transparency in public life who push hardest for the maintenance of privacy in private life. So no matter how much we struggle to accept the fact, secrets and secrecy are fundamental

components of our society. And in practical terms that means that much of the world remains out of bounds to the ordinary man and woman in the street.

But of course, that does not mean we have to like it! So if you have ever been tempted to push at a closed door or sneak a peak around a curtained-off area, or if a 'Keep Out' sign fills you with a burning sense of righteous indignation, this might be the book for you.

Contained herein are 100 places that are, to a greater or lesser extent, in the public sphere but physically off-limits. While the reasons for their being closed to

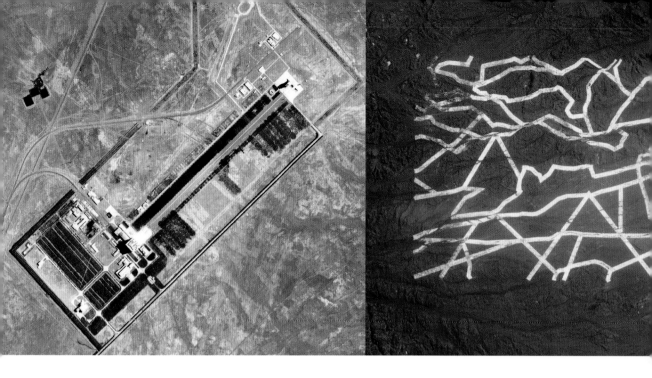

us vary from case to case, they collectively exemplify the enduring struggle between what we would like to know about and what others feel it is right or safe for us to know about.

We are denied access to some of them because of the nature of the work undertaken there, whether it be spies practising the dark arts of espionage or data centres building vast knowledge banks as they track our online activities. A few places are so secret that they are not even officially acknowledged, or their exact locations are unknown. Others are off bounds for security reasons – such as the room containing the English Crown Jewels – or because

they are simply too dangerous for us to enter (anyone fancy a day trip to the aptly named Snake Island?). Still others hold historical secrets, such as the legendary Amber Room that seemingly disappeared from the face of the Earth, or the Tomb of Genghis Khan, whose occupier ordered brutal measures to keep its location hidden. One site – the Great Pacific Garbage Patch – may even be described as a dirty big secret, an environmental disaster in the making that the world's governments scarcely acknowledge.

Whether you are driven by a raging belief in your right to know, or are simply a bit of a nosy parker, within these pages you can embark on a

tour of some of the most secret, hard to reach or closely guarded places on the planet (though of course, there may be a few still even more secret places that we simply haven't heard about yet!). Where else could you catch a glimpse inside the caves of Tora Bora, learn about the CIA headquarters or peek into the vaults of the Bank of England, all without having to get out of your armchair?

We start our tour far below the waves of the Pacific Ocean, looking at a submarine wreck that symbolizes all the intrigue of the Cold War. From there we gradually work our way eastwards around the globe, stopping off in locations as disparate as Washington, DC, the Vatican Secret Archives, a mountain lair in North Korea and a satellite station in the Outback of Australia.

Whatever our motives for wishing to uncover a secret, the process of discovery is a delectable one. The American poet, Robert Frost, neatly captured the frisson of excitement that a secret can inspire within us when he wrote: 'We dance round in a ring and suppose, but the secret sits in the middle and knows.' So sit back and strap in for the journey of a lifetime to places that you either never knew existed or couldn't hope to visit even if you wanted to.

Go on, push at the door. It's open...

Wreck of submarine K-129

LOCATION Beneath the Pacific Ocean
NEAREST POPULATION HUB Petropavlovsk, Russia
SECRECY OVERVIEW Location uncertain: a sunken submarine at the heart of a Cold War mystery.

The K-129 was a nuclear-equipped submarine that sailed as part of the Soviet Pacific Fleet. After sinking in unknown circumstances in 1968, it was located by US forces, who subsequently attempted to raise it in a covert 'black op'. While some of the wreckage was retrieved, much remains in the sea – exactly what the Americans found, and in what circumstances, remains a mystery to this day.

Launched in 1960, the K-129 was based at the Rybachiy Naval Base in Russia's far eastern Kamchatka region. On 24 February 1968, the vessel and her 98 crew set out on a scheduled patrol and, after undertaking a deep-sea test dive, the captain reported that all was well. Nothing more was ever heard from the sub.

In March 1968, Soviet naval headquarters implemented a massive search and rescue effort across the North Pacific. They failed to find the submarine, but their efforts attracted the attention of American intelligence. By analyzing data from its underwater Sound Surveillance System, the US pinpointed the resting place of the K-129, almost 5,000 metres (16,500 ft) beneath the waters of the Pacific.

Confronted with the opportunity to get his hands on one of the USSR's nuclear fleet, President Nixon authorized a top secret salvage attempt known as Project Azorian. A bespoke vessel, the *Hughes Glomar Explorer*, was built especially for the job. The cover story was that the ship was to be used for mining manganese nodules from the seabed.

The salvage operation, carried out during July and August 1974, had mixed results. Some of the vessel was recovered, but a large section fell back to the seabed when technical equipment failed. The exact location of the wreck and details of the operation remain top secret, but it has been speculated that the US left the scene with recovered nuclear warheads, code books and operations manuals.

Many believe the wreck lies some 2,800 kilometres (1,500 nautical miles) northwest of the Hawaiian island of Oahu and 2,200 kilometres (1,200 nautical miles) southeast of Petropavlovsk. Why K-129 sank has never been discovered, but theories include an accidental on-board explosion or even a collision with a US vessel. The full truth may come with the declassification of government files in decades to come, but might equally rest with the dead under the sea.

RUSSIA

UNITED STATES

Aleutian Islands

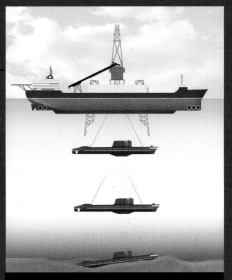

SECRET SCAVENGER *The* Glomar Explorer *was built by the US especially for the salvage operation. The vessel's cover story held that it belonged to a company owned by billionaire industrialist Howard Hughes, and was intended for use in projects to extract minerals from the ocean floor.*

MISSILE PLATFORM *Designed in the late 1950s, the Soviet Golf II submarine was a diesel-electric vessel with a top speed of 31 km/h (17 knots) on the surface and 22 km/h (12 knots) submerged. It carried three nuclear-armed ballistic missiles, each with a relatively short range of around 150 km (95 miles).*

The Great Pacific Garbage Patch

LOCATION North Pacific Ocean
NEAREST POPULATION HUB Honolulu, Hawaii, USA
SECRECY OVERVIEW Jurisdiction uncertain: the world's biggest rubbish dump.

Twice the size of Texas, a mass of non-biodegradable plastic has gathered in the waters of the northern Pacific Ocean. Brought together by ocean currents, this vast body of waste originates from countries all around the world and poses a major long-term threat to the ecosystem. Yet no nation state or major international body has formulated a comprehensive plan for dealing with it.

The responsibility of no single nation, the Great Pacific Garbage Patch is a truly dirty secret that few outside the community of environmental activists are ready to acknowledge and act upon. The patch has formed from countless tonnes of rubbish deposited into the sea, 80 per cent of it from mainland areas.

The Garbage Patch's location in the North Pacific is due to a gyre, an ocean current that is very calm at its centre but swirls round in a circle, drawing in ever-increasing volumes of floating debris. Ecologists have been forecasting the existence of such a feature since at least the 1980s, but it was only in 1997 that Charles Moore and his crew confirmed the existence of the Great Pacific Garbage Patch while competing in a yachting race. Moore subsequently set up a campaigning body to bring attention to the problem.

Plastic does not degrade like natural materials such as paper or cotton: instead, it breaks down into smaller and smaller harmful compounds over hundreds of years. Tiny bits of plastic found floating in the oceans are sometimes referred to as 'mermaid's tears' – surely a far more romantic name than they deserve. While many sea birds and mammals are killed when they become trapped in plastic debris, even more dangerous are the toxins that the plastics introduce into the food system, which then progress perniciously from the smallest plankton to the largest whale.

Scientists estimate that the Garbage Patch contains three-quarters of a million fragments of plastic per square kilometre (0.4 sq miles). Plastics account for 90 per cent of all the rubbish in the world's oceans, and as much as 70 per cent of it sinks, causing untold damage to life on the sea bed. Yet the Great Pacific Garbage Patch remains the floating landfill site that no government seems keen to discuss. It is a safe guess that if it were the Great Pacific Oil Reserve, there would be rather more of a clamour to establish sovereignty.

POISONED WATERS

Our increasing use of plastics has helped extend humanity's destructive footprint from the lands on which we live to the deepest parts of the distant ocean – a heavy price to pay for the added convenience of product packaging and the like.

UNITED STATES

PACIFIC OCEAN

North Pacific Gyre

Hawaii

DIRTY SECRET

The exact impact of the Garbage Patch on the Pacific Ocean's ecosystem is not known, but new research is constantly increasing our understanding of its effects. What is beyond doubt, however, is that the Garbage Patch poses a real threat of an environmental catastrophe.

3 HAARP research station

LOCATION Gakona, Alaska, USA
NEAREST POPULATION HUB Anchorage, Alaska
SECRECY OVERVIEW Access restricted: an atmospheric research facility under the jurisdiction of the US Department of Defense.

The High-frequency Active Auroral Research Program (HAARP) describes itself as 'a premier facility for the study of ionospheric physics and radio science'. Its stated aim is to 'further advance our knowledge of the physical and electrical properties of the Earth's ionosphere which can affect our military and civilian communication and navigation systems'.

HAARP is funded by the US Air Force and Navy, as well as DARPA (see page 70) to conduct research into the ionosphere – the part of the atmosphere between 55 and 800 kilometres (35–500 miles) above the Earth's surface. In this region, electrically charged gases can absorb, distort and reflect radio waves, with significant implications for military and civilian communications, navigation, surveillance and detection systems.

Depending on the Sun's activity at any given time, the Alaskan ionosphere can be characterized as mid-latitude, auroral or polar – thereby offering varying conditions to study. The Gakona region is also well served by transport links but far away from any built-up areas where electric lights and noise could interfere with experiments. The HAARP project began in 1990, and its main phase of construction ended in 2007.

HAARP's most important element is the Ionospheric Research Instrument (ISRI), a high-power, high-frequency radio transmitter that generates radio signals in the 2.8 to 10 MHz frequency range. The ISRI antenna consists of 180 towers, each 22 metres (72 ft) high and arranged in a large rectangular grid. Some of its signal is absorbed by the ionosphere (the rest bounces back to Earth or carries on up into space), and its effects on the relevant area of the ionosphere are then recorded and analyzed.

Though not a classified project (HAARP invites collaboration with universities throughout North America), entry to the site is restricted to 'those having a need to conduct business at the facility'. With its military funding and focus on the distant sky, HAARP has inspired numerous accusations of dark intentions. It has been variously accused of developing an anti-aircraft system through manipulation of the atmosphere, modifying the weather to cause climatic events, tsunamis and earthquakes, and even developing mind-control technology. Its reputation among conspiracy theorists is no doubt aggravated by ISRI's resemblance to a science-fiction death ray machine.

Bohemian Grove

LOCATION Sonoma County, California, USA
NEAREST POPULATION HUB San Francisco, California
SECRECY OVERVIEW Operations classified: host to an annual gathering of the secretive Bohemian Club.

Set amid beautiful redwood forest in Sonoma County's Monte Rio, each year Bohemian Grove becomes a holiday camp for some of the world's most powerful men. Allegations of debauchery and even paganism have been levelled at the events run by the Bohemian Club, while other critics highlight fears that major decisions affecting government and commerce are made in this entirely unregulated atmosphere.

The Bohemian Club is an all-male, private members' club whose clubhouse is on Taylor Street in San Francisco. It was established in 1872 by staff at the *San Francisco Chronicle* to serve as a hub for members of the city's cultural fraternity. However, within a short period it had opened its membership to a wider social strata, and was soon under the effective control of San Francisco's rich and powerful. The modern image of a Bohemian Club member is a wealthy, white man of a certain age – usually, though not always, with Republican proclivities.

There is currently a 15-year-plus waiting list for membership, which costs an initial US$25,000 and then a further US$5,000 in annual subs. More importantly, you must be approved for membership, which requires gold-standard connections and probably an Ivy League education behind you. Membership has included a formidable array of presidents, including Eisenhower, Nixon, Ford, Reagan and the two Bushes, along with a multitude of

other famous names, from Mark Twain and William Randolph Hearst to Clint Eastwood and the Rockefellers.

Bohemian Grove occupies some 1,100 hectares (2,700 acres) of land, though the section devoted to the Club's summer camp is much smaller. The first camp was held in 1893 on rented land that the Club eventually bought from a local logger in 1899. It now hosts between 2,000 and 3,000 attendees each summer, divided between smaller encampments according to rank and background. The programme for this two-week jolly includes a mixture of entertainments, talks and networking events, and begins with the curious Cremation of Care ceremony. As campers look on at the edge of a small lake, appointed members in hooded red robes 'sacrifice' an effigy called 'Dull Care', placing it inside a skull on a boat that is set alight and pushed off across the water. This is said to symbolize a dismissal of life's petty worries for the duration of the gathering. The entire ceremony occurs under the watchful

POWERFUL FRIENDS *Guests at the 1967 Bohemian Grove gathering included two future US Presidents, Richard Nixon and Ronald Reagan, seen here sat either side of the standing Harvey Hancock (once a campaign manager for Nixon). To the other side of Nixon is Glenn Seaborg, winner of the 1951 Nobel Prize in Chemistry.*

California

UNITED STATES

San Francisco

WISE HEADS *Bohemian Grove's overgrown Great Owl of Bohemia oversees the infamous 'Cremation of Care' ceremony, which is in reality nothing more than a bit of frivolity. For many years, the owl was voiced by famed journalist and long-time Grover, Walter Cronkite.*

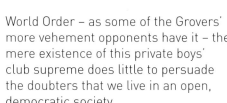

gaze of the club's mascot, a 12-metre (40-ft) concrete-cast statue known as the Great Owl of Bohemia.

For some, the Cremation of Care ceremony is a source of great concern, swollen with pagan, perhaps even Satanic, overtones. Some have wildly suggested that there is even a human sacrifice element to the ritual – an entirely unfounded assertion. Eyewitness reports suggest that the ceremony (and the camp in general) is all rather more redolent of frat-house high jinks. The concern seems less about playing out secret rituals than ensuring middle-aged and older men get to relive their youths – drinking too much, listening to Grateful Dead records, smoking fat cigars and freely weeing against trees.

Perhaps a more legitimate criticism is that the camp allows a clutch of the most influential politicians, businessmen and military figures in the Western world to have a get-together that is wilfully opaque. Legend has it, for instance, that the Manhattan Project, which led to the creation of the atom bomb, had an influential planning meeting at Bohemian Grove in 1942. Even if they are not busily establishing a New World Order – as some of the Grovers' more vehement opponents have it – the mere existence of this private boys' club supreme does little to persuade the doubters that we live in an open, democratic society.

One defence against allegations that the Club is an elite cabal directing national and international events is its motto, taken from Shakespeare's *A Midsummer Night's Dream*: 'Weaving spiders come not here.' Which is to say, members of the Club are not supposed to bring business through the door. Opponents might well respond with: 'They would say that, wouldn't they?'

The perimeter of Bohemian Grove is heavily guarded throughout the year and especially during the summer, although the odd unwanted guest (including a handful of journalists) has managed to find a way in during recent years. By jealously guarding its privacy, the Club provokes fears that Bohemian Grove is an arena for decisions to be made in our name but without our knowledge. The truth might equally be that the membership preserves the air of secrecy because they fear being left red-faced by their antics when let off the leash.

Skywalker Ranch

5

LOCATION Marin County, California, USA
NEAREST POPULATION HUB Novato, California
SECRECY OVERVIEW Access restricted: the private playground of the creator of *Star Wars*.

Skywalker Ranch covers some 2,000 hectares (5,000 acres) of land, of which only 6 hectares (15 acres) have been developed. George Lucas began accumulating this enormous estate in 1978, using early proceeds from the runaway success of *Star Wars*. It serves as a retreat for the film-maker – a place to conduct business privately and get his and his employees' creative juices flowing away from the public gaze.

Though Lucas himself does not live on site most of the time, security is tight. Members of the public are not welcome, though tours have occasionally been given to journalists, competition winners and a few other fortunate souls. The entrance to the ranch has a guard station and, perhaps unsurprisingly for a film director, banks of cameras to keep a close eye on proceedings (though for visitors, there is a strict 'no photography' policy). In short, unless you're a close buddy of George, a trusted employee or just plain lucky, this is not somewhere that you're going to get to see.

At the heart of the ranch is the three-storey Main House, built in a Victorian style and the site of Lucas's private offices. There are further buildings for various divisions of his company: the vast Research Library stands out for its huge, art nouveau stained-glass skylight. Elsewhere, there is the Stag Theatre for screenings, a guest house, a zoo and even the ranch's own fire station. For good measure, Lucas can stroll through a vineyard, visit his hill-top observatory or swim in the man-made Lake Ewok.

The ranch also encompasses the Lucasfilm Archives, an Aladdin's cave for any fan of modern cinema. Designed for the preservation and protection of items related to the great man's films, it includes props from the *Star Wars* movies, as well as from *Indiana Jones*, *American Graffiti*, *Willow* and many more. But as if to prove the ranch's exclusiveness, even President Ronald Reagan had a request to tour the site turned down.

6

Google Data Center, The Dalles

LOCATION Wasco County, Oregon, USA

NEAREST POPULATION HUB Portland, Oregon

SECRECY OVERVIEW High-security location: Google's first purpose-built data centre.

Google is one of the world's leading internet companies, helping to shape modern culture while making an awful lot of money. As proprietors of perhaps the world's leading search engine, the business requires vast banks of computer servers to keep things working. Its enormous Data Center at The Dalles was built amid great secrecy at a cost of US$600 million and opened in 2006.

Famously, Google was founded by Larry Page and Sergey Brin while they were still studying at Stanford University, and incorporated as a private company in 1998. Its mission, in its own words, is to 'organize the world's information and make it universally accessible and useful'. Since the initial launch of its search engine, this mission has seen Google diversify into software, social networking and even computer operating systems.

The company is, unsurprisingly, unwilling to divulge great detail about its server centres around the world, though estimates suggest there may be more than ten of these facilities spread across the globe, housing perhaps a million individual server units.

When Google came to construct its first custom-designed facility, a site on the Columbia River not far from the Dalles Dam offered not only suitable land on which to build and a local population to work there (employees number around 200), but also the possibility of plentiful and green hydroelectric energy. A business such as Google inevitably consumes enormous quantities of electricity, and the chance to build a more environmentally friendly facility fitted in neatly with the company's declared motto: 'Don't be evil'.

The Data Center, codenamed 'Project 02' in its early days, was shrouded in secrecy when it opened – even visiting journalists were required to sign confidentiality agreements. Although the secrecy level has since declined, security – both of the site itself and the data it contains – remains of paramount importance.

A full-time Information Security Team works to ensure the integrity of electronically held information, while the centre itself is surrounded by a perimeter fence that is patrolled by guards and constantly under closed-circuit surveillance. While Google wishes to make the world's information universally accessible, it clearly harbours no such ambitions for its own data centres.

Columbia River provides hydroelectric power

Crates Way

Four-storey cooling towers for ventilation of server farms

Steelhead Way

Main server buildings

Generator yard produces power for servers

Administration building

Hawthorne Army Depot

7

LOCATION Mineral County, Nevada, USA

NEAREST POPULATION HUB Sacramento, California

SECRECY OVERVIEW High-security location: the world's biggest ammunition storage facility.

Situated on the southern shore of Walker Lake, in the Great Basin region of west Nevada, this huge depot covers 59,500 hectares (147,000 acres) of semi-arid land and is scattered with almost 2,500 'igloos' storing army reserve ammunitions (for use after the first 30 days of a major conflict). Its other roles include renovating, demilitarizing and disposing of conventional ammunition.

The facility began operating in 1930 as the Naval Ammunition Depot Hawthorne. It came into being after enormous explosions in 1926 at the Lake Denmark ammunition depot in New Jersey led to high numbers of civilian casualties. The accident also badly damaged the neighbouring Picatinny Arsenal. A subsequent court of inquiry concluded that a new depot should be built to serve the Pacific area, in a remote area within 1,500 km (930 miles) of the west coast. Hawthorne was chosen, and building got underway in 1928. The facility was brought under army control in 1977, and in 1994 ended its previous supplementary duties as a centre for ammunition production.

Today, the Hawthorne Depot supports a mostly civilian community of some 4,500 people and is furnished with extensive railroad connections. At its peak towards the end of the Second World War, it employed more than 5,500 people. Hawthorne is now also used as a training base, boasting a large live-fire ordnance test facility and even a small, simulated Afghan town, used for the training of troops facing deployment to the region. The 'Afghan neighbourhood' is replete with multi-storey structures and dummy enemy soldiers, providing an unnerving setting amid the desert lands and mountains of Nevada. In 2005, Hawthorne was listed as one of several bases to be considered for closure, but it was later removed from the list, largely on account of the unique training opportunities it offered.

Security at Hawthorne is handled by a private contractor, Day and Zimmerman Hawthorne Corporation, although the depot was protected by the Marine Corps in its earlier days. As well as permanent on-site security, the depot has its own fire and emergency rapid response departments – this is one place where you really do get more bang for your buck.

Mine Road offers access to bunkers north of Hawthorne

Hawthorne City

Veteran's Memorial Highway

HEAVY METAL *One of the most important tasks undertaken at the Hawthorne facility is the disabling of obsolete or decommissioned ordnance. The depot's experience in handling dangerous chemicals means that it has also been selected as the major centre for the storage of US strategic mercury reserves. The toxic metal is kept in steel flasks within large UN-approved drums.*

2nd Avenue South offers access to bunkers south of Hawthorne

Mineral County, Nevada

UNDER COVER *The hummocky 'Igloo' bunkers at Hawthorne Depot are designed to store and protect enormous quantities of reserve munitions. A total of 2,427 bunkers are scattered across the site, providing some 56,000 square metres (600,000 sq ft) of storage space. Emergency services are permanently on hand to respond in the event of an accident.*

8 The Skunk Works

LOCATION Palmdale, California, USA
NEAREST POPULATION HUB Palmdale, California
SECRECY OVERVIEW Operations classified: a private facility for high-tech research, often with military applications.

The 'Skunk Works' is a widely used nickname for the home of Lockheed Martin's Advanced Development Programs (ADP), which has for decades been involved in landmark top-secret projects for the public and private sectors. Such is its fame that the name has since become a generic term for cutting-edge, often highly autonomous, technological projects.

Lockheed Martin came into being following a corporate merger in 1995 but the Lockheed part of the company traces its history back to 1912. In 1943, the US Air Force's Air Tactical Service Command opened talks with Lockheed executives about developing a jet fighter. A small team of engineers under Clarence 'Kelly' L. Johnson developed blueprints for what would become the XP-80 Shooting Star aircraft in less than a month. Their plans secured Lockheed the government contract, and the Skunk Works came into being, with Johnson at its head. The name is derived from Al Capp's *Li'l Abner* strip cartoon, which featured a

STEALTH FIGHTER *The Lockheed F-117 Nighthawk, developed at the Skunk Works, was a ground-attack aircraft operational between 1983 and 2008. Its unique shape allowed it to scatter radar waves off its surface without reflecting them back to enemy receivers.*

mysterious brewery, the 'Skonk Works', known for its strange concoctions.

Kelly put together small, hand-picked teams to work on a string of boundary-busting research projects in the years that followed. By the 1950s he had established 14 Rules & Practices, the thirteenth of which states that outside access to a project and its personnel must be strictly controlled by appropriate security measures. The organization regularly worked with the CIA and the Air Force, with testing often taking place at the legendary Area 51 (see page 30).

The Skunk Works quickly became renowned for its levels of secrecy and absence of official paperwork (contracts often followed long after projects began). It played an instrumental role in developing such ground-breaking technology as the U-2 spy plane in the 1950s and the 'Have Blue' project that led to the commissioning of the stealth fighter in 1978. It continues to develop breakthrough technologies including – in its own words – 'landmark aircraft that continually redefine flight'.

Although based in Burbank, California, for many years, Skunk Works is today located at US Air Force Plant 42 in Palmdale, California. It is estimated that Lockheed Martin receives somewhere in the region of 7 per cent of the US Department of Defense's annual budget. Skunk Works remains its most important and innovative division, with some 90 per cent of its work classified.

UNDER THE RADAR *The Darkstar unmanned aerial vehicle (above) was developed at the Skunk Works in the 1990s and built to fly for up to eight hours at a height of 14,000 metres (46,000 ft). Perhaps unsurprisingly, it was commonly mistaken for a UFO.*

US-Mexico drug smuggling tunnels

LOCATION Multiple locations along US-Mexico border
NEAREST POPULATION HUB San Diego, California, USA/ Tijuana, Mexico
SECRECY OVERVIEW Access restricted: secret underground routes for the movement of narcotics.

Stretching for more than 3,000 kilometres (1,860 miles), the long frontier between the United States and Mexico has a reputation as one of the world's most porous borders. Here, the governments of both nations have long been engaged in a bloody battle to stem the cross-border flow of illegal drugs, and in recent years the trade has literally been driven underground.

While the narcotics trade has clearly damaged communities on both sides of the border, it has effectively transformed some of Mexico's cities into war zones. Worth billions of dollars each year, the business is estimated to have accounted for some 40,000 Mexican lives between 2006 and 2011. After the government launched a crackdown in the mid-2000s, the drugs cartels arguably became even more efficient, better armed and organized with military precision.

Their ruthless pragmatism is reflected in the drug tunnels that ease the passage of narcotics from one country to the other. Some run for up to 800 metres (half a mile) and are equipped with sophisticated lighting and ventilation systems, wooden props to support the walls and even tracks for electric carts.

The tunnel floors are routinely lined with wooden boards and in some cases cemented over, while drainage systems counter the risks of groundwater. Access may be via a rope ladder, although some of the more sophisticated examples boast wooden staircases and even hydraulic lifts. Such impressive construction suggests cooperation from engineers and building professionals.

Entrances are centred around Tijuana on the Mexican side and San Diego on the US side. They are generally found in private properties, with Tijuana in particular amply endowed with disued warehouses.

California's clay soil seems particularly conducive to tunnel digging, although some tunnels have been routed into Arizona, where they link to an existing network of underground drainage canals. It is estimated that each tunnel takes on average six months to a year to construct, using a mixture of hand-held tools and pneumatic drills. According to official figures, more than 150 illicit tunnels have been discovered since 1990, leading to the recovery of hundreds of tonnes of marijuana alone. They are often found around the time of the marijuana harvest in October, suggesting a seasonal construction timetable.

ON THE BORDERLINE *Main: a Mexican soldier inspects a tunnel on the Tijuana side of the border following the discovery of 20 tonnes of marijuana in November 2010. Inset: a narrow fence and half a world separate teeming Tijuana from the heavily defended San Diego side of the US-Mexico border.*

Area 51

LOCATION Southern
Nevada, USA
NEAREST POPULATION HUB
Las Vegas, Nevada
SECRECY OVERVIEW
Operations classified:
US defence testing base
and alleged location of
extraterrestrial artefacts.

Area 51 is part of a United States' Air Force facility in Nevada, believed to be attached to the Edwards Air Force Base in California. As a centre for the development and testing of aircraft and weapons, you might expect it to be secretive. But Area 51 is perhaps the best-known 'secret place' on the globe, and for good reason. Conspiracy theorists hold that here you will find irrefutable evidence that aliens have visited Earth.

Situated roughly 40 kilometres (25 miles) from the nearest town, Area 51 covers 36,000 hectares (90,000 acres) of sparse Nevada desert and includes a large hangar, seven runways, radar antennae and an assortment of smaller administrative, accommodation and catering buildings. Its chief role is as a testing and training facility for new defence technologies and systems.

The large salt flat of Groom Lake, which lies entirely within Area 51, was used for testing bombs and artillery during the Second World War. In the 1950s, after the government entered into a partnership with the Lockheed Skunk Works (see page 26), it became the test site for the U-2 spy plane. It also hosted vital work on the development of radar systems and stealth bombers, and today remains a centre of cutting-edge military development. Captured Soviet aircraft were allegedly brought here in the Cold War to add greater reality to war games.

As such, confidentiality has always been highly prized. Employees must swear an oath of secrecy and buildings within the complex are said to be devoid of windows so that development teams do not have knowledge of each other's specific work.

However, the air of extreme secrecy that surrounds Area 51 has inspired those of a suspicious bent to claim that the base undertakes work beyond the bounds of our Earthly imagination – there have been claims of research programmes aimed at controlling the weather, mastering teleportation and even achieving time travel. Most famously, though, Area 51 has been identified by assorted conspiracy theorists as a place where scientists have studied unidentified flying objects and alien life forms.

Such arguments often centre on the claim that the wreckage of a spaceship and its alien occupants were brought to Area 51 after crash-landing near the town of Roswell, New Mexico, in 1947. In July of that year, the Army Air Field at Roswell put out a press release saying that it had recovered an unidentified

Groom Lake

GROOMED FOR SUCCESS *The US Army Air Corps built the first two runways at Groom Lake in the 1940s. A network of much larger runways emerged from the 1950s onwards, after Kelly Johnson, of Skunk Works fame, recognized the area's potential as a testing site.*

Main control tower overlooking all runways

New runway 14L/32R

New Base Headquarters Building (2005)

Old runway 14R/32L (no longer used)

Southern Taxiway and Runway 12/30

HIDDEN SECRETS *While UFO enthusiasts argue that Area 51's many hangars contain the remains of crashed or captured alien spacecraft, but in reality they probably house high-tech prototype aircraft. Many conspiracy theorists argue that Hangar 18, the largest on the base, is the last resting place for all manner of extraterrestrial booty.*

GeoEye

E.T. DRIVE HOME *Nevada State Route 375, a UFO sighting hot spot, was officially designated as the Extraterrestrial Highway by state authorities in 1996, with a dedication ceremony held in the nearby town of Rachel in April of that year. Rachel now supports a thriving trade in alien- and Area 51-related memorabilia.*

flying object. In the days and weeks before, various members of the public had reported seeing a disc-like object in the skies. A short while later, the army statement was retracted (in later years declassified papers suggested the object was actually a secret surveillance balloon) but by then the press had got hold of the story.

The legend of Roswell continued to grow until it reached a crescendo in the 1970s, fostering a small industry of conspiracy-laden books, reports, documentaries and films. An alien spacecraft was recovered, it was said – and its crew, too, according to others. There were even claims of conveniently lost film footage recording the autopsy of an alien corpse. In 1989, one Bob Lazar added fuel to the fire with an interview in which he claimed to have been a physicist at Area 51, and to have seen no less than nine alien spacecraft, which the authorities were attempting to reverse-engineer.

Some of the most ardent ufologists hold that Area 51 contains a complex of underground tunnels and warehouses (including the fabled Hangar 18) storing all of this extraterrestrial booty. A few even claim that aliens are actually

running the project. Inevitably, the veracity of such stories has not been (and is unlikely ever to be) proved. But it is an attractive tale for those who believe in little green men...

Whatever the truth, potential visitors should bear in mind that the US government treats the base as strictly off-limits to all but a few. Indeed, Area 51 received hardly any official recognition until Bill Clinton signed a presidential order in 1995 exempting it from certain environmental regulations. The site was declassified in 1997, though the projects undertaken there remain top secret.

Civilian and most military air traffic is forbidden from the airspace overhead, and it is a court martial offence for a military plane to purposefully breach the no-fly zone. Area 51 does not appear on any government-produced maps, and the site is adorned with signs warning trespassers that use of deadly force is authorized. Teams of imposing security guards keep vigilant watch over the perimeter fencing, which is liberally peppered with motion sensors: if you're intent on some alien action, your best bet might be to stay at home and tuck up with a DVD of *E.T.* instead.

Granite Mountain Records Vault

LOCATION Little Cottonwood Canyon, Utah, USA
NEAREST POPULATION HUB Salt Lake City, Utah
SECRECY OVERVIEW High-security location: the record vaults of the Church of Jesus Christ of Latter-day Saints.

The Mormon-run Granite Mountain Records Vault is built deep within a Utah mountainside, and visits by members of the public or journalists are rarely sanctioned. Over the years, this has led some to question why the Church of Jesus Christ of Latter-day Saints is so protective of its privacy at the facility. The Church, meanwhile, argues that its policies are less to do with maintaining secrecy than ensuring security.

Granite Mountain is a deep-storage facility containing a mass of materials related to the Mormon Church, its operations, organizational structure and history. It is also home to a stock of genealogical information perhaps unrivalled anywhere in the world. It is said to include upwards of 35 billion items of genealogical data stored on almost 2.5 million rolls of microfilm (a total that increases by around 40,000 rolls per year). The archive employs a staff of 50 to catalogue, store, copy and, since 2002, digitize the records.

The history of the Mormon Church began in New York in the 1820s, when a man named Joseph Smith claimed to have experienced a series of visions. These included one in which an angel directed him to a hillside, where a book inscribed on gold plates lay buried. In 1830 he published *The Book of Mormon*, which he said was the translation of these plates, and established a new Church based on their teachings. A little more than a quarter of Smith's original manuscript

remains in existence, but what is left is stored within Granite Mountain.

The movement soon spread, but often found itself in conflict with local populations over its unorthodox beliefs (which in its early days included polygamy). Indeed, Smith himself perished during a skirmish with a mob in Illinois in 1844. Leadership of the Mormons then fell to Brigham Young, who relocated a large group of his followers in 1847 to what is now Salt Lake City – Utah has remained the Church's spiritual home ever since.

Mormon beliefs emphasize ancestral connections, and as a result, the Church began to accumulate genealogical records from the 1890s onwards. From the 1930s, many of these records began to be transferred to microfilm, and within a decade there were more than 100,000 rolls in urgent need of a permanent home. Various sites in Salt Lake City were considered and rejected, until an architect from Little Cottonwood Canyon suggested tunnelling into the sheer face

HALL OF RECORDS

A rare photo from deep inside Granite Mountain reveals countless filing cabinets for the safe storage of microfilms capturing genealogical records from around the world in miniaturized form. At the last count, more than 35 billion such images were stored in the vault. Opposite: one of three imposing main entrances to the Granite Mountain Vault.

of Granite Mountain. Not only would this be an immensely secure location, he argued, but it would provide wonderful temperature regulation – a major concern for all archivists.

Building works commenced in May 1960, with arched tunnels excavated to a depth of 700 metres (2,300 ft), some 250 metres (820 ft) beneath the peak. Three main corridors into the archive, and a further four cross-tunnels, were constructed. The passages were lined with concrete and steel (and painted in tasteful pastel shades, by all accounts), while six storage chambers were also lined with steel – all at a cost of a reputed US$2 million to the Church. The whole complex today covers an area of 6,000 square metres (65,000 sq ft). Huge reinforced entrance doors, weighing between 9 and 14 tonnes and reputedly able to withstand a nuclear blast, help to protect the facility from uninvited guests.

Storage cabinets 3 metres (10 ft) high accommodate the wealth of archival material. The transfer of microfilm began in 1963, and the vault was fully operational by 1965. Its mountain home offers protection not only from nuclear attack but also from natural disasters such as fire and earthquakes. The Church itself maintains that the records are best protected by strictly limiting their exposure to humans. For this reason, public tours are prohibited, with finger marks, dust and clothing fibres all cited as potential threats to the well-being of the vault's contents. Since 2001, technological developments have allowed the archive to be kept at a permanent temperature of 13°C (55°F) and at 35 per cent humidity.

In 2010, some 300 million of Granite Mountain's genealogical records were made available online to researchers and members of the public in a major step forward towards openness. Nonetheless, the degree of security maintained at the vault leads many to wonder what other secrets might lie buried deep within its stone.

12 ADX Florence

LOCATION Fremont County, Colorado, USA

NEAREST POPULATION HUB Pueblo, Colorado

SECRECY OVERVIEW High-security location: the highest-security prison in America.

Sometimes referred to as the Alcatraz of the Rockies, Colorado's ADX Florence prison is home to many of America's most dangerous criminals. Its residents include seasoned terrorists and prisoners too violent to keep in regular facilities. Many of its inmates know that the only way that they will be leaving the penitentiary system is in a box.

Opened in November 1994 at a cost of some US$60 million, the prison lies off Highway 67 amid the sprawling foothills of the Colorado Rockies. It covers some 15 hectares (37 acres) and lies not far from the small town of Florence. With room for 490 inmates, the prison has a staff numbering almost 350. The land on which it stands was donated by the people of Florence in 1990, principally because the facility promised significant local employment.

To a large extent, ADX Florence owes its existence to events at a penitentiary in Marion, Illinois on 22 October 1983. On that day, two guards were killed in separate but virtually identical incidents, after the prisoners they were escorting were able to unpick their handcuffs and stab the officers with help from fellow prisoners. The violence highlighted the question of how best to handle dangerous prisoners already facing such stiff punishments that further loss of freedom holds few terrors. One of the answers was the 'control unit prison', of which ADX Florence is a prime example.

Here, the most dangerous prisoners in America are kept isolated from their guards and from one another as much as possible. Only around 5 per cent of inmates are sent here directly from the courtroom: most are redirected from other prisons where they have shown a propensity for violence. Security at the facility is rigorous, with each prisoner assigned one of six security levels.

The jail was designed jointly by LKA Partners (Colorado Springs) and the DLR Group. Cells are 2.1 x 3.6 metres (7 x 12 ft), and contain basic furniture manufactured from concrete. Toilets and sinks are designed so that attempts to back up water or flood cells are impossible, while windows have been installed in such a way as to prevent inmates from knowing their exact location within the facility, with views generally restricted to a bit of sky and some wall.

The main complex has high outer walls, and the entire site is surrounded by guard towers and razor-wire fencing

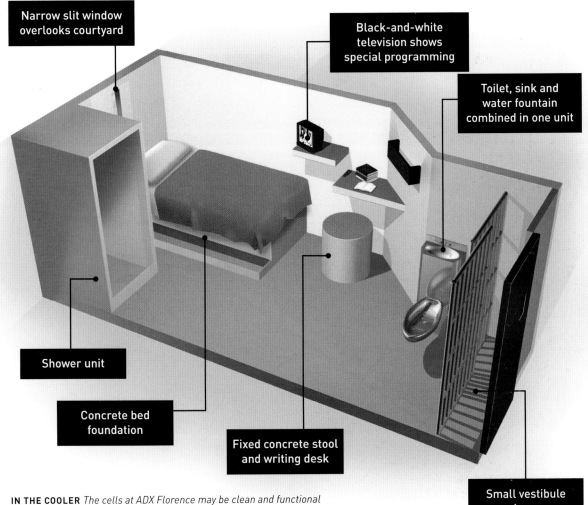

Narrow slit window overlooks courtyard

Black-and-white television shows special programming

Toilet, sink and water fountain combined in one unit

Shower unit

Concrete bed foundation

Fixed concrete stool and writing desk

Small vestibule area increases security of cell

IN THE COOLER *The cells at ADX Florence may be clean and functional but inmates lead a lonely existence in an oppressive atmosphere. As Robert Hood, a former warden, remarked on life at the facility: 'I don't know what hell is, but I do know the assumption would be, for a free person, it's pretty close to it.'*

to the height of two men, with regular patrols by guards and dogs. Inside the complex are almost 1,500 steel doors, activated via remote control, as well as surveillance cameras, motion detectors and pressure pads. When a guard manually unlocks a door, the key is quickly replaced in an aluminium shield for safekeeping and so that inmates are not able to visually memorize its configuration to later recreate it. There have to date been no successful escape attempts.

Prisoners are not allowed any telecommunications devices, but are permitted a single, monitored, 15-minute telephone call each month. They are locked in their cells for 23 hours a day in the first year of their sentence and do not eat or socialize together – food is hand-delivered to cells by the guards. A sunken, swimming pool-like exercise yard can be used by one prisoner at a time for short spells. Where appropriate after the first year, attempts are made towards greater socialization, including

NO WAY OUT *With a roll call that includes some of the most hardened criminals in the country, security around the prison is about as tight as it gets. It seems to be working, though, as there have been no break-outs in the two decades since it opened.*

a shared dining room. Inmates who respond well to the prison's programme may be allowed out of their cells for as much as 16 hours a day during their final year at the institution. Each cell has a small black-and-white television broadcasting 'improving' programmes.

Within the prison is an area known as Range 13, which has even more stringent security measures in place. Inmates here are considered so dangerous they

have virtually no human contact. Indeed, Range 13 rarely contains more than one or two inmates, and is frequently unoccupied for long spells.

The jail's roll call has included Timothy McVeigh (subsequently executed for his part in the Oklahoma bombings), Ted Kaczynski (the 'Unabomber'), Eric Rudolph (Atlanta's Olympic Park bomber), Ramzi Yousef (convicted of the 1993 World Trade Center terrorist attack, and occasionally resident in Range 13), and a number of people convicted of Al-Qaeda activities or associated with the Mob. To get into ADX Florence, you need to be seriously bad.

Dulce Base

LOCATION Rio Arriba
County, New Mexico, USA
NEAREST POPULATION HUB
Albuquerque, New Mexico
SECRECY OVERVIEW
Existence unacknowledged:
believed by some to be
home of an underground
extraterrestrial base.

Few places have captured the imagination of conspiracy theorists more than Dulce Base. A site for which there is little concrete evidence, believers nonetheless place it at the heart of a conspiracy between the powers-that-be and alien life forms intent on carrying out despicable research on human subjects. Whether it exists or not, Dulce Base is an instructive case study of the way conspiracy theories can take hold.

Rumours of a secret base beneath a New Mexico mountain can be traced back most clearly to Paul Bennewitz, a technological entrepreneur with a side line as an investigator of unidentified flying objects. Beginning in the 1970s, Bennewitz claimed that he regularly saw strange light displays in the sky, which he believed might be linked to the Kirtland Air Force Base a little outside his native Albuquerque.

The base had something of a reputation for classified development programmes – it was, for instance, used in the 1940s as a transportation hub by Los Alamos National Laboratory staff working on the Manhattan Project to develop the atomic bomb. It is also home to an Underground Munitions Storage Complex, believed to be the largest nuclear weapons storage facility in the world.

Bennewitz was not alone in claiming to have seen strange night-time light shows. Around this time, New Mexico threw up a number of other apparently

unexplained phenomena, including multiple instances of cattle maiming. Bennewitz is said to have made contact with a woman who, under hypnosis, described how she and her son were kidnapped by extraterrestrials and taken to an underground lab where she witnessed cattle being mutilated. The woman also claimed to have been fitted with an implant that left her subject to mind control.

Bennewitz was taken with her story and continued to compile evidence, including apparent video footage of lights in the night sky. He also constructed a system of radio receivers, and produced tapes that he said were UFO transmissions. Sometime towards the end of 1980, he contacted the authorities at Kirtland to make them aware of what he regarded as a potential UFO threat. His claims were met with a degree of scepticism, and received only limited follow-up.

However, Bennewitz was not to be dissuaded from his suspicions. Indeed, they developed until in 1982 they drew

UNITED STATES   **39**

the attention of the Aerial Phenomena Research Organization (APRO), a long-established and scientifically credible UFO-study group. William Moore, one of APRO's most senior figures, established a friendship with Bennewitz, who by now had concluded that two types of aliens had made it to Earth: good ones known as 'whites' and evil ones known as 'grays'. The grays were inhabiting a deep underground base, he told Moore, beneath Archuleta Mesa, near Dulce.

Dulce is a small town in the Jicarilla Apache Reservation, close to the New Mexico-Colorado border. With a population hovering around 2,500, it is, all in all, a quiet, out-of-the-way and unassuming sort of place. Nearby stands the impressive mountain of Archuleta Mesa, with a peak of 2,800 metres (9,200 ft). According to Bennewitz, the grays had reached agreement with the White House to carry out experiments on Earth-based life forms in a specially constructed base beneath the mountain.

Over the course of the 1980s, Moore provided Bennewitz with 'evidence' to back up his suspicions, and helped him publicize his story that aliens had arrived on Earth and, with the complicity of the US government, were experimenting on humans and perfecting forms of mind control. Needless to say, Bennewitz was treated by many as simply a crank.

Then, in 1989, Moore publicly declared that he had been part of a scheme (alleged by some to be in conjunction with staff at Kirtland AFB) to supply Bennewitz with disinformation. The only motive for this plot seems to have been to assist Bennewitz in utterly discrediting himself. Bennewitz, meanwhile, suffered deteriorating mental health until his death in 2003.

BIG BORE *A US Air Force tunnel-boring machine (or 'mole'), capable of drilling a tunnel several metres wide through hard rock, photographed at Little Skull Mountain, Nevada, in 1982. Those who believe that Dulce Base exists suggest that hardware of this kind could have been used in its construction.*

So Dulce Base, for which no one has ever produced hard physical evidence, seems like nothing so much as a figment of Bennewitz's imagination. But for many, a fundamental question remains – if Bennewitz was a crank, why go to all that effort of undermining him? Had he, some wonder, stumbled upon something that may have been wholly unrelated to extraterrestrials, but which the authorities didn't want him sniffing around? Was the misinformation really a case of misdirection, and the Dulce Base rumour a cover for something equally startling? For where better to hide a secret truth than in a great mass of incredible lies? Or, just maybe, Bennewitz was right all along...

Cheyenne Mountain Complex

14

LOCATION El Paso County, Colorado, USA
NEAREST POPULATION HUB Colorado Springs, Colorado
SECRECY OVERVIEW Operations classified: an underground centre tasked with maintaining the security of North America.

The Cheyenne Mountain Complex is home to the Alternate Command Center for NORAD and, latterly, USNORTHCOM. A joint enterprise between the United States and Canada, NORAD has been key to surveying the region's airspace and identifying potential threats to both countries. It then assesses the danger posed by any irregular activity, and raises the appropriate alarm.

NORAD (the North American Aerospace Defense Command) was established as a US-Canadian cross-border body in 1958, when the threat of attack from the USSR was the continent's most pressing concern. USNORTHCOM, meanwhile, is the United States Northern Command, established to protect homeland security following the attacks of 11 September 2001. NORAD's motto of 'Deter, Detect, Defend' neatly summarizes the job done inside Cheyenne Mountain. While the threat of mutual annihilation has proved enough to put off most would-be attackers, the detection element is achieved with the aid of extensive radar and satellite systems that pick up on any abnormal activity in the skies. Meanwhile, Air Force fighters and bombers and, as a last resort, missiles are all primed for defensive action should the call ever come.

Both NORAD and USNORTHCOM have their headquarters at the Peterson Air Force Base in nearby Colorado Springs. Many day-to-day operations are now carried out there, but Cheyenne Mountain nonetheless stays on alert to take over at short notice. Rising to almost 3,000 metres (10,000 ft) in the Rocky Mountains range, the mountain was chosen as NORAD's base because of its central location and stable tectonics, as well as its proximity to the US Air Force Academy and other military installations. Construction began in 1961, and it is estimated that more than 450,000 kilos (1 million lb) of explosives were used in the process of hollowing out the mountain. There are 4.5 kilometres (2.8 miles) of tunnels and chambers, covering an area of some 1.8 hectares (4.5 acres), where there was previously almost 700,000 tonnes of granite. By the time NORAD started its operations there in 1966, it was estimated that the project had cost US$142 million. A major upgrade scheme commenced in 1989, though by the mid-1990s it was hugely behind schedule and several hundred million dollars over budget.

The complex consists of around 15 free-standing, steel-built, multi-storey buildings (the majority are three storeys

COLORADO

Colorado
Springs

Painted Desert

Rocky Mountains

CONTROL ROOM *A rare glimpse inside the Cheyenne Mountain Complex reveals USAF and other military personnel at work. One of the base's more light-hearted tasks is its annual tracking of Santa Claus's Christmas Eve flight around the world.*

DOOMSDAY DOORS *These vast 25-tonne steel doors can be fully opened or closed in a relatively speedy three-quarters of a minute – long enough to make sure you don't get your fingers jammed. They are an integral part of the system that can seal off the mountain's interior from the outside world.*

high), each resting on huge springs (there are almost 1,400 in total, each weighing a tonne). In engineering parlance, this gives the structures 'independent bounce capability', making it possible for each building to sway as much as a foot in any horizontal direction, thus allowing the shock from a nuclear explosion or an earthquake to be largely isolated. A main thoroughfare constructed through the middle of the mountain from the north to the South Portal is another means of lessening the effect of shockwaves.

Entry to the complex is via 0.9-metre (40-in) thick, 25-tonne steel doors, which are designed to open and close within 45 seconds. In the event of a nuclear explosion, there are sensors at the main entrances that pick up on pressure waves, prompting blast valves to close and seal the complex off. In such an event, there are enough food reserves to see several hundred people safely through a stay of up to 30 days, while natural springs provide water stored in four huge excavated reservoirs. These vast tanks can hold up to 5.7 million litres (1.5 million US gallons), and it

has even been reported that workers sometimes use rowing boats to cross them. Meanwhile, a highly efficient ventilation system ensures a constant supply of fresh air. The mountain also has provision for many of life's other 'essentials', including medical facilities, barbers, gyms and saunas. On the surface, local attractions include a nearby zoo and a shrine to early 20th-century humourist Will Rogers!

Thankfully, Cheyenne Mountain has never reached its highest state of alert, although there have been one or two close calls as a result of human or technological error. Most famously, in 1980 NORAD's computers ran a test programme without realizing it was only a test. Fortunately, an eagle-eyed worker spotted the mistake before any jets were scrambled or missiles launched.

The mountain can also boast a notable cinematic career, most impressively as a setting for the classic 1983 film *WarGames*, a cautionary tale of a young hacker who unwittingly accesses a NORAD supercomputer and brings the world to the brink of nuclear war.

15 Waste Isolation Pilot Plant

LOCATION Delaware Basin, New Mexico, USA
NEAREST POPULATION HUB Carlsbad, New Mexico
SECRECY OVERVIEW Access restricted: a deep repository for America's nuclear waste.

The Waste Isolation Pilot Plant (WIPP), located in Eddy County, New Mexico, has served as a rubbish dump for much of the US's transuranic radioactive waste since 1999. Chosen for its stable tectonics and geological characteristics, it is expected to receive some 38,000 shipments of waste over 35 years. However, the site will remain off-limits to future generations for perhaps 10,000 years.

Transuranic waste consists mostly of clothing, tools, fabrics, soil and assorted other materials that have been contaminated with radioactive elements with atomic numbers greater than that of uranium (principally plutonium). This is the most dangerous waste produced as a by-product of the various US nuclear research programmes, and its disposal presents a significant challenge.

After a prospective location in Kansas for the storage of such waste was rejected, the site in New Mexico gained support. The Delaware Basin, a salt basin created in the Permian period of geological time (some 250 million years ago) by a shallow sea undergoing a series of evaporation cycles, was chosen because of its geological suitability and the absence of potentially dangerous groundwater. Congress authorized construction of the WIPP in 1979 and testing at the facility began in 1988. In March 1999, the first waste shipment arrived from the Los Alamos nuclear weapons research and development facility in Albuquerque.

Transuranic waste is given one of two major classifications: it is either 'Contact-handled' (CH), which means it can be handled by workers in controlled conditions without any extra shielding beyond the container it comes in; or it is 'remote-handled' (RH), which means it emits greater amounts of radiation and must be transported and handled using lead-lined containers. RH waste accounts for only about 4 per cent of the total brought to the facility.

Disposal rooms for the waste material are located about 600 metres (2,000 ft) beneath the Basin's surface (which is to say, about one and a half times deeper than the Empire State Building is high). RH waste canisters are stored in boreholes drilled into the walls of the store rooms, which are then capped with concrete. CH waste, meanwhile, is simply layered on the floors. Once the repository is full, it will eventually collapse in on itself and any gaps will be filled with salt until the WIPP is entirely encased, hundreds of metres below ground.

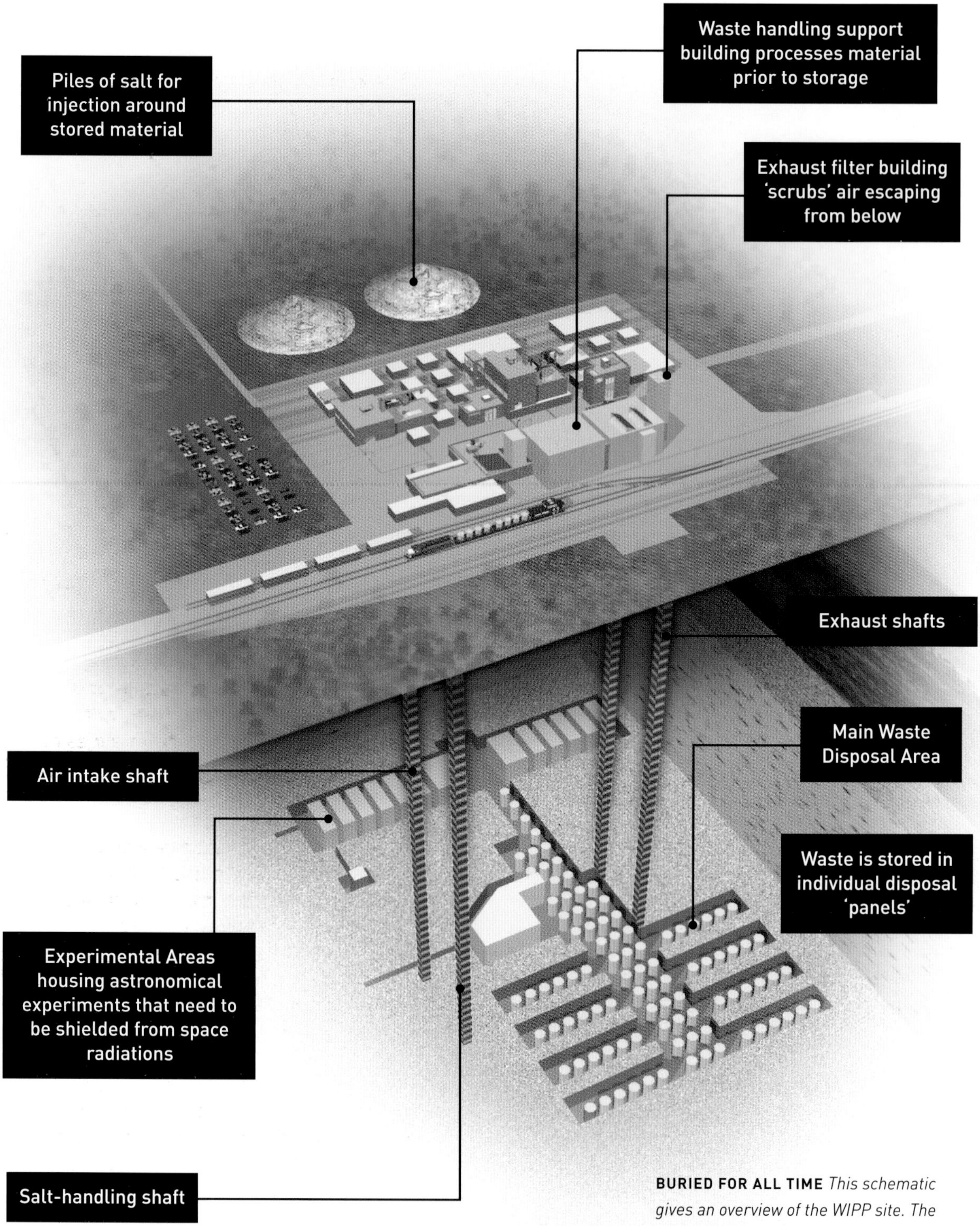

Piles of salt for injection around stored material

Waste handling support building processes material prior to storage

Exhaust filter building 'scrubs' air escaping from below

Exhaust shafts

Main Waste Disposal Area

Air intake shaft

Waste is stored in individual disposal 'panels'

Experimental Areas housing astronomical experiments that need to be shielded from space radiations

Salt-handling shaft

BURIED FOR ALL TIME *This schematic gives an overview of the WIPP site. The waste disposal area is contained within a sedimentary layer known as the Salado Formation, which consists of salt, clay and shale. The salt will eventually isolate the radioactive waste from the outside world.*

UNDER CONSTRUCTION *One of WIPP's underground tunnels, buried at a depth of some 650 metres (2,130 ft) in the middle of the thick salt bed. The first exploratory shaft at the New Mexico site was sunk in 1981, a full 18 years before WIPP received its first shipment of waste.*

While keeping people away from the site today is the immediate concern, it is equally important to ensure that future generations do not stumble upon it. For this reason, a think-tank of scientists, anthropologists and linguists has spent years developing a system to warn the people of the far future to keep away. The resultant plan employs 'Passive Institutional Controls', a series of verbal and non-verbal markers designed to indicate that the area is not safe.

So what does this mean in practice? Firstly, once the plant has been filled in, a sloped earthen hill (called a berm) will surround the facility's 50-hectare (120-acre) footprint, with a height of 11 metres (36 ft) and width of 33 metres (110 ft). Within the soil will be 128 equally spaced metal objects visible to radar, as well as magnets to give the area its own magnetic signature. Granite monuments, 8 metres (27 ft) high, will mark the perimeter of the berm, with another layer marking the outer edges of a control area covering some 10 square kilometres (4 sq miles).

In addition, an information centre will be built in the middle of the facility's footprint, constructed from granite and inscribed with messages in several languages as well as pictograms. Two further rooms containing the same information will be buried elsewhere on the site, and records will also be sent to archives throughout the world in order that maps, reference works and the like can be accurately maintained. Finally, 23-centimetre (9-in) discs made of granite, fired clay or aluminium oxide will be randomly buried across the site, each carrying a warning in one of seven languages (English, Arabic, Chinese, French, Russian, Spanish and Navajo). Rarely can a place that wants to keep people out have had so many indicators of its precise location.

The WIPP is regulated by a variety of agencies, of which the most important are the Federal Department of Energy and the New Mexico Environment Department. Access to the plant is necessarily tightly controlled, and the site is surrounded by a large fence.

Anyone visiting on official business must watch a safety film before entering and wear appropriate equipment (including emergency breathing apparatus and a radiation monitor, if going underground). All waste shipments are tracked by satellite from a central control centre, and all routes to the WIPP have stringent safety and security regimes, as well as some 25,000 trained responders in the event of an emergency.

Forensic Anthropology Research Facility

LOCATION Freeman Ranch, Texas, USA
NEAREST POPULATION HUB San Marcos, Texas
SECRECY OVERVIEW Access restricted: a 'body farm' for the study of human decomposition after death.

The Forensic Anthropology Research Facility (FARF) is maintained under the jurisdiction of the Forensic Anthropology Center at Texas State University (FACTS). This unusual outdoor research laboratory focuses on 'reconstructing the post-mortem interval to determine time since death and related studies on human decomposition'. It is perhaps more graphically described as a 'body farm'.

Opened in 2008, FARF looks at the way in which bodies decompose in open-air environments, an area of particular use in the field of criminal forensics. It is one of five such institutions across the United States (the first opened in 1981 at the University of Tennessee at Knoxville) and is by far the largest, taking up 10 hectares (26 acres) of the University's Freeman Ranch (the rest of the site is a working ranch). A range of environments are simulated across the site, including forested areas, scrubland and ponds.

The facility is governed by strict protocols concerning health, safety and security. It is surrounded by razor-wire perimeter fencing, and visits from the public are rarely permitted. There is no residential property within 1.6 kilometres (1 mile) of the site, although it is said that any odours dissipate within 15 metres (50 ft). Freeman Ranch was not the original intended site, but a previous location close to San Marcos Municipal Airport was vetoed over concerns that large numbers of vultures might be attracted by the corpses, putting air safety at risk.

Research is carried out on around six corpses at any one time by specially selected academics. Some of the bodies are buried in shallow graves, others left open to the elements, and some are even stored in car boots in a bid to closely replicate genuine homicide scenarios.

If you are so minded, you may make arrangements to donate your body to the centre. It is even possible to donate a loved-one's cadaver if you think it is what they would have wanted.

Lunar Sample Laboratory Facility
Johnson Space Center

LOCATION Johnson Space Center, Texas, USA
NEAREST POPULATION HUB Houston, Texas
SECRECY OVERVIEW High-security location: purpose-built labs for the preservation and study of lunar materials.

The Apollo lunar landing missions of 1969–72 brought back invaluable geological samples weighing some 382 kilograms (842 lb). The Lunar Sample Laboratory Facility, covering 1,300 square metres (14,000 sq ft), was constructed in the late 1970s to provide these precious Moon rocks with a permanent, secure and non-contaminating environment, and visitors from outside the scientific community are not welcome.

Around 100 specially screened educators and scientists visit the facility each year to examine samples, which are divided into two kinds: those that have been released to scientists for experimentation and then returned; and 'pristine' samples that have not been out of NASA custody since coming to Earth. If visitors are working with pristine samples, they must adhere to the strictest rules. On arrival, they are required to remove any jewellery and change into nylon coveralls (known as 'bunny' suits), hats, gloves and multiple pairs of overshoes. They are then given a minute-long air shower to remove any lingering potential contaminants.

Pristine samples are processed in stainless steel cabinets fitted with attached rubber gloves, into which workers insert their hands so that they can manipulate samples without direct contact. Inert nitrogen constantly flows through the airtight cabinets to ensure no build-up of reactive gases that might permeate through the gloves. Any tools that are used undergo a special cleansing regime and are stored in hermetically sealed bags. The only materials permitted to come into contact with pristine samples are stainless steel, aluminium and Teflon. All materials used in the building of the labs themselves were selected to avoid the risk of chemical contamination, and high-tech security systems are in operation at all times.

The Facility's vault, which contains NASA's 26,000 pristine samples, has a heavy door fitted with two combination locks. Transfers are made through an airlock, and a further watertight door can be bolted on if there's a hurricane threat. The vault is elevated above the maximum predicted sea-level rises that might accompany a hurricane. A small but significant proportion of the collection is kept in another secret location, in case disaster ever strikes the Johnson Space Center. Considering these fragments of Moon rocks might help us answer some of the fundamental questions of our Universe, it is easy to see why such measures are in place.

OUT OF THIS WORLD *The rock samples gathered during the Apollo Lunar missions are kept in Johnson Space Center's Building 31N, which officially opened for business in 1979. The Facility includes samples gathered from nine separate exploration sites on the Moon.*

ROCK OF AGES
Left: A sample of Moon rock awaiting study in the Lunar Sample Laboratory at JSC. Right: In 1972 Harrison Schmitt became the only geologist to walk on the Moon, when he served aboard the three-man crew of the Apollo 17 mission, the last manned landing on the Moon.

Fort Knox Bullion Depository

LOCATION Kentucky, USA
NEAREST POPULATION HUB
Louisville, Kentucky
SECRECY OVERVIEW
High-security location:
the world's most famous
gold bullion depository.

Although it is not even the largest gold bullion depository in the United States (an honour currently held by the Federal Reserve Bank of New York, see page 82), Kentucky's Fort Knox is legendary for its extraordinary levels of security. Indeed, during the Second World War the site became home to some of the most valuable treasures and important documents in the world.

A classified facility, the Fort Knox bullion depository was constructed in 1936 for storing US gold reserves. Built by the Treasury Department, it now falls under the jurisdiction of the US Mint. Its first gold deposits arrived here by railroad in January 1937.

Each gold bar in the Fort Knox vaults measures 17.8 by 9.2 by 4.5 centimetres (7 by 3.6 by 1.8 in), and weighs in at 12.5 kilograms (27.5 lb). Today, gold holdings total about 3.9 million kilograms (150 million troy ounces), down from a peak in the Second World War of more than four times that amount. The Fort has also variously housed such important items as the US Constitution, the Declaration of Independence and Lincoln's Gettysburg Address, along with the Hungarian crown jewels, a Magna Carta and a Gutenberg Bible. The Constitution and Declaration, moved for safekeeping in the early 1940s, were secured within a purpose-built bronze chest that weighed some 68 kilograms (150 lb) and made its journey under the watchful eyes of secret service agents and armed troops.

The depository is built over two storeys, with a footprint of roughly 32 x 37 metres (105 x 121 ft). The original construction of the building required 750 tonnes of reinforced steel, 670 tonnes of structural steel, 1,500 cubic metres (16,000 cu ft) of granite and 10,500 cubic metres (113,000 cu ft) of concrete. Entry into the vault is via blast-proof doors 53 centimetres (21 in) thick and weighing over 20 tonnes. The vault is subdivided into numerous compartments sealed with tape and wax that reveal tampering if they are broken.

The building is, as one might expect, all but impenetrable to the uninvited. As well as state-of-the-art security systems (the finer details of which are tightly guarded), two sentry posts guard the gateway to the building, which is set into a steel fence. There are further guard boxes at each corner of the building. The guards, who are all members of the United States Mint Police (founded in 1792), are highly trained and not especially keen on calm dialogue with would-be intruders. In the basement of the building a firing range offers the

Goodman Army
Air Field

GARRISON TOWN *The bullion depository lies on the edge of the Fort Knox Army Post, a 44,000-hectare (109,000-acre) military base with a population of more than 12,000 soldiers and other staff ready to defend the nation's gold reserves at a moment's notice.*

WELCOME TO
FORT KNOX

Lindsey
Golf Course

HEAVY DUTY *Construction of the Fort Knox Army Post began in earnest in 1918. This permanent camp was named after Henry Knox, a Bostonian officer in the Continental Army during the American War of Independence who became the new nation's first Secretary of War.*

Main entrance from
Bullion Boulevard

GOLDEN VISION *The Depository at Fort Knox is estimated to store something approaching 2.5 per cent of all the gold ever refined, although its holdings lag some way behind the Federal Reserve Bank in New York, which houses more than 4 per cent of the historical total.*

Kentucky Veterans'
Cemetery

HARD KNOX *The Bullion Depository's sophisticated defence systems include guard towers, security cameras and perimeter fencing. There is believed to be an escape tunnel, should anyone be accidentally locked inside the vaults, but access only goes one way.*

guards a chance for a little extra target practice during their lunch hour. What is more, the Fort Knox military base just up the road is ready to offer extra muscle should it be required.

Admission to the vaults requires a combination code that is not known to any one individual, so several members of staff must be present to dial the correct code. The vault has a 104-hour time lock, and there is an escape tunnel for anyone unlucky enough to find themselves trapped inside once the lock has been set. Employees are legally bound not to disclose any details of the security mechanisms in operation and visits from the public are prohibited, without exception.

Operating at such a high level of security, it is perhaps inevitable that Fort Knox has aroused the interest of conspiracy theorists. Indeed, their suspicions have been intensified by the complete absence

of large-scale movements of gold in or out of the facility for many years. The only gold that has been transferred has been in small samples to satisfy auditing protocols and purity control. So theories abound, ranging from claims that there is no gold left at Fort Knox because it was all moved to London, to suggestions that Fort Knox now stores objects belonging to little green men from outer space.

The idea that there may no longer be gold inside those granite and steel walls has particularly haunted the American psyche over the years. With the world then in financial meltdown, the idea that the vault was empty took hold in 1974 after the suggestion was made in a book attacking the broader financial system. Eventually a reluctant Treasury permitted a visit by selected members of the press to view the holdings and assuage the doubters. Needless to say, they were able to report that there was gold and plenty of it. It was the first time any member of the public had been allowed into Fort Knox's vaults since 1943 – and that member of the public had been the then-President, Franklin D. Roosevelt.

19 Coca-Cola's Recipe Vault

LOCATION Coca-Cola World, Atlanta, Georgia, USA
NEAREST POPULATION HUB Atlanta, Georgia
SECRECY OVERVIEW High-security location: repository of the secret recipe for the iconic beverage.

Coca-Cola might well be the world's favourite drink, with a reported 1.7 billion servings sold every day. Such is the mythology that has grown up around the Coca-Cola brand that its recipe is perhaps the most famous trade secret in history. Jealously guarded since first being committed to paper in the early part of the 20th century, it now resides in an extraordinary vault that doubles as a tourist attraction.

The Coca-Cola story begins in Atlanta, Georgia, in 1886 with a chemist called John Pemberton, creator of delights such as French Wine Coca (a heady mix of wine and cocaine) and Pemberton's Indian Queen Magic Hair Dye. Facing the spectre of prohibition, he set upon devising a non-alcoholic version of his Wine Coca. The result was a brownish syrup that he intended to market as a sort of 'cure-all'. Quite serendipitously, however, a batch of this syrup was mixed with carbonated water, creating the drink that is known and loved today.

But for all his talents as a potion-maker, Pemberton was deeply flawed as a businessman. In 1891, he sold his business to Asa Griggs Candler for what turned out to be a regrettably low $2,300. Candler was quick to realize that the value of his purchase lay in Coca-Cola's distinctive taste, and he forbade its recipe to be written down lest anyone copy it. In 1919, Ernest Woodruff led a team of investors who bought the company from the Candler clan. The purchase required a loan, which

Woodruff secured by offering the Coca-Cola formula as collateral. After finally persuading Candler to write it down for him, Woodruff deposited the recipe in the vault of the Guaranty Bank of New York. It remained there until 1925, when the loan was paid off, and was then moved to the Trust Company Bank in Atlanta Georgia, where it stayed until 2011 (by which time the bank had evolved into the SunTrust Bank).

Despite countless imitators on the market, Coca-Cola has made a policy of rarely filing trademark lawsuits against them, since doing so might force them to reveal the formula in court. That said, the basic recipe is believed to include a mixture of caffeine, caramel, coca, citric acid, lime juice, sugar, water and vanilla.

The part of the recipe that remains elusive is 'Merchandise 7X', the ingredient responsible for the drink's unique special flavour despite accounting for just 1 per cent of its volume. Over the years, many have claimed to have uncovered the secret.

NOT-SO-SECRET LOCATION *Coca-Cola CEO Muhtar Kent (right) invites Georgia governor Nathan Deal and Atlanta Mayor Kasim Reed to inspect the custom-built vault for the secret formula, during the opening ceremony at the World of Coca-Cola exhibit, Atlanta, in December 2011.*

For instance, in 2011, US radio show *This American Life* announced the rediscovery of a story published in the *Atlanta Journal Constitution* in 1979. Alongside the article was a photo of a recipe from an old notebook that, it was claimed, belonged to a friend of John Pemberton. Nonetheless, Coca-Cola remains adamant that no one has yet come up with the correct formula.

Company legend has it that only a tiny band of people know the recipe, and they are not allowed to travel together for fear of an accident in which the formula might be lost forever. In December 2011, the recipe was retrieved from its vault at SunTrust Bank and, under high security, was transferred a few minutes down the road to a new purpose-built vault at the company's World of Coca-Cola exhibition. The decision to move the formula was apparently unrelated to SunTrust's decision to sell off its Coca-Cola stock holdings in 2007.

In front of the watching media, a metal box believed to contain the recipe was placed into a newly constructed 2-metre (6.6-ft) high steel vault. This vault is never opened, and is protected by a barrier that keeps the viewing public several metres away. The area is kept under surveillance, with guards on hand to deal with any troublemakers. By the door stands a keypad and a hand-imprint scanner, although officials have refused to confirm if these are simply for show.

Centers for Disease Control and Prevention

20

LOCATION Druid Hills, DeKalb County, Georgia, USA
NEAREST POPULATION HUB Atlanta, Georgia
SECRECY OVERVIEW Access restricted: one of only two places in the world known to store the smallpox virus.

With a goal of improving public health and carrying out research into disease prevention, the US Centers for Disease Control and Prevention (CDC) is one of only two facilities approved to hold samples of the smallpox virus, now fortunately extinct in the wider world. Debate rages as to whether it is time to destroy the virus for good, or to retain small stocks for research purposes.

The CDC originated in 1942 as the Office of National Defense Malaria Control Activities. Atlanta was selected as a base for the organization, which was originally focused on reducing the mosquito-borne disease that was then endemic in the Southern States. The organization subsequently underwent several name changes, and the scope of its work broadened, so that today it employs some 15,000 people and has an annual budget of several billion dollars.

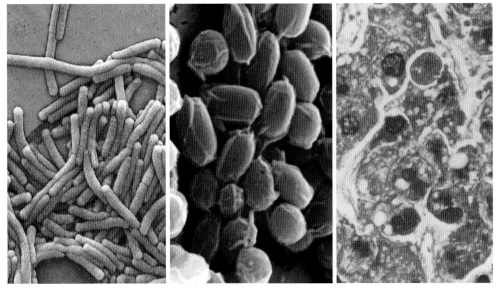

MICROSCOPIC KILLERS *Scientists at the CDC undertake investigations into some of the deadliest viral and biological threats known to humanity. Pictured here are electron micrographs of tissue affected by, from left to right,* Legionella, Anthrax *and* Ebola.

The CDC also happens to be home to one of a small number of Biosafety Level 4 laboratories, a designation that reflects stringent precautions for storing certain harmful biological agents. It is because of these exacting safety and security standards that it is allowed to keep a stock of smallpox virus. Only a handful of other viruses – including Ebola and the Marburg virus – are subject to such high-level protective measures.

Smallpox accounted for the death of millions across the globe over many centuries, and seemed beyond control until the English physician Edward Jenner discovered the first ground-breaking vaccine in 1796. In 1980, after a global vaccination programme running for several decades, the World Health Organization (WHO) declared that smallpox had become the first disease to be completely eradicated from the world. The last person to naturally contract it (as opposed to being infected in a laboratory accident) was an unvaccinated Somali hospital worker.

A scheme was set up whereby existing smallpox stores were to be surrendered and destroyed. However, the United States and the then Soviet Union argued that they should be allowed to keep small stocks in high-security environments so that further research work might be undertaken. CDC was to be one of these secure environments and the VECTOR State Research Center of Virology and Biotechnology in Koltsovo, Russia, the other.

CDC is home to around 450 samples (some of which have reportedly been given nicknames depending upon their origins – for the record, these include 'Harvey', from a British patient who contracted the bug in Gibraltar, 'Yamamoto' from Japan and 'Garcia' from South America). Stored in a chained and padlocked freezer in a high-security building, no more than ten scientists have access to the samples. On the rare occasions when they are accessed, staff must wear protective suits and breathing apparatus.

The WHO regularly reviews whether the remaining samples should be destroyed, and have so far decided against it. While those in favour of getting rid of the stockpiles suggest that a renewed outbreak is only possible while the virus is preserved, advocates of retention argue that it is impossible to know whether these really are the only reserves left on the planet. While it is hoped that no country surreptitiously retained a small sample when the global stocks were disposed of in the 1980s, we cannot know for certain. Furthermore, the population born since the 1980 WHO announcement has gone unvaccinated, while evidence suggests even those who have been vaccinated can expect only a decade of immunity. In an age when bioterrorism is a perpetual threat, the supporters of retention contend that it would be madness to destroy our best hope of responding to a new outbreak.

SUITED UP *Two CDC laboratory workers carrying out research in one of the facility's top-security Biosafety Level 4 labs. The scientists' air supply comes from overhead lines that plug directly into their protective suits. A complex airflow system ensures pathogens do not escape from the experimental area.*

Iron Mountain, Boyers

LOCATION Boyers, Pennsylvania, USA
NEAREST POPULATION HUB Pittsburgh, Pennsylvania
SECRECY OVERVIEW High-security location: a secure storage facility built into a disused mine.

Iron Mountain Incorporated is one of the world's leading data management companies, and its most famous high-security storage facility lies more than 60 metres (200 ft) underground in the former mining town of Boyers, Pennsylvania. Among the priceless materials stored in the former mine is the Corbis photographic collection, now owned by Bill Gates.

The Iron Mountain company was founded by Herman Knaust, a businessman who had made his fortune in mushroom farming and marketing. In 1936, he forked out US$9,000 to purchase a defunct iron ore mine and 40 hectares (100 acres) of surrounding land in Livingstone, New York. It was, Knaust was convinced, the ideal setting for mushroom cultivation on an industrial scale. But by 1950 the bottom had fallen out of the mushroom market and Knaust spotted a new opportunity. The Second World War and the Cold War had focused attention on the need to preserve official records in locations secure from military attack or other disasters. The one-time 'Mushroom King' renamed his mine and founded Iron Mountain Atomic Storage, Inc.

Meanwhile, the town of Boyers in Butler County, Pennsylvania, was a once-thriving mining community that had dug all it could out of the ground. From 1954 onwards, various organizations began to use its former limestone mines as storage facilities. After Iron Mountain went through a rapid phase of expansion in the 1980s and 1990s, the company bought one of these sites in 1998 from National Underground Storage for a little short of US$40 million. It is in many respects the company's flagship branch.

About 53 hectares (130 acres) of the mine are now devoted to climate-controlled storage, with clients ranging from the Corbis photographic library to US government departments, and from film companies to the National Archives. The facility is entirely protected from the elements, geologically stable and resistant to bombing.

On the approach to Iron Mountain, visitors are greeted by armed guards, who check their credentials and give their vehicles a thorough inspection. Entry to the complex is via large, steel gates, and guests must be accompanied by an official escort at all times. Security systems, including extensive surveillance, are in operation throughout the facility – not even Bill Gates gets into Iron Mountain on a nod and a wink!

Mine entrances for access to storage facilities

Boyers village

Main parking lot

FILED AWAY *The Iron Mountain Corporation is just one of several organizations who use Boyer's abandoned mines as ready-made storage facilities. For instance, the US Office of Personnel Management and the US Patent and Trademark Office both run their own facilities.*

ICONIC IMAGES *The Corbis archive contains original images of many famous events such as the destruction of the German airship Hindenburg at Lakehurst, New Jersey, in 1937.*

Mount Weather Emergency Operations Center

LOCATION Blue Ridge Mountains, Virginia, USA
NEAREST POPULATION HUB Washington, DC
SECRECY OVERVIEW Existence unacknowledged: secret installation to house US government officials in the event of a disaster.

Straddling the Loudon and Clarke counties of Virginia, the facility at Mount Weather comprises two main parts – one above ground, concerned with the management of national disasters, and a more mysterious subterranean section. This hidden, unacknowledged complex is widely believed to serve as a 'continuity of government' base, a home for key Washington personnel in times of crisis.

The Mount Weather site was historically used for launching weather balloons, and later came under the aegis of the US Bureau of Mines. During the 1950s, an extensive programme of drilling into the mountain was undertaken with a view to the military building a subterranean complex of tunnels and bunkers.

Today the complex, covering several acres, is believed to include high-tech ventilation systems, computer rooms, a broadcasting studio, a hospital, reservoirs and accommodation quarters. It is widely speculated that Mount Weather would be used as an alternative command centre by the President and other senior government officials as well as members of the Supreme Court in the event of a disaster. Much of Congress was rumoured to have been transferred here in the immediate aftermath of the 11 September attacks in 2001.

Sited inconspicuously off Route 601, the centre first came to public attention in 1977, after a Boeing 727 crashed nearby in bad weather. Towards the end of the 1970s, the Federal Emergency Management Agency (FEMA), now part of the Department of Homeland Security and charged with disaster response, opened above-ground training facilities. It is also rumoured that the US National Gallery of Art has an emergency plan to deposit at-risk works of art here.

While FEMA's operations are in the public domain, the underground part of the complex retains its mystique. No journalists or members of the public have ever been granted a tour, and all personnel associated with it in an official capacity maintain a strict code of silence. The area is surrounded by razor-wire fencing and barriers, while signs warn 'US Property. No Trespassing'. Armed guards patrol the environs and protect the main entrances, which are believed to include 3-metre (10-ft) thick blast doors weighing over 30 tonnes each. Some conspiracy theorists have become convinced that the complex houses a 'shadow government' pulling Washington's strings, although there is little evidence to back this up.

PANIC STATIONS *FEMA was constituted in 1979 and has run a facility at Mount Weather since its inauguration. The organization received fierce criticism for its response after 2005's Hurricane Katrina devastated New Orleans. Pictured left is a search-and-rescue flyover during that operation.*

Helipad control tower

FEMA main operations building

Restricted Area with access to underground facility

Cafeteria building

HIgh-frequency communications antennae

Old Blueridge Road

PRESIDENTIAL BOLTHOLE *In the event of a catastrophe such as the outbreak of full-scale war, the underground complex beneath Mount Weather would offer a possible shelter for the US President and senior government officials, arriving aboard military helicopters such as the President's Marine One.*

Raven Rock Mountain Complex

23

LOCATION Pennsylvania, USA
NEAREST POPULATION HUB Camp David, Maryland
SECRECY OVERVIEW Operations classified: Alternate Joint Communications Centre for the US government.

Sometimes known as the 'underground Pentagon', or simply as 'Site R', the Raven Rock facility is a communications hub built into a mountain, running dozens of systems and providing information technology services to, among others, the National Command Authority (i.e. the President and the Secretary of Defense), the Joint Chiefs of Staff and assorted other agencies in the Department of Defense.

Raven Rock was initially constructed with the intention that it should serve as an alternative operations base for the government in the event of a military emergency such as a nuclear strike. With the threat from the Soviet Union growing ever more pressing in the late 1940s, it was decided to locate the base amid the natural defences of Raven Rock, which is formed of greenstone – one of the hardest forms of granite known to man. The complex lies a few kilometres away from Camp David, which is over the state border in Maryland. However, Raven Rock spent long spells under the jurisdiction of Camp Albert Ritchie in Maryland.

Building on Raven Rock began in 1951, during the presidency of Harry S. Truman, and the facility became operational three years later. Hewn out of rock some 200 metres (650 ft) beneath the mountain's peak, the complex is thought to boast some 65,000 square metres (700,000 sq ft) of space and room for up to 3,000 people. According to informed conjecture, the

Air intakes and cooling towers

East entrances D and C

site contains five main buildings, each three storeys high, with rooms full of computers and even a giant underground reservoir and a helipad. Above ground, the site is surrounded by a forest of communications antennae, towers and satellite dishes.

There are thought to be perhaps four or five entrances into the complex, constantly under guard by the Raven Rock Military Police Company and closed-circuit surveillance. Some of its metal-clad ingresses are visible from nearby Route 16. However, anyone who stumbles across the complex will encounter razor-wire fencing and conspicuous red warning signs.

Nonetheless, Raven Rock is a product of its times. Many of its technological features soon became obsolete, and rumours of its existence quickly spread – something of a problem for a secret base. Plans to overhaul the complex for modern operations were drawn up in the late 1970s, but were abandoned before the decade was out.

Even more damaging to its prospects in the 1980s was the rise of Mikhail Gorbachev through the political ranks of the USSR. With the collapse of the Soviet Union and the end of the Cold War in the early 1990s, it seemed as if Raven Rock had come to the end of its useful life – a mothballed future appeared its most likely fate.

But there was to be another twist. Dick Cheney, Vice-President to George W. Bush, reputedly stayed in Raven Rock

UNDER THE ROCK *An overview of the Raven Rock Mountain Complex, built amid the pressure-cooker atmosphere of the early Cold War. While the odd driver along Route 16 may glimpse one of the entry portals, they are given little clue as to the vast infrastructure that lies within the mountain.*

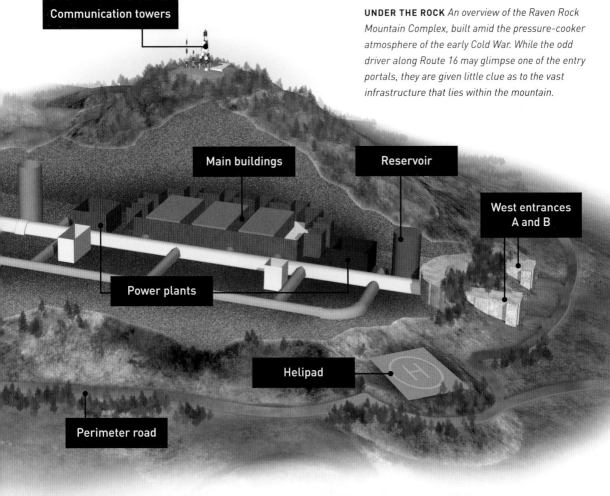

Communication towers

Main buildings

Reservoir

West entrances A and B

Power plants

Helipad

Perimeter road

AERIAL VIEW *The complex boasts an impressive array of communications hardware, including a forest of antennae or aerials on top of the mountain. As early as 1951, local newspapers were speculating about the construction of a 'Second Pentagon' at the site, though some have argued that the facility was out of date almost as soon as it was completed.*

for one or more spells after the terrorist atrocities in New York and Washington on 11 September 2001. Never had there been such a direct attack on the nation's heart of government as when the Pentagon, the core of the nation's defence system, was hit by a hijacked aeroplane. Suddenly the world seemed far less secure than it had the day before, and the need for an alternative operations base in case of a future, even more devastating hit on Washington seemed more important than ever. The future of Raven Rock was, for the short- to mid-term at least, secured.

Today, the majority of operations carried out at Raven Rock are still highly classified. Access is strictly monitored and confidentiality is a prerequisite for all staff and visitors. It is illegal to photograph, map or sketch the site without prior permission, and cellular mobile phones and other modern communication devices are not allowed. In fact, even if a phone did find its way in, it would be useless as there is no service. However, anyone found guilty of breaching security can expect to experience the full force of the law, whether in the form of a hefty fine or a spell in prison.

For a no-longer-secret secret base, covertness remains high on the agenda and no one can be too sure what is going on inside that mountain – it can only be hoped that it need never be used as an emergency base for the US government.

24

CIA Headquarters

LOCATION Langley, Fairfax County, Virginia, USA
NEAREST POPULATION HUB Washington, DC
SECRECY OVERVIEW Operations classified: the home of the CIA, the USA's intelligence agency.

The US Central Intelligence Agency (CIA) is responsible for providing intelligence on matters of national security to Washington's policy-makers. As well as operating an unrivalled network of spies around the world, it also engages in covert action when required to do so by the President. The George Bush Center for Intelligence, the CIA's home at Langley, Virginia, is among the most secure buildings on the globe.

Ever since evicting the British from America in the 18th century, the government of the United States has been involved in intelligence gathering at home and abroad – yet the CIA is relatively new on the scene. By the 1880s, both the navy and army had their own independent spying operations, and in the aftermath of the First World War their respective duties fell under the remit of the Bureau of Investigations (forerunner of the FBI). In 1941, with the US poised to join the Second World War, President Roosevelt appointed a Coordinator of Information, William J. Dawson. Within a year, Dawson was heading up a new Office of Strategic Services (OSS). Though disbanded after the war, the OSS provided the blueprint for the CIA, which was founded under President Truman in 1947.

Today, the CIA has four major divisions: the National Clandestine Service, overseeing the work of a web of spies; the Directorate of Science and Technology, which scans the media, satellite photography and the like

to glean intelligence; the Directorate of Intelligence, which assesses the findings of the first two groups; and the Directorate of Support, which handles everything from personnel matters to administration.

The George Bush Center – situated to the west of the national capital – covers an area in excess of 100 hectares (250 acres), encompassing the Original Headquarters Building (OHB) and the New Headquarters Building (NHB). Though the Center's postal address is Langley (it was to here that President Madison and his wife fled during the 1812 Siege of Washington), Langley itself is now a neighbourhood of McLean, a large conurbation founded in 1910.

The OHB, designed by the Harrison & Abramovitz partnership, was built between 1959 and 1961. The NHB, meanwhile, was constructed between 1984 and 1991, in accordance with plans drawn up by Smith, Hinchman and Grylls Associates. It is set into a hillside behind the OHB and the two buildings

INTELLIGENCE HUB *Above: the New Headquarters Building, designed by Smith, Hinchman and Grylls Associates, opened for business in 1991. Opposite: the CIA's seal on the lobby floor of the Original Headquarters Building. The design was approved by President Harry Truman in 1950 and features the iconic American bald eagle.*

almost melt into one another. The NHB consists of two connected six-storey office blocks and includes a vast, four-storey-high glass atrium. A Cornerstone Ceremony was held during the building's construction phase in 1985, during which a box of Agency-related paraphernalia was sealed into the cornerstone to be opened at a later date. The box contained, among other items, a copy of the CIA Credo, an iconic CIA medallion and a miniature spy camera and cryptography microchip.

Some have noted the name of the complex with a wry smile – the most recent President George Bush was not always known for his intellectual pronouncements (though that is perhaps to 'misunderestimate' him). In fact, the CIA complex is named for George W.'s father, George H.W., who became the first director of the CIA to hold the highest office in the land when he took the presidency in 1988. He had been head of Central Intelligence from 1976–7, and the building was renamed in his honour in 1999.

Everything associated with the CIA is covert, even down to the size of its staff and annual budget. Some have suggested that its budget is effectively unlimited, though officials deny this. The last figures in the public domain, which date to the late 1990s, revealed a healthy annual figure in excess of US$26 billion set aside for intelligence spending. It is likely that the CIA's funding only increased following the 11 September terrorist attacks of 2001 (after which the CIA came in for heavy criticism because of alleged intelligence failings).

Security provisions at the George Bush Center are highly classified, and access to the Center is for authorized personnel only. The organization's website explains that no members of the public are allowed 'for logistical and security reasons'. It is fair to assume that anyone found intruding at the site can expect punishment beyond a simple stern talking-to.

The CIA inspires many mixed emotions. For some people, its work is the foundation upon which US national security rests. For others, its reputation is dogged by failure, from the OSS's lack of foreknowledge of Japan's attack on Pearl Harbor, to lapses highlighted by the assaults of 11 September. For yet others, there are difficult questions as to just who is guarding the guards, and how efficiently. Somebody within the walls of the George Bush Center for Intelligence could probably tell them – but they won't.

25 DARPA Headquarters

LOCATION Arlington, Virginia, USA
NEAREST POPULATION HUB Washington, DC
SECRECY OVERVIEW Operations classified: home of US Department of Defense thinktank

The Defense Advanced Research Projects Agency (DARPA) is a government agency charged with pushing back technological frontiers. Its aim is 'to maintain the technological superiority of the US military… by sponsoring revolutionary, high-payoff research bridging the gap between fundamental discoveries and their military use'. It is a body for whose work the term 'highly classified' might have been invented.

DARPA was founded in 1958 as the Advanced Research Projects Agency, spurred by the need to meet the challenges set by the unexpected launch of the Soviet Sputnik satellite in 1957, and the beginnings of the Space Race. The 'Defense' part of the agency's name was added later. With an annual budget in excess of US$3 billion, DARPA is regarded by many as the Department of Defense's 'Chief Innovation Agency'. Teams of experts are brought together on a project-by-project basis, and the organization prides itself on its independence.

Among its most significant achievements is the creation of ARPANET, a computer network that was originally developed to connect up DARPA's various affiliated university and research laboratory partners. This was the first network to use packet switching, a technique that has become the foundation of the modern communications age, and is widely regarded as the forerunner of the internet. Other stand-out achievements include the Project Vela nuclear test monitor system, and the development of Stealth fighter technology.

Necessarily enveloped in a cloak of secrecy, DARPA is a prime target for those concerned at what might be developed by a brains trust that does not have to worry about public accountability. This has led some to make claims that certain DARPA achievements could only be the result of reverse-engineering of captured alien spacecraft. One might be tempted to say that if that is the case, then well done for being so clever!

In 2009, ground was broken on DARPA's new headquarters at 675 North Randolph Street, a short step away from its old Virginia Square address. The new site is 13 storeys high, has a footprint of 3.2 hectares (8 acres) and is the first structure in Arlington to be built in line with the Department of Defense's Minimum Anti-Terrorism Standards for Buildings, boasting cutting-edge security. If you fancy a peek inside, be warned: only technological geniuses with a maverick streak need apply.

INNOVATIONS
DARPA's search for designs for a tactical flying car saw the AVX Aircraft Company come up with this vertical-take-off concept.

IN A FLAP
DARPA's Nano Air Vehicle is a tiny robotic hummingbird equipped with an on-board camera that can relay images back to its operator. It offers a method of assessing potential threats at a safe distance.

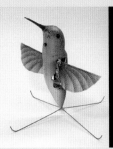

TAKING THE STRAIN The Legged Squad Support System (LS3) is a robot developed to carry 180 kilograms (400 lb) of equipment for overburdened marines or soldiers.

3701

CA

26 The Pentagon

LOCATION Arlington County,
Virginia, USA
NEAREST POPULATION HUB
Washington, DC
SECRECY OVERVIEW
Operations classified: the
heart of the United States'
defence network.

The Pentagon is the iconic headquarters of the US Department of Defense and, in terms of area, the world's largest office building. It has regularly been the target of attacks, culminating in the 11 September 2001 atrocity, in which a hijacked passenger plane was flown into it. The already tight security has since been upgraded and today the Pentagon is one of the world's most heavily protected buildings.

In the early days of the Second World War, it became clear that the rapidly expanding US Department of War needed new headquarters to consolidate its operations. The Department's chief engineer at the time, Brigadier Brehon B. Somervell, came up with the basic designs for what would become the Pentagon after what he described as 'a very busy weekend' in July 1941. Several locations were earmarked as potential sites before President Roosevelt decided on the plot of the recently closed Washington-Hoover Airport.

The breaking of ground for the new headquarters occurred on 11 September 1941. Several concessions to wartime circumstances were made in the construction process. Principally, the architects employed limited use of steel, which was then in short supply. This meant, for instance, that ramps were built between floors rather than lifts being installed. The Pentagon's basic fabric is reinforced concrete, with Indiana limestone used on the façade (Roosevelt forbade the use of Italian marble). The

site was conveniently located on what was essentially waste ground and swampland by the Potomac River, which was dredged for sand and gravel to be used in cement-making.

The building rises 23 metres (75 ft) into the air and each side is 281 metres (922 ft) in length, covering an area of 14 hectares (34 acres) including the central courtyard and providing work space for 24,000 employees. It consists of five concentric pentagons of five floors each, joined by ten interconnecting 'spoke' corridors. There are more than 28 kilometres (17 miles) of corridors, yet the clever design means that no two points are more than seven minutes' walk apart. The original construction phase took only 16 months, and was completed at a cost of US$83 million. When it was officially opened on 15 January 1943, the Pentagon consolidated some 17 Department of War offices.

In 1998, the Pentagon Renovation Program began – the first major overhaul in the building's history. Work

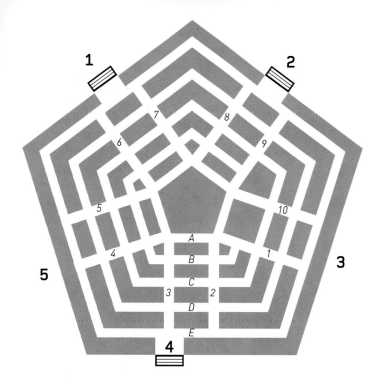

was carried out in phases over 13 years, and among its provisions were the installation of improved security systems and steel reinforcements to strengthen the building's concrete structure. Blast-resistant windows were also fitted.

On 11 September 2001, exactly 60 years to the day after ground was broken for the building of the Pentagon, the hijacked American Airlines Flight 77 was crashed into its west side. The attack killed all 64 people on the flight (including the five hijackers) plus 125 office workers. It has been suggested that the death toll could have been much higher, but for the fact that many staff were not occupying their normal offices because of the planned renovations. Somewhat ironically, the Pentagon's central courtyard was informally known as 'Ground Zero' prior to the 11 September attacks, since it was always assumed that the complex would be a key target in any Cold War Soviet missile attack.

While always of high importance, the 2001 attack served only to further focus concentration on security. In early 2002, the Defense Department established the Pentagon Force Protection Agency (PFPA), a direct successor to the Federal Protective Service and the United States Special Policemen. While focusing on law enforcement, the PFPA's remit has extended to include security, surveillance, crisis-prevention and anti-terrorism operations around the complex. The first line of defence for the Pentagon and its environs is the PFPA's Pentagon Police.

Other security measures added in recent years include the removal of all direct access into the Pentagon from the Metrorail station that serves it, and the filtering of road traffic away from the building. Members of the public are permitted to tour the Pentagon but must book a time in advance, undergo a security screening, provide identification and pass through metal detectors.

The highly secret work done inside the Pentagon continues to mould the world around us and set the geo-political agenda. From here, wars are fought and, thankfully more often, avoided. It remains the intention of the Department of Defense to avoid turning the Pentagon into a fortress, isolated from the public that it is there to serve. But the experience of 2001 has ensured that even if it doesn't look like a fortress, its defences are just as difficult to breach.

27 # The Oval Office

LOCATION The White House, Washington, DC, USA
NEAREST POPULATION HUB Washington, DC
SECRECY OVERVIEW High-security location: the American President's office and the heart of US government.

The Oval Office is synonymous with the American presidency to such an extent that it is often used as shorthand for the presidency itself. Famous around the world as the setting for countless presidential addresses and for its depiction on television and film (has there ever been a more noble occupant than President Jed Bartlett of *The West Wing*?), only a select few ever get to see the room in real life.

The Oval Office is the principal office of the President of the United States and, perhaps above any other location, can claim to be the central hub of US government. It covers about 76 square metres (820 sq ft) and is located on the first floor of the West Wing of the White House, at 1600 Pennsylvania Avenue NW. Its location offers the Commander-in-Chief easy access not only to the most important members of his staff but also to his residential quarters.

The first Oval Office was built in 1909, according to designs drawn up by Nathan C. Wyeth for then-president William Howard Taft. Originally, it was decorated in a vivid green. After the office was gutted by fire in 1929, President Herbert Hoover oversaw a refurbishment that included the installation of air conditioning for the first time.

However, the Oval Office of today was designed by Eric Gugler as part of the major West Wing expansion undertaken by President Franklin D. Roosevelt in 1934. At this time, the room was moved from its previously central location within the wing to the southeast corner.

Architecturally, the room references a range of traditions, including Georgian, baroque and neoclassical styles. Access is via any of four doors, with the east door opening out onto the picturesque Rose Garden.

Roosevelt worked closely with Gugler on many of the office's design features, including an instantly recognizable ceiling medallion that incorporates elements of the Presidential Seal. While many presidents have gone in for a little redecorating, few have tampered excessively with its iconic features, such as the large south-facing bow windows (though during the Cold War, these windows are said to have been fitted with devices to hinder Soviet eavesdropping through detection of vibrations caused by sound waves impacting on the panes). Most have made do with little more than an update of the famous carpet, which has always featured the Presidential Seal since the days of Harry Truman.

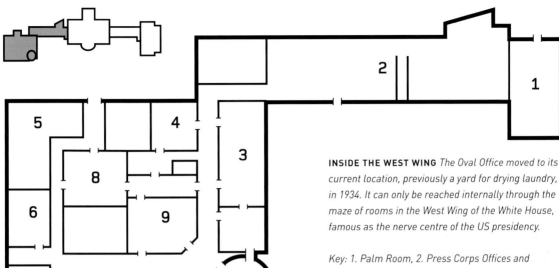

INSIDE THE WEST WING *The Oval Office moved to its current location, previously a yard for drying laundry, in 1934. It can only be reached internally through the maze of rooms in the West Wing of the White House, famous as the nerve centre of the US presidency.*

Key: 1. Palm Room, 2. Press Corps Offices and briefing room, 3. Cabinet Room, 4. Press Secretary, 5. National Security Advisor, 6. Vice President, 7. Chief of Staff, 8. Lobby, 9. Roosevelt Room, 10. Oval Office.

For much of its history, the White House was remarkably open to its citizens. As recently as the 1990s tenure of Bill Clinton, an occasional open-house policy operated. However, the threat of attack has ensured that security considerations have long taken precedence.

The White House itself is surrounded by a perimeter fence, with the entire complex under the protection of the United States Park Police and the Secret Service. In recent years, road traffic has been diverted away from the building and there are police barricades in several surrounding streets. The White House airspace is a strict no-go area for unauthorized aircraft, and the skies around Pennsylvania Avenue are vigilantly guarded by a Norwegian Advanced Surface-to-Air Missile System. Other security systems (including radar and bullet-proof windows) are regularly reviewed and updated.

Yet for all of the White House's security provisions (or perhaps because of them – some people like nothing better than a challenge), there has been no shortage of interlopers over the years. For instance, in 1974 alone there were two major incidents. In the first, an army private stole a helicopter and landed it on the White House lawn. Then, on Christmas Day, a man with a Messiah-complex crashed his car through the perimeter fencing and ran towards the building itself, telling negotiators (falsely as it turned out) that he was wearing explosives.

Fast forward 20 years to 1994, and a light aircraft crash-landed in the grounds while apparently headed for the building itself. A couple of months later saw the attempted assassination of Bill Clinton when an attacker fired 29 rifle rounds at the White House from the perimeter fence. Even after security was upped in light of the 11 September 2001 attacks, intruders have scaled the fence and generally made a nuisance of themselves on several occasions. None, though, has ever made it into the Oval Office.

28 Centralia

LOCATION Columbia County, Pennsylvania, USA

NEAREST POPULATION HUB Philadelphia, Pennsylvania

SECRECY OVERVIEW Access restricted: a former mining town left to burn for 50 years.

Centralia was once a thriving mining town, with a population of 2,000 or more. But in 1962, a fire broke out underground. After fire-fighting attempts failed, the decision was taken to let the blaze burn itself out – a process that may take another 250 years. That left little future for Centralia, whose population now hovers around ten. For those left behind, it is a town their government has chosen to forget.

Centralia was laid out in 1854, and was originally called Centreville until 1865, when the post office insisted on a change of name to avoid confusion with another Centreville already in the area. For a century, the town relied on its anthracite coal mines for employment. Then came a fateful night in May 1962 when local sanitation workers burnt rubbish over an old mine entrance, igniting the coal that lay below.

Several attempts were made to stem the blaze, but all failed or were deemed economically unviable. As the fire continued to burn, air quality in the area declined, and numerous residents reported the damaging effects of high carbon monoxide and carbon dioxide levels. Despite this, up until 1981 there was still a resident population of about a thousand. That year, however, a young boy fell down a sinkhole that opened suddenly in the ground, and was almost killed amid a cocktail of noxious fumes. It was clear that something more needed to be done to safeguard the town's citizens.

In 1984, the federal government set aside a budget of US$42 million for the relocation of Centralia's citizens. Most of the townsfolk took the money on offer, and moved out to other nearby neighbourhoods. A few doughty souls decided to stick it out, however, and in 1992, the government opted to claim legal powers over Centralia and condemn its remaining buildings. A decade later the post office, which had once insisted on the town's name change, withdrew Centralia's postcode altogether. Then in 2009, Pennsylvania's State Governor began to evict the last remaining population. Centralia, it seemed, was simply to be erased from the record.

Yet still a few houses remain occupied, amid scattered signs warning of the underground fire and of land collapses. Smoke and sulphurous steam can still be seen emerging eerily from the ground in places, including sections of Route 61 that used to serve the town. Alas, the road into Centralia is now closed for business.

Columbia County,
Pennsylvania

ROAD TO HELL
Smoke still seeps from fissures in the tarmac of Pennsylvania's Route 61, some 50 years after Centralia's underground coal reserves were first accidentally ignited. The town long ago stopped receiving traffic in any significant volume.

Mount Carmel

Anstes

Centralia township

HOLY SMOKE *The Assumption of the Blessed Virgin Mary Ukrainian Catholic Church sits on a hillside overlooking the main part of Centralia. The church celebrated its centenary in 2011, bringing a swell of people to the usually deserted town to take part in a commemorative mass.*

Ashland

Harvey Point Defense Testing Activity Facility

LOCATION Perquimans County, North Carolina, USA
NEAREST POPULATION HUB Hertford, North Carolina
SECRECY OVERVIEW Existence unacknowledged: a suspected CIA training school.

Originally built by the US government as a Navy airbase, recent decades have seen a great deal of speculation as to Harvey Point's current purpose. The *New York Times*, among numerous other respectable newspapers, believes that it has been used as a secret paramilitary and counter-terrorism training centre, operated by the CIA, since the early 1960s.

Harvey Point is named after the well-to-do Harvey family, who first settled here in the 1670s and provided North Carolina with its first governor. In 1942 the 490–hectare (1,200-acre) site was transformed into an air station, from where seaplanes flew during the Second World War. In the late 1950s, the base briefly became the testing centre for an ill-fated long distance bomber project, but in 1961, the Navy closed off pubic access to Harvey Point and announced that it would henceforth be used as a weapons testing facility.

In 1975, a Presidential Commission on CIA Activities revealed that the agency had been using Harvey Point for training both domestic and foreign personnel in bomb detection and disposal. Interest in CIA activities at the base increased over the years that followed. In 1998, the *New York Times* reported that, during the previous decade, the CIA had provided counter-terrorism training at Harvey Point and elsewhere to a total of 18,000 foreign intelligence officers from some 50 countries.

Today, the facility is surrounded by a 40-kilometre (25-mile) no-fly zone, and all civilian staff are sworn to secrecy about what happens there. No land records for the site have been made available since 1942, and the base is surrounded by security fencing, while thick enclaves of cypress trees offer further defence from prying eyes. However, locals have reported seeing helicopters and buses with blacked-out windows regularly arriving and leaving. There have also been numerous complaints of loud explosions – occasionally strong enough to shake nearby houses and rattle windows. It has been speculated that these are controlled explosions conducted during simulated terrorism training exercises.

Some commentators have even alleged that Harvey Point alumni include individuals who have since used the skills they were taught here against American interests. Assuming that there really is a CIA training centre at Harvey Point, it is a school whose graduates do little to advertise their qualifications.

Federal Reserve Bank of New York's vaults

LOCATION New York City, USA

NEAREST POPULATION HUB New York City, New York

SECRECY OVERVIEW High-security location: home to the world's largest accumulation of gold.

One of a dozen regional banks in the US Federal Reserve System, the New York 'Fed' is housed in a 22-storey concrete and limestone edifice, in lower Manhattan. But the really interesting stuff is underground – for that is where the gold vaults are hidden. As of 2008, the Bank stored 5.6 million kilograms (216 million troy ounces) of the shiny stuff, equating to over a fifth of the world's official monetary gold reserves.

Designed by Philip Sawyer and built at a cost of US$23 million, the Federal Reserve's present site at 33, Liberty Street opened in 1924. The vaults lie on the bedrock of Manhattan Island, some 24 metres (80 ft) below street level and 15 metres (50 ft) below sea level. The bedrock here was considered to be one of the few places where it was possible to lay foundations strong enough to support the vault and its contents. The vault walls themselves are made from steel-reinforced concrete.

The value of the initial gold deposits in the Fed totalled some US$26 million. and by 2011 they were estimated at US$411 billion. The vast majority of the Bank's holdings belong to the central banks of foreign nations, though the identity of each deposit's owner is kept on a strictly need-to-know basis.

Uniformed guards keep the Bank and its vaults safe, and must annually prove their skill with firearms on the Bank's own firing range. CCTV and electronic surveillance systems record all goings-on within the walls, while a central control room receives alerts every time the vault is opened or closed. Should an alarm be triggered, security staff can seal off the entire building in less than half a minute.

Access to the vaults is not by a traditional door but via a short passageway, cut through an upright steel cylinder that revolves through 90 degrees around its vertical axis within a steel and concrete frame. A variety of time and combination locks govern when the vaults can be opened, and no single employee is in possession of all the codes.

The gold itself is stored in 122 separate compartments in the main and auxiliary vaults. When new bars are deposited – laid down in an overlapping, brick-wall design – the relevant compartment is locked with a padlock, two combination locks and an auditor's seal. Storage is free, but the Bank charges a per-bar fee for moving the gold. It's safe to assume that few of the depositors face major problems in paying for this service.

MANHATTAN LANDMARK
The New York Fed at 33 Liberty Street on Manhattan Island is the largest of a dozen US Federal Reserve Banks. While top-level economic policy might be decided in Washington, DC, the Big Apple is still the beating heart of the US financial system.

Manhattan

Hudson River

TEMPLE OF CAPITALISM
The Bank moved to its current downtown location in 1924, in a building designed by York & Sawyer architects. Occupying a city block all of its own, the construction's neo-Renaissance facades were to influence bank design for decades.

East River

Governors Island

31

AT&T Long Lines Building

LOCATION Thomas Street, New York City, USA
NEAREST POPULATION HUB New York City, New York
SECRECY OVERVIEW High-security location: a communications hub that is among the most secure buildings in all New York.

Tourists walking the streets of New York frequently spend much of the time craning their necks to stare up at the jungle of skyscrapers that soar into the heavens above. However, 33 Thomas Street is a tower unlike any of the others – with 29 floors rising 170 metres (550 ft) towards the clouds, it certainly has stature. But a second glance reveals its most remarkable feature – a complete lack of windows.

Nestled in the Tribeca district of Manhattan and owned by the AT&T telecommunications company, the building was designed by John Carl Warnecke & Associates and was completed in 1974. Its purpose was to house telephone switching equipment and it plays a crucial role in the smooth running of the American telephone system, as well as air traffic control for a large part of the country. While it retains these functions, it now also operates as a secure data-storage centre.

In Warnecke, the building was blessed to have one of the more notable architects of 20th-century America. By the time he turned his attention to Thomas Street, he was already well known as a favourite of the Kennedy clan. Having initially made his name in Chicago, he was responsible for such high-profile designs as the grave site of John F. Kennedy at Arlington, consecrated in 1967.

Perhaps his greatest gift, and one conspicuously evident in the AT&T Long Lines Building, was to marry beauty with the most functional requirements. To contain all the necessary technical equipment, each floor of the Thomas Street building measures around 6 metres (20 ft) high, about twice the height of floors in a standard skyscraper. The building is considered a fine example of Brutalist architecture, with its exterior consisting of huge precast concrete panels adorned with pink Swedish granite facades. In a city dominated by glass, you might think that it would stand out as some sort of monstrosity, but in fact it blends discreetly into its environment.

More importantly, it is an incredibly resilient structure. It was designed so that it could be self-sufficient for up to a fortnight in the event of a nuclear attack, and its floors are reinforced to withstand up to 1.5 tonnes of pressure per square metre (300 lb per sq ft). It is a construction of rare strength, as you might expect for one so crucial to the nation's communications systems. And of course, no one is going to break in through an open window.

The Tomb
Yale University

LOCATION Yale University, Connecticut, USA
NEAREST POPULATION HUB New Haven, Connecticut
SECRECY OVERVIEW Access restricted: headquarters of the notorious Skull and Bones Society.

Of all the secret societies associated with American universities, none is more famous than Skull and Bones, whose members meet in a building known as the Tomb. The society boasts a list of alumni that includes some of the most influential people on the planet, leading some commentators to see Skull and Bones as a training camp for an all-powerful cabal.

The society was founded in 1832 by Alphonso Taft and William Huntington Russell as the Order of Skull and Bones. Its members, called Bonesmen, have been selected since 1879 by a process known as tapping. In this ceremony, held each April, the Society's senior figures walk among the members of Yale's junior class who gather on the grass at Branford College. Fifteen candidates who are considered to be the *crème de la crème* are then chosen by being tapped. Known members include several US presidents and assorted high-ranking figures from Wall Street and Washington.

The Tomb is the commonly used name for the Skull and Bones Meeting Hall, located on New Haven's High Street. It is an imposing, windowless, sandstone building in the Greco-Roman style. There is some debate as to the identity of its original architect, but the first wing was built in 1856, with a second following in 1903. Castellated towers from a condemned local brownstone building designed by A.J. Davis were added in 1911, forming a small courtyard.

The lack of windows begs the question of what lies inside, and reports suggest a somewhat overwrought gothic interior, the walls strewn with portraits of esteemed former members (George W. Bush being a recent addition), medieval armour and human and animal skeletons. It has been alleged that the Tomb also holds the stolen gravestone of Elihu Yale, one of the University's principal early benefactors, and the man after whom it was named. Another unproven rumour says that the Tomb contains the skeleton of the Apache chief Geronimo, pilfered in the early years of last century. A locked room, the Inner Temple, stores treasures including the Society's founding documents. Clocks in the Tomb are also said to be set five minutes fast, adding to the sense of isolation from the normal world.

Amid claims of mysterious initiation ceremonies, coded nicknames and oaths of secrecy – plus an unfaltering air of elitism – Skull and Bones seems an organization quite at ease with its exclusivity.

New Haven,
Connecticut

EXCLUSIVE CLUB
*The Skull and Bones
Meeting Hall stares
blank-faced onto the
High Street of New Haven,
Connecticut. Its imposing
design entirely hides the
interior from the view of
passers-by, which only
adds to the Society's
mysterious and semi-
mythological status.*

Mill River

Old Campus
Courtyard

Yale Campus

Yale University
Art Gallery

ONLY A NUMBER *The figure 322
in the Society's emblem has been
a subject of great debate. One
theory suggests a connection to the
death in 322 BC of the Greek orator,
Demosthenes.*

Long Wharf

33

Air Force One

LOCATION Stationed at Joint Base Andrews, Maryland, USA

NEAREST POPULATION HUB Washington, DC

SECRECY OVERVIEW High-security location: the US President's personal aircraft.

Strictly speaking, Air Force One is not an aircraft but merely the call-sign of any Air Force jet in which the President happens to be flying. In practice, however, it normally refers to either one of two Boeing 747-200 series jets (with tail numbers 28000 and 29000) that are at the President's disposal. As the 'flying White House', Air Force One is about as highly protected as a means of transport can be.

Franklin D. Roosevelt became the first serving President to travel by aeroplane on official business when in 1943 he flew to Casablanca, Morocco, to discuss the progress of the Second World War with Winston Churchill. Roosevelt's security advisers were unhappy at having to use commercial airliners with all their attendant security risks, and it was subsequently decided to convert a military plane for the President's use alone. While a suitable aircraft – nicknamed 'Sacred Cow' – was soon adapted, Roosevelt himself would use it only once, to reach the Yalta Conference of 1945.

In 1944, Roosevelt had established the Presidential Airlift Group as part of the White House Military Office. This group

FLYING WHITE HOUSE *This cutaway view of Air Force One reveals its two decks. Journalists, security personnel and guests sit towards the back of the plane while the President's suite nestles in the nose, in front of the President's office and a medical office. The conference room can be seen over the wing.*

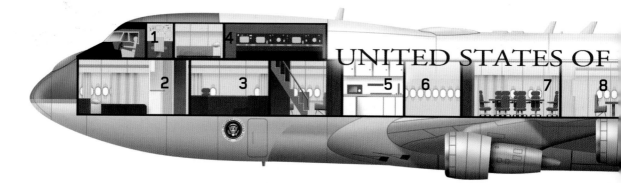

is responsible for maintaining and operating presidential aircraft to this day, working out of the Air Force's Joint Base Andrews in nearby Maryland. The designation 'Air Force One' itself did not come about until 1959, during the Presidency of Dwight Eisenhower. Three years later, John F. Kennedy became the first US president to use a jet aircraft, a customized Boeing 707.

The present Air Force One was widely featured in the media following the 11 September terrorist attacks of 2001. With his advisers uncertain of where best to keep him safe, President George W. Bush spent much of that day in the air. At one stage, his pilot would later reveal, there was real concern that the aircraft itself would come under attack.

The plane's facilities are split over three levels, providing over 370 square metres (4,000 sq ft) of floor space. With room for around 70 passengers on board, the guest list tends to be pretty exclusive, and anyone going aboard can expect to undergo stringent security screenings. Aside from the President, the passenger roster may include members of the

President's family and other specially invited guests. George W. Bush, for instance, occasionally took his pet cats and dogs for a spin.

As one might expect, the plane's plushest quarters are reserved for the President himself. His suite, which is towards the front of the jet, includes a bedroom, bathroom, office and mini-gym. There is plentiful office space for members of the presidential staff, as well as a fully functioning conference room. Meanwhile, selected journalists are permitted on most trips. The press pool typically numbers around 13, with the composition varying from flight to flight. Reuters keeps a designated correspondent and photographer on all presidential flights. Media personnel occupy a seating area accessed through the plane's rear door.

Aside from the pilot and co-pilot, there is a crew of some 26, selected from among the most highly regarded military personnel. The pilots themselves are at the very peak of their chosen profession. There is also a staff doctor who travels

Key: 1. Flight deck and crew area, 2. Presidential suite,
3. President's office, 4. Communications, 5. Main galley,
6. Senior staff, 7. Conference room, 8. Office staff,
9. Guest section, 10. Security staff,
11. Press and support crew seating.

28000

9   10   11

CRICA

IN-FLIGHT CONFERENCE *President Barack Obama meets with key members of his staff in Air Force One's conference room on 3 April 2009, during a short flight from the UK to France.*

everywhere with the President. Armed Secret Service agents, meanwhile, take responsibility for the aircraft's security: indeed, Air Force One claims the same degree of security and technology as the Oval Office. Even foreign dignitaries invited to accompany the President on a flight are not allowed access to every area of the aircraft.

Air Force One is equipped with its own anti-missile defence systems, and has infrared countermeasures situated around the tail and the engines, designed to confuse heat-seeking weapons. There is also shielding to protect the plane's electronics from an electromagnetic pulse attack. With over 350 kilometres (218 miles) of wiring on board, and some 85 telephones, all communications in and out are encrypted.

Before each flight, Secret Service agents check and seal the jet's fuel supplies, as well as inspecting the relevant runway for any safety risks. In the event of a threat to the President as he boards or disembarks the plane, agents have orders to shoot. Several agents fly ahead of Air Force One to safety-check the destination airport, where an armoured limousine is prepared for the President's transfer. One of the agents on board Air Force One is entrusted with 'the football' – the briefcase that contains the presidential nuclear activation codes. The jet always taxis to a halt with its left side facing towards any public areas, leaving the on-board presidential quarters as protected as possible.

In 2006 a rare – and thankfully low-level – security breach was reported when a detailed plan of the aircraft mistakenly appeared on the website of Robins Air Force Base in Georgia. Nonetheless, Air Force One is as secure as you could ever hope to be when you're flying in a tin can miles up in the sky.

The Oak Island Money Pit

34

LOCATION Southern Nova Scotia, Canada
NEAREST POPULATION HUB Halifax, Nova Scotia
SECRECY OVERVIEW Site of historic mystery: the legendary home of an unclaimed treasure trove.

In 1795, according to a long-standing Nova Scotian legend, 18-year-old Daniel McGinnis, investigating mysterious lights seen on the south-eastern part of Oak Island, found a depression in a clearing. Upon closer inspection he discovered a deep pit, apparently man-made. The so-called 'money pit' has been excavated regularly ever since, but all attempts to discover the secrets buried within have been thwarted.

Oak Island is one of several hundred uninhabited islands in Canada's Mahone Bay, 200 metres (660 ft) out to sea. It covers about 57 hectares (140 acres) and its highest point lies 11 metres (36 ft) above sea level. The island is privately owned, and permission must be gained before landing there.

After McGinnis made his discovery, he returned with two friends to begin excavating. They dug down through about 10 metres (33 ft), apparently uncovering a level of flagstones and then layers of logs every 3 metres (10 ft) or so. There were also marks in the pit wall, seemingly made by a pickaxe – that is to say, evidence of a human hand.

Having exhausted themselves and found nothing, McGinnis and his cohorts left the dig. A group called the Onslow Company took up the gauntlet in 1803, digging to around 30 metres (100 ft). They too found regularly spaced layers of logs, along with sections of charcoal and coconut fibre. Most significantly, towards the end of the dig it was claimed that a stone was discovered, bearing a strange inscription of symbols. The stone later mysteriously went missing, but by then the symbols had supposedly been faithfully recorded on paper and were circulating among a number of treasure-seekers. One researcher eventually translated the inscription as 'forty feet below, two million pounds lie buried', though much mythology surrounds all aspects of this part of the story.

Alas for the Onslow Company, their work came to an end when the pit flooded. New attempts to make progress occurred frequently throughout the 19th century and into the 20th. In 1849, some gold chain links were said to have been found. The pit regularly flooded or collapsed over the years, and claimed its first life in an accident in the 1860s. Debate rages as to whether these floodings were the result of a purpose-built flood tunnel (quite a masterful feat of engineering if that is the case) or occurred naturally as a result of the island's peculiar geology and tidal pattern.

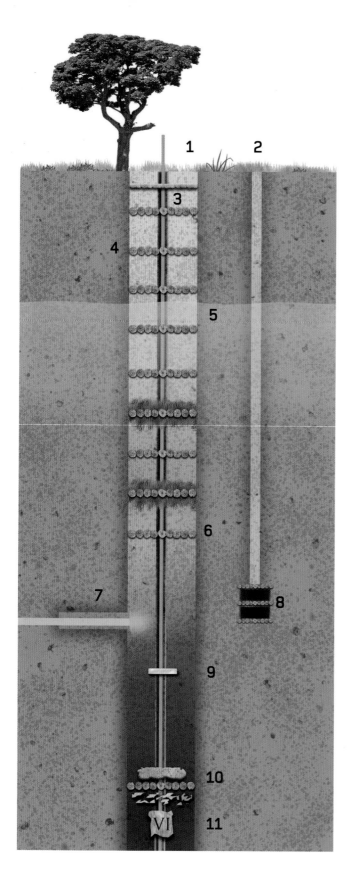

DEEP MYSTERY *Treasure hunters and archaeologists have dug down into the Money Pit for more than 200 years, with varying degrees of success.*

Key: 1. Top of original pit, dug in 1795, 2. Secondary shaft excavated in 1849, 3. Shaft dug through original pit in 1897, 4. Oak platforms, 5. Level of 1804 flood, 6. Level at which inscribed stone was discovered in 1804, 7. Flood tunnel, 8. Layers of metal and wood discovered in 1849 shaft, 9. Iron sheet discovered in late 1890s, 10. Stone and wood layers at base of 1898 shaft, 11. Parchment fragment recovered from base of pit.

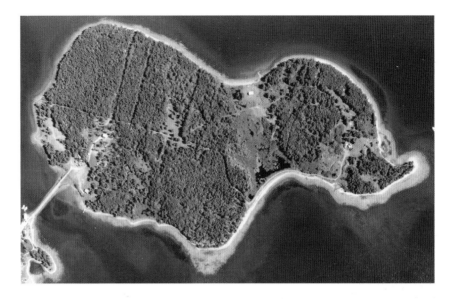

UNTOLD RICHES *The densely forested Oak Island has kept treasure hunters occupied for over two and a quarter centuries. Mahone Bay, in which the island sits, laps the east coast of Nova Scotia's Lunenburg County, and is a popular area for fishing and pleasure cruising.*

A team working under the name of the Old Gold Salvage Group got to work in 1909 and counted future US President Franklin D. Roosevelt among its number. A dig by William Chappell in 1931, meanwhile, took the pit down to 50 metres (165 ft), and came upon all sorts of artefacts, including a Cornish miner's pickaxe – but whether these dated from post-1795 excavations or an earlier date altogether is not certain. As the decades passed, increasing amounts of debris accumulated, and even the location and structure of the original shaft was becoming unclear.

In the late 1960s, a new company called Triton Alliance acquired most of the island, and by 1971 they had succeeded in descending to 72 metres (235 ft). This team claimed to have lowered cameras into a cavern beneath the pit, producing pictures they said showed evidence of wooden chests and human remains, though the images are not of sufficient quality to tell for sure. Legal wrangles and environmental concerns have held up new digs in recent decades, but the 2011 Oak Island Act allows the treasure hunt to continue under licence from the Canadian government.

There are several exotic theories as to what might lie at the bottom of the pit. Some say that it is the treasure of the pirate Captain Kidd, others the treasure of Edward Teach (better known as Blackbeard). The latter theory is reinforced by Blackbeard's public proclamation that he had buried his stash 'where none but Satan and myself can find it'. Other stories claim that it contains treasure found by Spanish sailors on a wrecked galleon, or that it houses riches moved by the British during the American Revolution or the Seven Years War. Still others suggest it is the lost treasure of the Knights Templar, or the jewellery of Marie Antoinette, smuggled out of Paris as the guillotine beckoned. And of course, wherever there is the promise of unknown treasure, there are those who speculate that it is nothing less than the Holy Grail itself.

Others, though, prefer a more rational solution. They do not believe the pit is a man-made construct at all but simply a natural sinkhole or underground cavern. What is for sure is that until there is conclusive evidence either way, the search for the secret treasure of the Oak Island Money Pit will go on.

Guantánamo Bay Detention Centre

LOCATION Guantánamo Province, southern Cuba
NEAREST POPULATION HUB Guantánamo, Cuba
SECRECY OVERVIEW Operations classified: home of a notorious US prison camp established after the attacks of 2001.

Established in 2002, following the terrorist attacks on the World Trade Center and the Pentagon, Guantánamo (sometimes known colloquially as Gitmo) was set up to detain terror suspects captured during fighting in Afghanistan and, later, Iraq. The US has come under international pressure to close it down, with human rights group Amnesty International describing it as 'the gulag of our times'.

There has been a US naval base on the banks of Guantánamo Bay ever since 1898, when the country took control of Cuba following the Spanish-American War. In 1902 Cuba won independence, and the following year its government agreed to lease Guantánamo Bay to the Americans in perpetuity (though the communist regime in place since the Cuban revolution of 1959 does not recognize the agreement as legal).

The naval base covers 120 square kilometres (46 sq miles) and is the only US base situated in a country with which it does not share diplomatic ties. After the 2001 attacks in New York, Washington and Philadelphia, George Bush famously declared a 'War on Terror' and set up a detention camp at Guantánamo for individuals considered a potential threat to American security. Natural defences including sea and surrounding swampland, combined with nearby minefields and a permanent military guard, makes Guantánamo one of the most secure detention facilities on the planet.

Many of the inmates held here were captured during US military action in Afghanistan and Iraq in the early 2000s, but a large number came from elsewhere, and were handed over by third parties in exchange for rewards. Guantánamo's main detention camp, Camp Delta – with room for over 600 prisoners and perched on a cliff overlooking the sea – opened in April 2002, taking over duties from Camp X-ray, which closed in the same month.

Images of manacled prisoners in orange jumpsuits, kneeling on the ground in outdoor cages as guards watched over them, rapidly became one of the most enduring images of the early 21st century – particularly among those concerned that Washington was dispensing with acceptable judicial practice in respect of terror suspects.

The Bush administration categorized the Guantánamo detainees as 'unlawful enemy combatants' – a status that denied them the rights of prisoners of war set out under the Geneva Convention but

UNITED STATES

ATLANTIC OCEAN

Florida

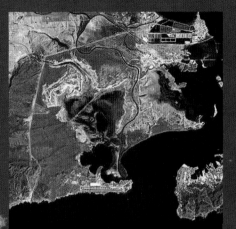

AMERICAN ENCLAVE *Surrounded by steep hills on all sides, Guantánamo is the largest bay on Cuba's southern coast. Christopher Columbus landed here in 1494 during his exploration of the 'New World', and it has been a de facto American possession, by virtue of a perpetual lease, since 1903.*

CUBA

CARIBBEAN SEA

CAMP DELTA
Joint Detention Group

Honor Bound to Defend Freedom

HARD TIME *Camp Delta, the permanent detention camp that replaced the temporary Camp X-ray in 2002, is divided into a number of sub-camps, with some running a moderately more relaxed regime than others. Nonetheless, conditions here remain a concern for human rights groups.*

did not require that they be put through the US criminal justice system. Instead, a system of military commissions was put into operation. According to Amnesty International, as of 2009 almost 800 prisoners had been held at the camp, but only 26 had been charged for trial by military commission and just three had been convicted.

Within a very short time of opening, Guantánamo was attracting international attention as inmates were held indefinitely without trial. There were also regular reports of alleged mistreatment, ranging from excessive use of solitary confinement to beatings, sleep deprivation, prolonged exposure to extreme noise and light, and mishandling of the Koran by guards. Some former inmates even alleged sexual degradation. The United Nations

called for the closure of the camp, but Washington insisted it was necessary for the defence of the nation and denied allegations of inhumane treatment.

The camp's defenders claim that it has produced intelligence key to preventing further terrorist attacks in the US and elsewhere. However, questions over techniques used to interrogate prisoners prompted a debate as to the definition of torture. For instance, there have been widespread claims that 'waterboarding' was used on certain inmates, in which an immobilized prisoner has water poured over them, causing them to feel like they are drowning.

Some have argued that waterboarding constitutes a form of coercion that falls outside the definition of torture, though many others – including President Obama – concluded that it does indeed qualify, rendering any intelligence it produces as without legal merit. (It should be noted that Donald Rumsfeld, the former US Secretary of Defense, has dismissed the allegations that waterboarding took place at the camp as a 'myth').

Guantánamo has been the subject of fierce courtroom debate for years, principally concerning the legal status of inmates. During his bid for the presidency in 2008, Barack Obama referred to the camp as a 'sad chapter in American history'. He would later say that his administration would have failed if within two years of coming to power it had not 'closed down Guantánamo in a responsible way, put a clear end to torture and restored a balance between the demands of our security and our constitution'. However, plans to transfer prisoners to high-security facilities on the US mainland met significant domestic opposition, and as of 2012 the camp was still operating.

WHO GOES THERE? *Detainees at Guantánamo are kept under constant surveillance by US military personnel. To date, there have been no recorded instances of escapes from the Cuban enclave. The chances of success for such an enterprise are minimal, given the camp's physical position and its state-of-the-art security systems.*

36 Snake Island

LOCATION Atlantic Ocean, off the coast of São Paulo State, Brazil
NEAREST POPULATION HUB São Paulo
SECRECY OVERVIEW Access restricted: a snake-infested island off-limits to visitors.

Lying just off the coast of Brazil, the island of Ilha da Queimada Grande is populated by a unique and highly venomous species of lancehead viper. Perhaps unsurprisingly, this small island has become known as Snake Island – an ophidiophobic's vision of hell, only doughty scientists and crazed adventurers dare set foot on its ground.

Snake Island is home to a vast colony of golden lancehead pit vipers (*Bothrops insularis*), among the most poisonous snakes on the planet. The golden lancehead is only to be found on this one particular island, so it is understandably rather protective of its territory. Its venom is about five times as potent as that of its cousin, the *fer-de-lance*, which is itself responsible for more South American snakebite deaths than any other species.

Just getting to the island, which covers about 45 hectares (110 acres), takes considerable determination. It is first necessary to cross a 30-kilometres

(19-mile) stretch of choppy water from the coast of the Brazilian state of São Paulo, and there are few local sea captains willing to make the trip. Once at the island, there is no beach to speak of, and access is via a steep, rocky slope covered in hand-mincing barnacles. All of which is somewhat academic, given that the Brazilian Navy expressly forbids civilians from landing there anyway. Only accredited scientists are occasionally given special dispensation to visit.

There are at least 5,000 snakes writhing around the place, with conservative estimates suggesting one for every square metre (10 sq ft): they have even taken over a now-defunct lighthouse. Being lighthouse keeper here surely ranked high among the worst jobs in the world. Legend has it that the last keeper lived there with his family until snakes got into their cottage. As they tried to flee, they were taken out one by one by vipers dangling from the branches of overhanging trees. Myth or not, the best advice is to leave their home as it is – a secret serpentine paradise.

Surtsey

LOCATION South of the Icelandic coast
NEAREST POPULATION HUB Reykjavik, Iceland
SECRECY OVERVIEW Access restricted: arguably the world's most pristine natural habitat, unspoilt by human intervention.

The North Atlantic island of Surtsey is among the planet's youngest places, having emerged from the sea during an underwater volcanic eruption that lasted from 1963 until 1967. The territory was quickly declared a nature reserve, and only a small band of accredited scientists has ever been allowed to land there to record how life on Earth spontaneously develops.

The infant island lies around 20 kilometres (12.5 miles) southwest of Heimaey, the largest of the Westman Islands. The first indications of a volcanic eruption underway here came on 14 November 1963, when changes in the surrounding water temperature, a rising plume of smoke and the smell of hydrogen sulphide were all observed. However, the eruption is thought to have begun several days earlier, some 130 metres (430 ft) beneath the sea.

The eruption followed the line of a tectonic fissure, and emerged from the sea in columns of dust and ash that reached heights of several kilometres. Within a week, an island had formed. It was named Surtsey, after Surtr the fire giant of Nordic mythology. Although the sea immediately began to erode some of its territory, continuing eruptions that added to the land mass more than kept pace. The island achieved its maximum diameter of more than 1,300 metres (4,300 ft) in the early part of 1964. Iceland quickly asserted dominion over it, and declared it a nature reserve.

By the time the eruptions came to an end in June 1967, Surtsey covered an area of 2.7 square kilometres (1 sq mile). It consisted of roughly two-thirds tephra (rock fragments thrown up during an eruption) and one-third rapidly cooling lava. While the tephra has gradually washed away over the years, the hard lava core has proved far more resilient. It has been estimated that the wind-battered island will not be returned to the sea before 2100 at the earliest, and it may survive for several centuries. However, two smaller sister islands that appeared during the original eruption were soon eroded to nothing by the Atlantic waves.

Scientists were quick to realize that Surtsey offered a unique opportunity to study geological and biological evolution on virgin land. If man can be kept at bay, the island's remote location means there are few threats to its well-being other than the sea itself. The first vascular plant was discovered as early as 1965, although the first bush, an altogether more complex and demanding form of

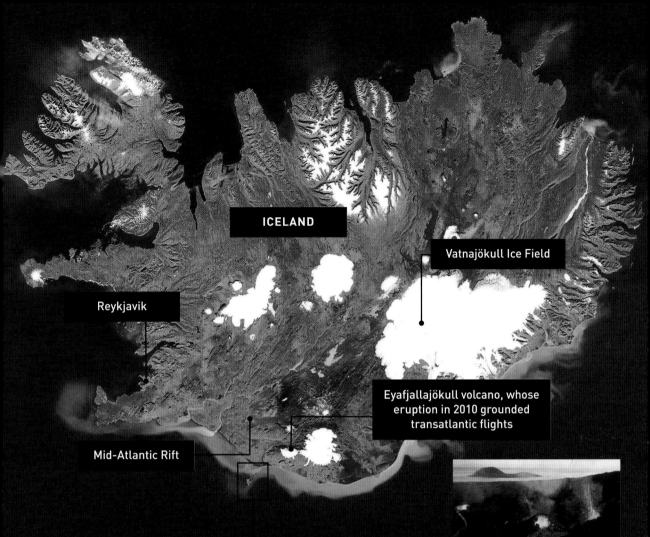

ICELAND

Vatnajökull Ice Field

Reykjavik

Eyafjallajökull volcano, whose
eruption in 2010 grounded
transatlantic flights

Mid-Atlantic Rift

VOLCANIC ISLAND
*Surtsey's geography
has changed
considerably since it
first emerged from
the sea. For instance,
it lost about a metre
in height in the 20
years following the
original eruption. The
island is still subject
to volcanic activity,
as evidenced in the
close-up photo.*

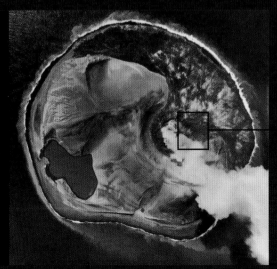

LONELY OUTPOST *The only concession to mankind on the island is a rudimentary hut that serves as home to visiting scientific personnel. It is administered by the Surtsey Research Society, which works hard to ensure that the landscape remains unspoiled for the species that have gradually colonized it.*

plant life, was not to appear until 1998. The island's poor-quality soil was quickly improved by the guano from birds that started flocking there around 1970. The first resident bird species were the fulmar and guillemot, and the soil can now support complex life forms, such as earthworms. Seals started breeding on Surtsey in 1983.

As for humans, landing on the island is strictly forbidden, unless you are a scientist who has been awarded a permit by the Surtsey Research Society, which supervises all activity on the island on behalf of the Icelandic Environment and Food Agency. Diving in the island's environs is not allowed, nor is disturbing any of its natural features, introducing any organisms, soils or minerals, or leaving any waste. It is also forbidden to discharge a firearm within 2 kilometres (1.2 miles) of the coast.

While most of the species so far found on Surtsey have clearly been brought here by natural 'vectors', human-imported crops were discovered (and promptly removed) on two occasions during the 1970s. In the first instance, a tomato

plant was found: it is thought that a researcher must have had a hearty lunch and then been caught short, prompting an instance of unregulated seed dispersal! In 1977 a crop of potatoes was discovered dug into the ground, and the finger of blame was firmly pointed at some spirited young boys from the nearby Westman Islands who had rowed out to Surtsey during the spring.

The island was inscribed on UNESCO's list of World Heritage Sites in 2008. By 2004, the assorted life recorded on the island included 69 vascular plants, 71 lichen, 24 fungi, 14 bird species and 335 species of invertebrates. In 2009 it was widely reported that a Golden Plover was found nesting on the island, the first wading bird to do so. Each year, somewhere between two and five new species are discovered.

The one nod to human comforts is a basic prefabricated hut where scientific researchers are stationed. It contains little more than a few bunks, a solar panel to produce energy and a radio for use in emergencies. There is also a dartboard to provide entertainment.

The Royal Mint

LOCATION Llantrisant, South Wales
NEAREST POPULATION HUB Cardiff, Wales
SECRECY OVERVIEW High-security location: where people literally make money.

Since the late 1960s, responsibility for minting all of the UK's money has fallen on the Royal Mint's operations at Llantrisant in South Wales. Able to produce 5 billion coins each year, it is now the world's leading exporting Mint as well, manufacturing coins for some 60 other countries. With all that cash floating around, it is no surprise that the Mint does not welcome uninvited guests.

The Royal Mint was established as early as AD 886, and by the 16th century was the sole producer of coinage in the realm. By that time, its home had long been at the Tower of London. One of the Bank's most famous Masters was Sir Isaac Newton, who held the post from 1699–1727 and did a great deal to combat the counterfeiting of coins that was rife at the time.

In 1809, the Mint relocated to new premises at East Smithfield in London, where there was far more room to accommodate the large, state-of-the-art mechanical coin presses then being introduced. However, by the 1960s even this location was becoming inadequate. With decimalization scheduled to come into force in 1971, it was decided that a new site would have to be found to cope with producing the mass of new coins and notes due to come into circulation. Areas in the northeast of England and near Glasgow in Scotland were rejected in favour of the green, green grass of Llantrisant, tucked into a corner of the Rhondda Valley. Some

have rather unkindly described it as 'the hole with a Mint' – a play on the famous advertising slogan for Polo mints: 'the mint with a hole'.

Queen Elizabeth II officially opened the Mint's new home at Llantrisant in 1968. The last coin to be minted in London was produced in 1975, and all the Mint's operations have been in Wales since 1980. Llantrisant is also home to the Mint's museum of more than 70,000 coins, which although not open to the public, actively participates in putting on displays elsewhere.

Covering around 12 hectares (30 acres), the Llantrisant site employs more than 750 people and cost £8.5 million to build. Its buildings are clad in panels of lightweight concrete that sit on brick podiums. The site is surrounded by perimeter fencing and there is a permanent deployment of armed Ministry of Defence Police. You could try crossing their palms with silver, but in a place already full of coinage, don't rely on it making much impact.

Guardian Telephone Exchange

LOCATION Subterranean Manchester, Lancashire, England
NEAREST POPULATION HUB Manchester
SECRECY OVERVIEW Access restricted: a long-secret communications network beneath the city streets.

Originally constructed in the 1950s during the Cold War, this complex of underground tunnels was designed with a view to safeguarding communications in the event of a nuclear strike. It mirrored similar enterprises undertaken in other major British cities such as London and Birmingham. Today the tunnels house a vast network of telephone cabling, though rumours about the Exchange's exact status continue.

The tunnels that housed the Exchange are thought to cover around 3 kilometres (1.8 miles), stretching from Manchester's city centre to the Ardwick and Salford areas. The complex was built in 1954 by a workforce consisting largely of Polish immigrants. It was said to be able to withstand an atom bomb blast equivalent to that which befell Hiroshima, and in its heyday was reputedly staffed constantly, equipped with its own water supplies, food and emergency generators capable of sustaining a small workforce for several weeks.

Constructed at a depth of 35 metres (115 ft), the tunnels are about 2 metres (80 in) in diameter. The main entrance was purported to be on George Street, beneath a huge concrete slab designed to offer blast protection. The enterprise cost somewhere in the region of £4 million (partly funded by NATO partners) and included such luxuries as a recreation room for staff, complete with pool table and piano. The Exchange's existence was only acknowledged in 1968, and it was subsequently abandoned by its troglodyte population in the 1970s, when it was then given over to telecommunications cabling.

In 2004, an electrical fire broke out during refurbishment of the tunnels, knocking out some 130,000 telephone lines in the northwest of England. A few conspiracy theorists barked that this was somehow evidence of a government-inspired information blackout, though most regard such a notion as fanciful. A year later, theft of equipment from the tunnels sparked a full-scale terror alert (the break-in followed shortly after the 2005 terrorist attacks on London).

While there is little to suggest that the tunnels are used today for anything other than running cables, official information regarding the network's extent and access points remains sketchy. This lack of transparency has led some to suspect that the complex could be reactivated if required. Others, however, hold that it is nothing more than a Cold War relic, unsuitable for human access on health and safety grounds.

Government Communications Headquarters

LOCATION Cheltenham, Gloucestershire, England
NEAREST POPULATION HUB Cheltenham
SECRECY OVERVIEW Operations classified: home of the branch of the British intelligence service known as GCHQ.

The Government Communications Headquarters (GCHQ) facility, operating under the remit of the UK's Joint Intelligence Committee, is responsible for providing the British government and armed forces with intelligence by monitoring and intercepting communications throughout the world. It is housed at a highly secure complex known as 'the Doughnut'.

GCHQ can trace its roots to 1919, when the Government Code and Cypher School (GCCS) was established as a code-breaking body. During the Second World War, GCCS was based at Bletchley Park near London, where it was involved in the crucial and highly secretive effort to break the German Enigma and Lorenz cyphers, developing some of the first automated computers in the process. Details of this work only emerged into the public domain decades later. In 1946, the organization was renamed as GCHQ and relocated to Eastcote in London until 1951, when it moved to a split site (Oakley and Benhall) at Cheltenham, Gloucestershire.

GCHQ faced twin challenges in the 1990s. Firstly, the end of the Cold War brought into question its very reason for being. Secondly, the internet posed new technological challenges. However, the 'War on Terror' ushered in by the attacks of 11 September 2001 gave it a new purpose, and GCHQ staff now exert as much energy monitoring emails and chat rooms or surveying the output of websites as they ever did on intercepting phone calls and postal mail.

To cope in this new era, GCHQ moved into custom-built premises at Benhall in 2003. The circular, steel-reinforced building – which cost £337 million to build – soon garnered the affectionate nickname of 'the Doughnut'. However, that may make it sound like a much more inviting place than it actually is.

Within its walls, a staff of 5,500 is focused on identifying and monitoring potential threats to national security. Specific details of the work undertaken are highly classified, with members of staff not even permitted to divulge their surnames. Attempted visits by members of the public are not well received (a boundary fence is regularly patrolled and kept under constant surveillance) and external telephone calls are not normally connected unless the caller has a specific name or extension number to offer the operator. In other words, they have far more ability to monitor you than you do to monitor them.

LISTENING POST *GCHQ's satellite ground station at Bude on the north coast of Cornwall in southwestern England is littered with radar dishes and domes. The base, on the site of the Second World War airfield RAF Cleave, is alleged to be part of the ECHELON signals intelligence network.*

HOME SWEET HOME *GCHQ's move into 'the Doughnut' in 2003 consolidated staff from some 50 smaller offices spread across Cheltenham. The new complex is constructed from concrete, glass, steel and Cotswold stone and incorporates an underground road for the secure delivery of sensitive materials.*

Defence Science and Technology Laboratory
Porton Down

LOCATION Porton Down, Wiltshire, England
NEAREST POPULATION HUB Salisbury, Wiltshire
SECRECY OVERVIEW Operations classified: home of a controversial government biological and chemical research centre.

One of Britain's most secretive research sites, the laboratory at Porton Down, has been a focus of chemical and biological warfare research for almost a century. It has been accused of carrying out unauthorized experiments on servicemen, leading to an unspecified number of fatalities and claims of long-term serious medical conditions among veterans.

The First World War was the first to see widescale use of gas as an offensive weapon. Work on Britain's chemical weapons capability began in a few scattered huts on the downs close to the quiet Wiltshire village of Porton in March 1916. Initially known as the War Department Experimental Ground, the centre has undergone numerous name changes over its life, and since 2001 has been called the Defence Science and Technology Laboratory (Dstl), Porton Down. It is ultimately answerable to the Ministry of Defence.

From the outset, the Porton Down establishment relied on volunteers from the armed services for assistance in its research. In its earliest days, the facility was principally engaged in work on chlorine, phosgene and mustard gas. While much of the early focus was on developing these offensive weapons, since the 1950s the laboratory claims to have been engaged only in research to establish the hazards of chemical warfare, in order to develop suitable defensive strategies.

However, Porton Down's post-Second World War testing programme was to culminate decades later in legal arguments over alleged unethical practices: in short, the laboratory was accused of recklessly endangering British servicemen by exposing them to highly dangerous chemical agents without their full knowledge.

Perhaps the single most infamous case concerned the death of Leading Aircraftman Ronald Maddison on 6 May 1953. Maddison, just 20 years old, had a nerve agent, Sarin, dripped onto his skin and died as a result. Maddison had been led to believe that he was taking part in an experiment to find a cure for the common cold (volunteers reportedly received a £2 fee and three days of extra leave) but a closed inquest held shortly after his death returned a verdict of 'misadventure'. It was only in 2004, following a lengthy campaign by members of his family, that the inquest was reopened, this time returning a verdict of unlawful death.

Andover–Salisbury
railway line

Dstl Facility

Tetricus Science Park

Edge of 2,800-
hectare (7,000-acre)
Test Range

Health Protection
Agency Facilities

CABINET OF CURIOSITIES

Porton Down is one of a select group of institutions operating facilities with the maximum biosafety rating of 4. Researchers work at sealed, air-filtered cabinets, inserting their arms into specially fitted gloves to avoid contact with harmful elements.

PERFECT CHEMISTRY *Troops modelling the latest in chemical warfare suits and hardware at Porton Down in 1988. While questions about historic conduct at the facility linger, few doubt that it has played a crucial role in protecting British forces serving in disparate theatres of war over the years.*

Other disturbing cases include volunteers being given the hallucinogen LSD during the 1950s, causing long-running mental problems for some. In the following decade, a vehicle left the facility and drove through local villages to the outskirts of Bristol, depositing zinc cadmium sulphide into the atmosphere as it went. It was part of an experiment to see how a germ cloud might spread, but while the scientists involved were equipped with protective suits and gas masks, the local population had no such precautions. Authorities would later insist the release represented 'no danger to public health'.

The suspicion that Porton Down has regularly used unknowing human guinea pigs for experimentation has proved difficult to shift. In 1999, Bruce George, Chairman of the House of Commons Defence Committee, admitted the facility's operations were '... too big for us to know... there are many things happening there that I'm not even certain Ministers are fully aware of, let alone Parliamentarians.' Yet In the period 1916–2008, more than 25,000 servicemen are thought to have undergone tests at the facility. In 2008, the Ministry of Defence paid £3 million in compensation to a group of 369 who had brought a joint action against the government, claiming that tests carried out over a period of several decades had left them with permanent health problems. Their allegations included claims of exposure to mustard gas, nerve gas and tear gas.

The Porton Down site has a footprint of 2,800 hectares (7,000 acres) and is among the most highly secure in the Ministry of Defence's portfolio. In an age when the threat of terrorists using biological or chemical agents has never been greater, it is unlikely that the Dstl will open its doors to closer scrutiny in the near future.

Many others told similar stories of having unknown substances dripped on their arms until their skin blistered or reddened, at which point ointments were applied. Others have spoken of being herded into gas chambers. A common thread is that volunteers were not made aware of the specific risks to which they were being exposed. Many have subsequently discovered that their service records show no evidence of their ever having even been at Porton Down.

42 RAF Menwith Hill

LOCATION North Yorkshire, England

NEAREST POPULATION HUB Harrogate

SECRECY OVERVIEW Operations classified: a US-run base purported to be part of the ECHELON surveillance system.

RAF Menwith Hill is a base belonging to the UK Ministry of Defence, but made available to the US Department of Defense, who are responsible for many elements of its running. As part of America's global defence communications network, Menwith's stated mission is to provide intelligence support for the United States, UK and their allied interests. However, some question the extent of its powers.

Built on land owned by the British War Office, RAF Menwith Hill became operational in 1960, at which time it was known as Menwith Hill Station. The nearest town is Harrogate, a well-to-do spa town whose genteel air is about as far from an atmosphere of international subterfuge as you could hope to get.

From the beginning, however, Menwith Hill was staffed by US military personnel under the remit of the US Army Security Agency. In 1966, the US National Security Agency (NSA) took over administration. Today, the base primarily serves as an NSA field station, with US staff working alongside employees of the Ministry of Defence and GCHQ (see page 104).

GOLF BALLS *The radomes (a portmanteau of radar and dome) at Menwith Hill give the station the appearance of a huge golf driving range. There are now more than 30 such domes at the base, and the technology they contain is allegedly crucial to the smooth running of the purported ECHELON signals intelligence network.*

Menwith Hill has always been at the technological cutting edge, and in its early days was used to monitor communications coming out of the Soviet bloc. It was also an early adopter of IBM computer technology. Today, the site is home to large numbers of multi-faceted radar domes or 'radomes' (there are currently more than 30), crucial to the ability of the US and UK to intercept and monitor communications. The US National Reconnaissance Office (NRO) – established in 1961 and based in Virginia, with responsibility for building and running spy satellites – also has a permanent presence on site.

Menwith Hill is widely believed to form part of the fabled ECHELON global surveillance network. ECHELON is said to be able to 'eavesdrop' on all types of modern communication, from telephone conversations to email exchanges. It is alleged that the network operates under the agreement of the governments of Britain, the US, Australia, Canada and New Zealand. A 2001 report by the European Parliament into the alleged network concluded that Menwith Hill was its single biggest facility.

While the gathering of such information to thwart terrorism or organized crime may seem attractive, many fear that other information gleaned can be too easily abused. Some have suggested it could be used for industrial espionage, while others are concerned about the implications for civil liberties. Several journalists have cited instances of American companies gaining commercial advantage over European counterparts, though none of these cases were ever conclusively proved.

Indeed, there has never been official confirmation of ECHELON's existence. Furthermore, the Ministry of Defence insists that all operations undertaken at the base are 'managed in a way that accords with the law, including the European Convention of Human Rights and the Human Rights Act 1998'. That, however, is insufficient reassurance for many of Menwith's critics.

In 2007, the base drew further unwanted attention after the British government confirmed that it would be upgraded to provide early warning of missile attacks as part of a planned US missile defence system. Not only were peace campaigners enraged, but the scheme provoked ire from Moscow, amid claims that the system, aimed at intercepting incoming enemy missiles before they reach US or NATO airspace, breached arms control agreements. Some critics hold that the defence shield could prompt a new arms race. While Des Browne, the British Secretary of Defence at the time, insisted that there were no imminent plans for interceptor missiles to be based in Britain, opponents voiced fears that Menwith Hill could put the UK on the front line of a future war.

As the focus of so much speculation and public wrath (Menwith Hill has regularly been besieged by peace campaigners for decades), security at the base is tight. A perimeter fence is dotted with watchtowers and patrolled by guards and trained dogs, doing little to calm the righteous rage of those who consider the base to be a largely unaccountable US enclave on British soil.

In the popular imagination, this facility is filled with spies scanning our private conversations and intruding on the intimate details of our daily lives. Whether deserved or not, Menwith Hill has a reputation as the ultimate Big Brother, listening in on what everybody else is saying, but with not a lot to say for itself.

The Queen's bedroom
Buckingham Palace

LOCATION Westminster, London, England
NEAREST POPULATION HUB London
SECRECY OVERVIEW High-security location: the private chamber of the Queen.

Buckingham Palace is the British Queen's official London residence, and one of the most iconic buildings in the world. Yet despite attracting hordes of tourists, large swathes of the labyrinthine palace remain under the highest security and off-limits to the world at large. Most private of all is the Queen's personal bedroom, once the scene of a notorious break-in.

Buckingham Palace was originally plain old Buckingham House, built as the London pad of the Duke of Buckingham in 1705. The location he chose had once been a mulberry garden where King James I had attempted to rear silkworms (unsuccessfully, as he had planted the wrong type of mulberry bush). The house took the fancy of King George III, who purchased it as a residence for his wife, Queen Charlotte. It only became a palace in the 1820s, after spendthrift monarch George IV ordered extensive renovations from the architect, John Nash.

George, though, would never live in it, and so Queen Victoria became the first monarch to take up residence when she moved in during July 1837. After the young queen married Prince Albert in 1840 and started a family, it was soon clear that the palace needed to be extended – a job that fell to the architect Edward Blore and his builder, Thomas Cubitt. Their greatest contribution was the addition of the East Wing, complete with the famous balcony from which the royals wave to their subjects at times of

celebration. One such occasion marked the end of the Second World War, during which the Palace had received nine direct hits from German bombers.

Today, the Palace encompasses some 775 rooms, of which 52 are royal and guest bedrooms. When in residence (signified by the raising of the Royal Standard), the Queen and Prince Philip occupy a suite of rooms in the Palace's North Wing. By rights, this should be the single most impenetrable part of the building. But being such a famous landmark, Buckingham Palace has tempted many to test its security over the years, from naked paragliders to undercover journalists, and from paternal rights campaigners dressed as Batman to Osama bin Laden look-alikes. One man found on the grounds in 1990 even ambitiously claimed to be Prince Andrew and that he was there to visit his 'Mum'. But the most serious breach came on 9 July 1982, when the Queen found herself engaged in conversation in her bedroom for a good ten minutes with an intruder named Michael Fagan.

Constitution Hill

Palace Gardens

Private Apartments
including the Queen's
bedroom

Original Buckingham
House, remodelled 1826

The Quadrangle

East Facade,
built 1847,
remodelled 1913

Forecourt

Main Gates

Queen Victoria
Memorial

ATTENTION! *A member of the Queen's Guard on sentry duty at Buckingham Palace. The company is also responsible for guarding St James's Palace in London. Their famous uniform is recognized around the world, but despite their old-fashioned appearance, these are highly trained armed soldiers.*

been on guard outside her room was apparently out walking the dogs, and his replacement had not yet got to his position.

The first the Queen knew of a strange man in her bedroom was when she noticed the curtains twitch. Showing admirable calm, she proceeded to chat amicably with him as he walked across her chamber and perched on the end of her bed. After a while, he requested a cigarette but, perhaps unsurprisingly, the Queen did not have a packet to hand, so she requested some be brought in. This provided her with the opportunity to raise the alarm and a footman dutifully appeared on the scene, holding Fagan until the police arrived to arrest him.

Fagan was subsequently charged with civil offences and spent several months in a high-security mental health facility. It was the first time that an intruder had made it into the private royal apartments since the reign of Queen Victoria (though during the Second World War the Queen Mother had stumbled upon an army deserter in her bathroom).

The incident brought the issue of the Queen's security under blazing scrutiny, and the level of protection surrounding her became even greater. As well as armed guards throughout the Palace – presumably now issued with clear instructions on when they can take the corgis out – there are regular police dog patrols and a permanent detachment from the Queen's Guard, instantly recognizable in their red tunics and bearskins. In 2004, Scotland Yard took over responsibility for security at royal sites from the security services. The same year, an electric fence was erected around the Palace, administering a shock strong enough to disable an intruder until they are apprehended.

In fact, this was not Fagan's first visit to the Palace, since he had successfully scaled the barbed-wire-topped perimeter wall several weeks earlier. On that occasion, on 7 June, he had wandered around the palace unhindered, even stopping to enjoy some wine, cheese and biscuits. When he returned in July, he shinned up a drain pipe into the Queen's private apartments. It was reported that his activities did trigger an alarm, but a palace employee assumed the alarm system was faulty. The armed police officer who should have

MI5 Headquarters, Thames House

LOCATION Millbank, London, England
NEAREST POPULATION HUB London
SECRECY OVERVIEW Operations classified: home of the UK Security Service.

Thames House in Millbank, situated on the north bank of the River Thames in central London, is the imposing headquarters of MI5, the British Security Service. As the spiritual home of Britain's community of spooks, its spectacular facade can be enjoyed by all, but its inner workings are destined to remain unknown to the vast majority of us.

MI5 is the popular name for the Security Service, which is responsible for the United Kingdom's internal security, counter-terrorism and counter-intelligence activities. Falling under the jurisdiction of the Home Secretary, it was established in 1909 to counter infiltration of British organizations by foreign powers at a time when Europe's nations were ferociously jockeying for power and influence. The service underwent a number of reorganizations in the lead up to the First World War, when it formally became the War Office Directorate of Military Intelligence, Section 5. Despite being renamed as the Security Service in 1931, the MI5 moniker stuck.

The Service played a vital role in countering espionage during both World Wars, in the inter-war period and then in the Cold War. However, among its successes were notable failures, such as the one that saw the 'Cambridge Five' spy ring passing secrets unhindered to the Soviet Union for years. From the late 1960s, the Service became increasingly active in counter-terrorist work as the Northern Irish Troubles flared. Despite relative peace in Northern Ireland in recent times, the growth of Islamic extremist terrorism (resulting in attacks on the London transport system in July 2005 that killed 56) has ensured that the Service has been busier than ever in the last decade.

MI5 was previously based in buildings on Curzon Street and Gower Street, but by the 1980s it was increasingly clear that these were no longer meeting requirements. Thames House, meanwhile, stood empty in Millbank, on a stretch of the Thames that extends roughly from Vauxhall Bridge to Parliament Square.

The Millbank area can trace its modern incarnation to the devastating Thames Flood of 1928. Amid the extensive damage caused by a disaster that claimed 14 lives, some 25 metres (80 ft) of the Chelsea Embankment was washed away. The area where Millbank stands today had hitherto been filled with run-down dwellings and warehouses.

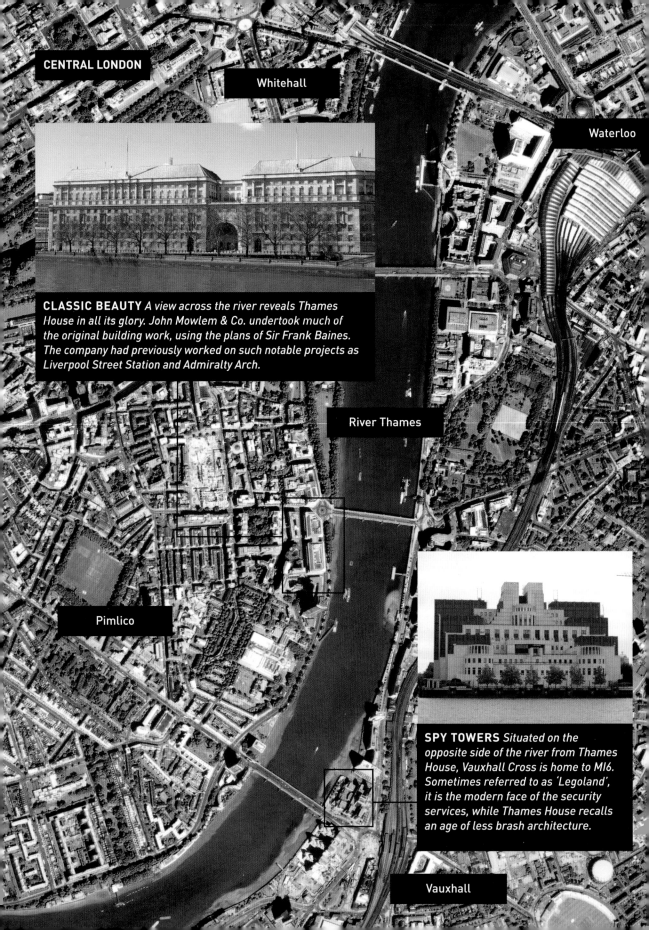

CENTRAL LONDON

Whitehall

Waterloo

River Thames

Pimlico

Vauxhall

CLASSIC BEAUTY *A view across the river reveals Thames House in all its glory. John Mowlem & Co. undertook much of the original building work, using the plans of Sir Frank Baines. The company had previously worked on such notable projects as Liverpool Street Station and Admiralty Arch.*

SPY TOWERS *Situated on the opposite side of the river from Thames House, Vauxhall Cross is home to MI6. Sometimes referred to as 'Legoland', it is the modern face of the security services, while Thames House recalls an age of less brash architecture.*

HOUSE OF SECRETS *The imposing Millbank entrance to Thames House shows evidence of the extensive development work undertaken in the 1990s, linking the main wings of the original building in preparation for the arrival of MI5.*

One positive outcome of the flood was the area's regeneration, spurred by the construction of assorted new office and apartment blocks.

Thames House was designed by Sir Frank Baines, and constructed during 1928 and 1929 on the corner of Millbank and Horseferry Road. Baines produced work in the imperial neoclassical style, and was greatly influenced by Sir Edwin Lutyens (1869–1944), the architect responsible for projects such as the Cenotaph war memorial in Whitehall, and much of the Indian capital, New Delhi. On the Portland stone façade of Thames House are patriotic sculptures of Britannia and St George, created by Charles Sargeant Jagger.

Among the building's early occupants were the industrial giant ICI and the International Nickel Company of Canada. Former Prime Minister David Lloyd George also had an office here. By the 1980s, the building housed ICI in one of its two main blocks and the Department of Energy in the other. After Thames House was sold to the British government in the late 1980s, it was earmarked as the new headquarters for MI5. Among the most significant changes made during an extensive overhaul was the addition of a new block that connects the two existing wings and lies behind the building's iconic archway. MI5 eventually moved in during 1994.

While it is a less obvious citadel than the sprawling Vauxhall Cross building across the river (headquarters of MI6, the Secret Intelligence Service involved in espionage abroad), Thames House underwent numerous structural alterations to improve security at an estimated cost of £227 million. The fabric of the building was strengthened to resist attack, and all windows have secondary glazing for bomb blast protection. Glass panels behind the windows in the lower floor make it impossible for anything to be left on the sills. Car parking is in a secure underground garage and there is an armed police presence, along with the expected array of surveillance equipment, secure entry systems and electronic defences.

As MI5's classified work carries on inside, there are those who fear that the activities commissioned from Thames House are not always in the national interest. For instance, in 2006 it emerged that the organization held 272,000 files on British citizens. Norman Baker, a Liberal Democrat MP, commented: 'I don't believe there are 272,000 people in this country who are subversive or potentially subversive. It suggests to me that there are files being held for not very good reasons.' The British public will probably never know one way or another.

45 Whitehall tunnels

LOCATION Beneath the streets of Whitehall, London, England
NEAREST POPULATION HUB London
SECRECY OVERVIEW Existence unacknowledged: a network of tunnels built in the Second World War.

During the Second World War, London was peppered by bombing raids, and tourist attractions such as the Cabinet War Rooms show how the city rapidly developed a subterranean alter ego. Yet the existence of a tunnel network running between Parliament and Trafalgar Square and accessible to those who work in Whitehall, the heart of British government, remains an unconfirmed rumour.

In late 1939, with the Second World War in its infancy, the Post Office undertook a scheme known by the reference number 2845. It involved constructing a tunnel system at a depth of about 30 metres (100 ft) to protect cabling and secure the government's telephonic and telegraphic systems. It is thought that the system may have grown to between 1.6 and 3.2 kilometres (1 and 2 miles) in length, with access via a series of lifts and stairways. Staff are believed to have had access via the Whitehall exchange in Craig's Court, with another entrance in the old Trafalgar Square Underground Station.

The first significant section of tunnel was in operation by 1941, linking the War Office, the Air Ministry and the Admiralty. A later extension would lead to the Cabinet War Rooms. It is not a huge leap of the imagination to suggest that, with overground London so vulnerable, these tunnels and their associated service passages could have been adapted to cope with the transfer of large numbers of government workers in the case of an emergency such as a gas attack. Indeed,

it has been widely reported that in 1955 the network, known as Q-Whitehall (the name may possibly derive from a GPO site engineering code of QWHI), was used to test how a gas attack within the tunnels might affect the buildings above.

While the Post Office scheme was discussed in some detail in a 1946 GPO publication called *The Post Office Electrical Engineers Journal*, the government quickly clamped down on such talk in the new Cold War climate: most of the country still remembered the Second World War slogan 'careless talk costs lives'. However, it is known that in the 1950s the GPO tunnels received extensive upgrade work (and possibly expansion) though the files relating to this lie in the National Archives awaiting declassification, which will not occur until 2026 at the earliest. Understandably given the evidence, some believe that Q-Whitehall remains very much in use today as a quick and convenient means for government officials and their civil servants to access government buildings.

The Mall, leading to Buckingham Palace

St James's Park

Admiralty House, formerly the command centre of the Royal Navy

Horse Guards, former Army headquarters

Downing Street, home of the British Prime Minister

Former War Office Building on Horse Guards Avenue, still used by the Ministry of Defence

HEART OF GOVERNMENT *A view from the air of London's Whitehall, home to many of the key institutions of British government. An obvious target for enemy bombers in the Second World War, it was essential to develop plans so that government could function even in the event of direct hits.*

Ministry of Defence Main Building, built between 1938 and 1959

Bank of England vaults

LOCATION Beneath Threadneedle Street in London, England
NEAREST POPULATION HUB London
SECRECY OVERVIEW High-security location: the safest place to store gold bullion in Europe.

The central bank of the United Kingdom, the Bank of England was founded in 1694. Since 1734, it has been based at Threadneedle Street in the heart of the City of London, and from 1797 it has had the nickname of the Old Lady of Threadneedle Street. Beneath its floors are cavernous vaults that store not only the gold reserves of the UK but also the wealth of countless other countries.

Gold is a curious material. While it is undeniably attractive to look at and remarkably stable as an element, it can be dug out of the dirt in its pure form, and is far from the rarest or most useful of metals.

Yet since the earliest days of mankind it has commanded adoration, symbolizing love, beauty and wealth. Perhaps most importantly, it has become the foundation of most of the world's economic systems. We might have chosen coal or coffee beans or salmon or anything else you care to think of, but it is gold against which the value of virtually every currency is measured.

In 1844, Britain officially adopted the 'gold standard', by which the value of sterling was directly linked to a fixed weight of gold. Even after Britain abandoned the standard in 1931, gold remained the safest bet in town, and as economic crisis gripped the world in the late 2000s, it became an even more attractive investment proposition. As of 2011, the UK government held

gold reserves of around 312 tonnes (1 million troy ounces) in the Bank of England, which roughly equates to 23,000 bars of 24-carat gold. Billions of pounds worth of gold belonging to other countries is held here too, often deposited by governments who don't have access to a suitably large and secure vault in their own nation.

When the Bank moved home in 1734, its new premises were the first purpose-built bank buildings in the world. Sir John Soane added greatly to the edifice in the late 18th and early 19th centuries, with additions including a windowless wall.

However, Soane's buildings were controversially pulled down between the First and Second World Wars, and Sir Herbert Baker designed new premises that rose several storeys higher above ground and descended three storeys below ground for good measure. The modern building has a defensive curtain wall, no windows on the ground floor and no other connecting buildings.

SAFE AS THE BANK OF ENGLAND *An aerial view of the Sir Herbert Baker-designed Bank of England complex. The Bank sits on a plot of land surrounded by Threadneedle Street, Princes Street, Bartholomew Lane and Lothbury. The building with pillars visible at top right is the Royal Exchange.*

The vaults themselves are vast, with a floor area large enough to accommodate the pitch of Wembley Stadium four times over with room to spare. Since much of London, including the site of the Bank, lies on clay, the vaults cannot possibly bear the weight of gold bars stacked floor to ceiling, so there is always some unused capacity within them. In fact, gold is rarely stored in columns higher than four bars in a bid to avoid damaging the stocks. The walls are designed to withstand bomb blasts, and for this reason the vaults took on the role of air raid shelter for bank employees during the Second World War.

Nonetheless, Bank legend has it that security was not always as tight as it should have been. It is rumoured that in 1836, the board of directors were called to a midnight assignation in the vaults, where they were greeted by an honest sewerman who discreetly told them that he had discovered a way into the hallowed caverns. For his public-spiritedness, he was given a princely reward of £800 by the grateful bankers.

Access these days is via huge doors that are opened by keys 90 centimetres (3 ft) in length (not the sort of thing to slip into a pocket unnoticed). As the key is inserted into the lock, the person attempting entry must give a password via a microphone next to the doors.

The identity of staff who work in the vaults is a closely guarded secret in order to lessen the chance of an employee's family being kidnapped and the employee being blackmailed into granting access. (Incidentally, one worker is specifically charged with giving the gold stocks a good dusting every now and then.) The Bank has become so synonymous with security that whenever an Englishman wishes to emphasis the safeness of something, he will tell you that it is 'as safe as the Bank of England'.

While all that gold is securely tucked away in the Bank's vaults, visitors to the Bank's museum are given the opportunity to handle a gold bar for themselves. Anyone wishing to get their hands on more of the vaults' contents is unlikely to succeed, and should perhaps make do instead with a copy of John Guillermin's 1960 heist movie, *The Day They Robbed the Bank of England*.

47 PINDAR Bunker

LOCATION Whitehall, London, UK

NEAREST POPULATION HUB London

SECRECY OVERVIEW Existence unacknowledged: secret underground bunker and alternative control post for the British government.

Pindar is a 'protected crisis management facility', designed to provide a place of safety for the British government in the event of an emergency. Although it is officially unacknowledged and details are scarce, a few scraps of information emerged from a 1994 parliamentary exchange between Jeremy Hanley, then Secretary of State for Defence, and Harry Cohen, then Member of Parliament for Leyton.

Construction on PINDAR, which sits beneath the main Ministry of Defence building in Whitehall, began in 1987, following eight years of planning. The new bunker is believed to incorporate elements of a previous shelter that was used during the Second World War. It is designed for use in the event of a major military strike or civil unrest, and became operational in 1992, having cost in excess of £126 million. It is on a permanent state of stand-by, and has a full-time staff which may be augmented as required at times of crisis.

Among its rumoured design features are blast-proof doors, extensive accommodation and catering quarters, and a broadcasting studio. There is also believed to be a situation room, complete with the latest communications equipment and fully protected against potentially crippling electromagnetic pulses. Reassuringly, there are also 'sufficient toilet facilities provided for the full complement of the site... usable as long as power within the site is maintained for pumping waste'.

Each year, at least one major exercise and several minor tests are scheduled to run at the site, mimicking real-life crisis situations. In the event of a building collapse above the bunker, there are several escape routes, although the bunker is not officially connected to any transport system. The facility is named in honour of the ancient Greek poet Pindar of Thebes, who died around 443 BC. When Alexander the Great sacked Thebes in the third century BC, the great warrior declared that the house of the celebrated poet should be the one building that was spared.

In 2006 and 2007, artist David Moore was given access to a secure military underground location for a photographic project called 'The Last Things'. While he never formally identified the location, it is commonly accepted that he was documenting PINDAR, and his images were subsequently made available for public consumption. As Moore's website notes, one Ministry of Defence official wryly commented: 'I don't understand how you've got this far.'

Tower of London Jewel House

LOCATION Tower Hill, London, England
NEAREST POPULATION HUB London
SECRECY OVERVIEW High-security location: the modern high-tech home of the English Crown Jewels.

The English Crown Jewels are estimated to be worth somewhere close to £13 billion, putting them high on the list of targets for master criminals. They have been kept under heavy guard at the Tower of London for centuries, and in 1994 were moved to a new home within the castle boundaries, a state of the art jewel house designed to keep them protected while being viewed by thousands of tourists each day.

From the King's Crown, adorned with over 3,000 jewels, to the Royal Sceptre that includes the Cullinan diamond (a 530.20-carat stone cut from the largest diamond ever mined), the Crown Jewels are an unrivalled collection. They have been stored at the Tower of London since 1303, having previously resided at Westminster Abbey until they were subject to an attempted theft.

The nearest anyone has come to successfully snatching them from the Tower was a notorious 1671 heist led by Colonel Blood. At that time the jewels were held in the Martin Tower, protected by a custodian, Talbot Edwards, who would allow visitors to inspect them for a small consideration. Blood and a female accomplice duly befriended Edwards and his wife over a period of weeks.

By early May 1671, Blood had persuaded the Master of the Jewel House to let him see the collection with a small troop of friends. He then led an ambush, the gang beating Edwards and seizing whatever valuables they could. Although they were apprehended before they could get away, Blood somehow secured himself a royal pardon – some say as the reward for his astonishing bravado.

The chances of such a ruse proving successful today are more remote than ever. The Jewels were moved to the Tower's neo-Gothic Waterloo Barracks in 1967, but by the early 1990s it was clear that the basement room in which they were kept was unable to cope with the crowds of tourists. A new jewel house was thus built within the Barracks, with capacity for 2,500 people each hour.

Opened in 1994, the building includes a raft of safety and security measures that cost more than £3 million. Today the jewels lie on cushions of French velvet protected by 5-cm (2-in) thick reinforced glass. They are kept under 24-hour surveillance from a nearby control room while Yeoman Warders (Beefeaters) and members of the Tower Guard stand ready to step in should the need arise. So you are welcome to look, but don't even think about touching.

Rosslyn Chapel vaults

LOCATION Roslin, Midlothian, Scotland
NEAREST POPULATION HUB Edinburgh
SECRECY OVERVIEW Site of historic mystery: vaults beneath a medieval church that have become a focus for conspiracy theories.

The elaborate chapel of Rosslyn near Edinburgh has long been linked to rumoured activities of the Knights Templar and Freemasons, but the speculation went into overdrive after it featured prominently in Dan Brown's 2003 novel, *The Da Vinci Code*. Many stories linked to the chapel have been convincingly debunked, but conspiracy theorists continue to be drawn to an underground chamber sealed for centuries.

Rosslyn Chapel is the common name for the Collegiate Chapel of St Matthew the Apostle. It sits amid the beautiful and spectacular setting of Roslin Glen in the Esk Valley. The name derives from the Gaelic words for 'rock' and 'foaming water' (and is not, as some have supposed, etymologically linked to the 'Rose Line' made popular by certain bestselling fiction writers).

Rosslyn was founded as a Roman Catholic chapel in 1446, by the Norman-descended William St Clair, First Earl of Caithness. However, building work was not completed until the 1480s. It was the third chapel in the immediate area, the first being in the nearby Rosslyn Castle and the second having long since been destroyed. After the Scottish reformation in the latter part of the 16th century, the church closed to the public until the 1860s, although in 1650 it was apparently used for stabling horses by Cromwellian troops during the Civil War. In 1861, an extensive restoration began, and Rosslyn came under the jurisdiction of the Scottish Episcopal Church.

What makes Rosslyn so distinctive is its amazing stonemasonry – a mixture of theological subjects and flights of fancy. Perhaps the single most notable feature is the 'Prentice Pillar', supposedly carved by a humble apprentice who was slaughtered by his master in a fit of professional jealousy when he saw how grand it was. The Chapel also contains some 120 carvings of bearded green men, as well as 213 cubes carved around the ceiling and engraved with mysterious symbols. Some modern musicologists believe it to be an obscure musical notation system. What is clear is that the architects and stonemasons were given free rein to express their creativity.

The most enduring rumour concerning the chapel is that Sir William St Clair was a prominent Freemason and a Knight Templar to boot, and that the church is home to treasures and important documents from one or both organizations. The Knights Templar was an elite religious military order famed for its escapades during the Crusades. It acquired immense wealth over the

UNFINISHED BEAUTY *Amazingly, the spectacular Chapel forms only a small part of William St Clair's ambitious original plan for a much larger, cruciform church.*

SCOTLAND

Edinburgh

IRELAND

WALES

ENGLAND

GREEN MAN
More than 100 bizarre faces are scattered around the Chapel, surrounded by intricately carved greenery that often emerges from their mouths. These 'Green Men' are thought to be ancient pagan fertility symbols, and may be placed to represent the progression of a year from the east to the west end.

FRANCE

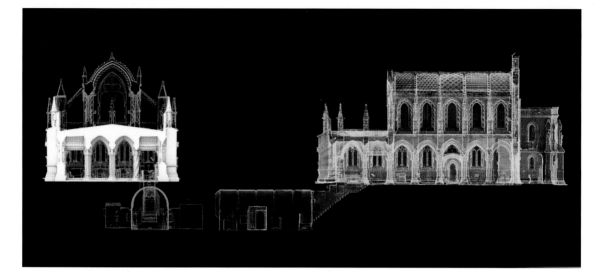

ANOTHER DIMENSION *This computer rendering shows Rosslyn Chapel's structure in 3-D. Researchers have used detailed laser scanning in a bid to establish if there are hidden treasures lying beneath the church floor. So far they have found scant evidence of Holy Grails or entombed Knights Templar but the quest continues.*

years and won a reputation among some as the guardian of the Holy Grail. But the fact is, Rosslyn was not built until the middle of the 15th century, a good 130 years after the Knights Templar had been dissolved at the command of the papacy, and 200 years *before* the first recorded evidence of the Freemasons.

However, the myth that has perhaps attracted more attention to Rosslyn than any other in recent times is that the Chapel is the resting place of the Holy Grail itself, a theory propounded in *The Da Vinci Code*. Most historians, though, believe there is little evidence to back up such an assertion (and especially some of the wilder claims as to what actually constitutes the mysterious 'Grail' itself). Given that most experts now disregard the Chapel's Knights Templar links, it is perhaps wisest to regard the whole story as fictional.

Nonetheless, the most avid conspiracy theorists hold that the evidence for even

their most outrageous claims lies buried by the St Clair family in secret vaults not examined for centuries (and, of course, a 'secret vault' at Rosslyn has a vital role in the *Da Vinci Code* denouement). Indeed, there are chambers deep beneath the church that have long been unopened and non-invasive seismic surveys carried out in the 1980s suggested the presence of metal objects within them. A proposed underground excavation of recent times was halted when the excavation team encountered an impassable wall.

The fact that the Chapel's owners have refused requests to open the vaults for fear of undermining the Chapel's medieval foundations is merely grist to the mill for those convinced that they have something to hide. The vaults' most likely contents are the bodies of several generations of the St Clair family, many of whom were reputed to be buried in full armour until the practice stopped in the early 18th century. A little macabre, perhaps, but not indicative of any historical conspiracy. However, until such a time as the St Clair-controlled Rosslyn Chapel Trust decides to open the vaults up to public inspection, the market in Rosslyn conspiracies is likely to remain bullish.

Wildenstein Art Collection

LOCATION Stored around the world. Headquartered in Paris.
NEAREST POPULATION HUB Paris, France
SECRECY OVERVIEW Location uncertain: said to be the most valuable private art collection in the world.

Many art collectors are more than willing to show off their prized pieces, but that is not something that could be said of the Wildenstein family. These French multi-millionaires jealously guard the precise details of a collection that has been built up over more than a century, despite their position as perhaps the most famous family in the art world.

The Wildenstein art dynasty began with Nathan Wildenstein in the 1870s. A French cloth merchant by trade, he educated himself in 18th-century painting, and took advantage of a sleeping market to earn a fortune. From his base in Paris, he had extended his empire of galleries to New York, London and Buenos Aires by the end of the 1920s. After Nathan's death, his son Georges moved the family's centre of operations to the USA in 1940.

The family has been long established as one of the leading suppliers to major galleries and museums throughout the world, but details of the Wildenstein's total holdings (and their locations) are scant. It has been speculated that the collection is split between secure locations in New York, Paris, London, Buenos Aires and Tokyo, and may include some 10,000 works.

Divorce proceedings in 1999 between Alec Wildenstein (grandson of Georges) and his wife Jocelyn (infamous for her attempts to give herself a feline appearance through plastic surgery) estimated the collection's value at US$10 billion. It is thought to include works by Giotto di Bondone, Vermeer, Caravaggio, Rembrandt, Monet and Van Gogh.

Further sketchy details about the collection have emerged in recent years during further legal battles between family members, and in 2011 a police raid at the Wildenstein Institute in Paris reportedly uncovered many works previously listed as stolen or missing. The Wildensteins came under renewed scrutiny as a result, but it is unlikely the public will get to view their remarkable collection at any point in the near future.

La Basse Cour

LOCATION West Flanders, Belgium
NEAREST POPULATION HUB Ghent
SECRECY OVERVIEW Access restricted: home to the First World War's largest unexploded mine.

La Basse Cour (which translates as 'The Farmyard') is a 60-hectare (150-acre) privately owned farm close to the town of Ypres. Amid the push-and-pull of the First World War's Western Front, its location on the Messines Ridge put it on the front line of hostilities. Today the farm sits on a massive 22,500-kilogram (50,000-lb) mine that has yet to detonate.

The Messines Ridge fell under German control in the early months of the First World War, and remained so until 1917. It was a major target for British forces stationed in the area and, as it became increasingly clear that trench warfare was producing only stalemate, a radical new plan was put into action.

From January 1916, British troops began digging underground tunnels from their lines around the Ypres Salient towards the German encampments at Messines. The idea was to lay a series of mines that could be exploded shortly before a major troop offensive. In fact, the scheme was put on hold until 1917, when 25 mines and 450,000 kilograms (1 million lb) of explosives were laid underground along an 11-kilometre (7-mile) front after a heroic period of subterranean burrowing.

British forces under the command of General Sir Herbert Plumer began a heavy bombardment of German positions towards the end of May 1917. On 7 June, Plumer gave the order to detonate the mines, creating a blast that claimed between 6,000 and 10,000 enemy lives and which was reputedly loud enough to be heard in London. Within a week, the British had secured the Messines Ridge.

However, six of the British mines survived the operation intact. Five of them were left undetonated for strategic reasons, while the sixth was lost during a German counter-mining attack and never recovered. It lay beneath a farm then known as Le Petite Douve, which was renamed as La Basse Cour by its owners, the Mahieu family, in the aftermath of the conflict.

And there the mine survives to the present day. While another of the Messines mines exploded spontaneously in 1955 during a lightning storm, the bomb beneath La Basse Cour remains buried some 24 metres (80 ft) beneath the Mahieus' property. Its exact location was pinpointed in the 1990s by British researchers using historical maps of the area, but only the foolhardy are likely to want to prod and poke at this sleeping but potentially deadly brute.

UNDERGROUND WORLD *Specialist tunnelling companies dug subterranean trenches across much of the Western Front, such as those preserved in the Wellington Quarry beneath Arras in northeastern France. The mine tunnels were among the most ambitious of all.*

NETHERLANDS

Ypres Salient

BELGIUM

Somme Battlefield

BIG BANG *A rare photograph captures the explosion of the mine under Hawthorn Ridge Redoubt, packed with 18 tonnes of explosives, at the beginning of the Battle of the Somme in June 1916.*

FRANCE

Line of the Western Front in 1916

LASTING IMPACT *The 24-tonne Lochnagar Mine, detonated at the beginning of the Battle of the Somme, left behind a crater some 91 metres (300 ft) across and 21 metres (70 ft) deep, which has been preserved in commemoration of the battle.*

Bilderberg Group Headquarters

LOCATION Unknown, believed to be in Leiden, the Netherlands
NEAREST POPULATION HUB Leiden
SECRECY OVERVIEW Operations classified: hosts to an annual private meeting of global figures.

The Bilderberg Group takes its name from the Bilderberg Hotel near Arnhem in the Netherlands, where its first meeting occurred in 1954. Held strictly behind closed doors, its annual meetings offer an opportunity for a cast of mostly European and American power-brokers to debate world issues. For sceptics, however, the group is a secretive cabal plotting a New World Order.

The Bilderberg Group was established by Prince Bernhard of the Netherlands, the international banking guru David Rockefeller, Polish diplomat Joseph Retinger and British politician Dennis Healey. Its underlying aim was to bring together the transatlantic great and good to reinforce the liberal, free-market philosophy of the free world. Interviewed years later, Healey freely admitted: 'To say we were striving for a one-world government is exaggerated, but not wholly unfair. Those of us in Bilderberg felt we couldn't go on forever fighting one another for nothing and killing people and rendering millions homeless. So we felt that a single community throughout the world would be a good thing.'

Over the years, the Group has garnered a remarkable record of inviting guests at the beginning of their careers who go on to become world leaders. This has led some to believe that Bilderberg has had a hand in moulding their professional lives to its own ends. However, it is the Bilderberg emphasis on privacy that most infuriates its critics. Even when

the group is being ostensibly open, it is at best opaque, they argue. The list of meeting attendees it releases is routinely incomplete, for instance, and while the Group has a website, it includes no details of its head office (widely believed to be located in Leiden)

Most devastatingly, the meetings themselves are aggressively protected by a mixture of private and official security forces. Protesters and journalists who discover the location of meetings – held in high-end hotels at a new location each year – regularly complain of intimidation from hired heavies, and a few claim to have been the victims of more sinister and heavy-handed treatment.

Bilderberg's defenders say that tight security is essential when you bring together so many important people. Its accusers argue that it's symptomatic of an over-powerful cabal plotting the world's future away from the scrutiny of the masses. Alas, you are unlikely ever to find your way to the Group's head office to get its own take on the question.

The Large Hadron Collider

LOCATION Beneath the Franco-Swiss border
NEAREST POPULATION HUB Geneva, Switzerland
SECRECY OVERVIEW Access restricted: the world's largest particle accelerator, studying the creation of the Universe.

The Large Hadron Collider (LHC) is a huge scientific instrument that smashes together subatomic particles called protons at speeds close to the speed of light, in order to replicate conditions that occurred in the trillionth of a second after the Big Bang. However, sceptics are concerned that in searching to understand the origins of the Universe, the experiment could bring about its end.

The LHC is run by CERN, the European Organization for Nuclear Research. which authorized funding for the project in 1994. It began operating in 2008, having cost in the region of US$10 billion to build, and consists of a 27-kilometre (17-mile) ring buried 100 metres (330 ft) below ground on the Franco-Swiss border, in an area between the Jura and Alps mountain ranges. The facility makes use of a tunnel previously used for CERN's Large Electron Positron Collider (LEP), an experiment that was dismantled in 2000.

The big idea behind the LHC is to expand our scientific knowledge beyond that laid out in the Standard Model – a framework that for several decades has provided the most widely accepted explanation for how subatomic particles function. For all its strengths, it has long been realized that the Standard Model leaves many fundamental questions unanswered. The LHC looks to fill some of these gaps by crashing together two beams of 'hadrons' – consisting of protons or lead ions – by firing them in opposite

WEIRD SCIENCE
A view of the Compact Muon Solenoid (CMS), a giant detector instrument designed to observe an array of particles and phenomena resulting from the LHC's high-energy collisions. Scientists hope it will provide crucial data to help explain the fundamental structure of the Universe.

directions around the accelerator, the hadrons gaining in energy as they increase in speed with every lap. The powerful magnetic field required to propel these energy-rich particles is provided by 1,750 superconducting magnets kept just a couple of degrees above absolute zero by several hundred thousand litres of liquid helium provided by a series of above-ground refrigeration plants.

After some initial hiccups, the LHC started its experiments in earnest in 2010. At full power, it sends trillions of protons around the accelerator ring at a speed equivalent to 99.9999991 per cent of the speed of light, achieving 600 million collisions every second. The effects of these crashes are captured and recorded by one of four vast detectors located at intervals around the accelerator. Each detector weighs several tonnes and building and fitting them into the LHC was a remarkable feat of engineering. For instance, just one of the detectors – the Atlas detector, which at 7,000 tonnes is by no means the largest – took a full two years to locate in a specially excavated cavern as deep as a 12-storey building.

With some 10,000 scientists from 40 countries involved in the project and huge attendant media coverage, it may hardly be said that CERN has undertaken its work on the LHC on the quiet. One of the project's chief aims is to detect the hitherto theoretical Higgs Boson, believed to be responsible for providing

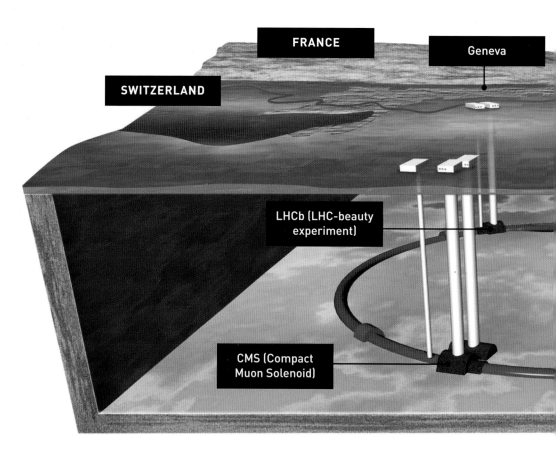

FRANCE

Geneva

SWITZERLAND

LHCb (LHC-beauty experiment)

CMS (Compact Muon Solenoid)

the mass to other subatomic particles. In late 2011, the LHC team tentatively suggested that the Higgs Boson may have been glimpsed for the first time, prompting a surge of excitement among the world's physicists, scientific journalists and interested laymen.

But for some observers, the LHC poses frightening and largely unknowable risks. Almost as soon as the project was first approved, startling Doomsday scenarios were being prophesied. Principal among these was the suggestion that the collider might produce black holes that could swell and ultimately consume the Earth. However, most experts agree that even if a black hole was produced, it would pose no risk as it would be microscopic in scale and

would evaporate almost immediately. Another theory warns of the creation of 'strangelets', prompting a runaway fusion process that could turn everything on the planet into 'strange matter'. Still others suggest that 'vacuum bubbles' will be created, stabilizing aspects of our universe that are inherently unstable and in the process rendering Earth uninhabitable for the human race.

Naturally, the safety of the LHC has been endorsed by numerous independent scientific authorities – and as you read this, the world has presumably not yet come to a premature end. But sceptics continue to argue that any experiment always involves some uncertainty over results – so why carry out an experiment that poses such large potential risks?

SUPER COLLIDER

The tunnels and experimental chambers of the Large Hadron Collider are buried at depths of 50 to 175 metres (160 to 574 ft) beneath the Franco-Swiss border. Particles are boosted to high speeds by the LINAC and SPS accelerators before they are injected into the LHC itself.

Main CERN surface facility

LINAC Linear Accelerator generates initial high-energy particles

ALICE (A Large Ion Collider Experiment)

ATLAS (A Toroidal LHC Apparatus)

SPS (Super Proton Synchrotron) accelerates particles prior to injection

Swiss Fort Knox

LOCATION Bern Canton, Switzerland
NEAREST POPULATION HUB Bern
SECRECY OVERVIEW High-security location: a secret bunker used to store confidential documents and data.

There are, in fact, two Swiss Fort Knoxes. Both are high-security secret bunkers built deep into the mountains of the Swiss Alps near the high-class ski resort of Gstaad. Run by a company called MOUNT10, which specializes in the secure storage of both physical and electronic information, Swiss Fort Knox I opened in 1996, while its companion entered operation some seven years later.

The company leases the bunkers from the Swiss military, which oversees a network of some 26,000 fortresses and bunkers throughout the Alps. While these defences were essential to protecting Swiss neutrality during the Second World War and then the Cold War, in more recent years they have become a drain on the public purse. But MOUNT10 has given at least these two sites a new lease of life.

The two bunkers are guarded 24 hours a day and protected by constant CCTV surveillance and motion sensors. Entry is strictly limited – visitors must be verified by advanced retina-scan technology and accompanied by security personnel at all times. Access in the first instance is past bullet-proof gates, and via camouflaged 3.5-tonne doors.

The company claims the bunkers are 'resistant against any military and civil threat' and offer the highest possible protection against chemical, biological or nuclear attack, as well as safeguarding computer servers from the potentially devastating effects of electromagnetic pulses. Meanwhile, unique access to subterranean glacial waters is used to maintain strict climate control within the depositories.

Among the most important information stored here is a 'digital genome' – a store of information brought together by a group of academics, designed to ensure that future generations will be able to read data on technological formats (such as USB sticks or floppy disks) that might by then be obsolete. The project has been described as a 21st-century version of the Rosetta Stone, the archaeological discovery that made it possible to decipher ancient Egyptian hieroglyphs.

Harry Lime in *The Third Man* once famously concluded that Switzerland's chief contribution to the world after 500 years of democracy and peace was the cuckoo clock. We might now add the protection of a key so that the people of the future might better understand our present.

HALL OF THE MOUNTAIN KING

The impregnable Swiss Fort Knox complex at Saanen is designed to preserve valuable data and artefacts against all disasters up to and including nuclear war.

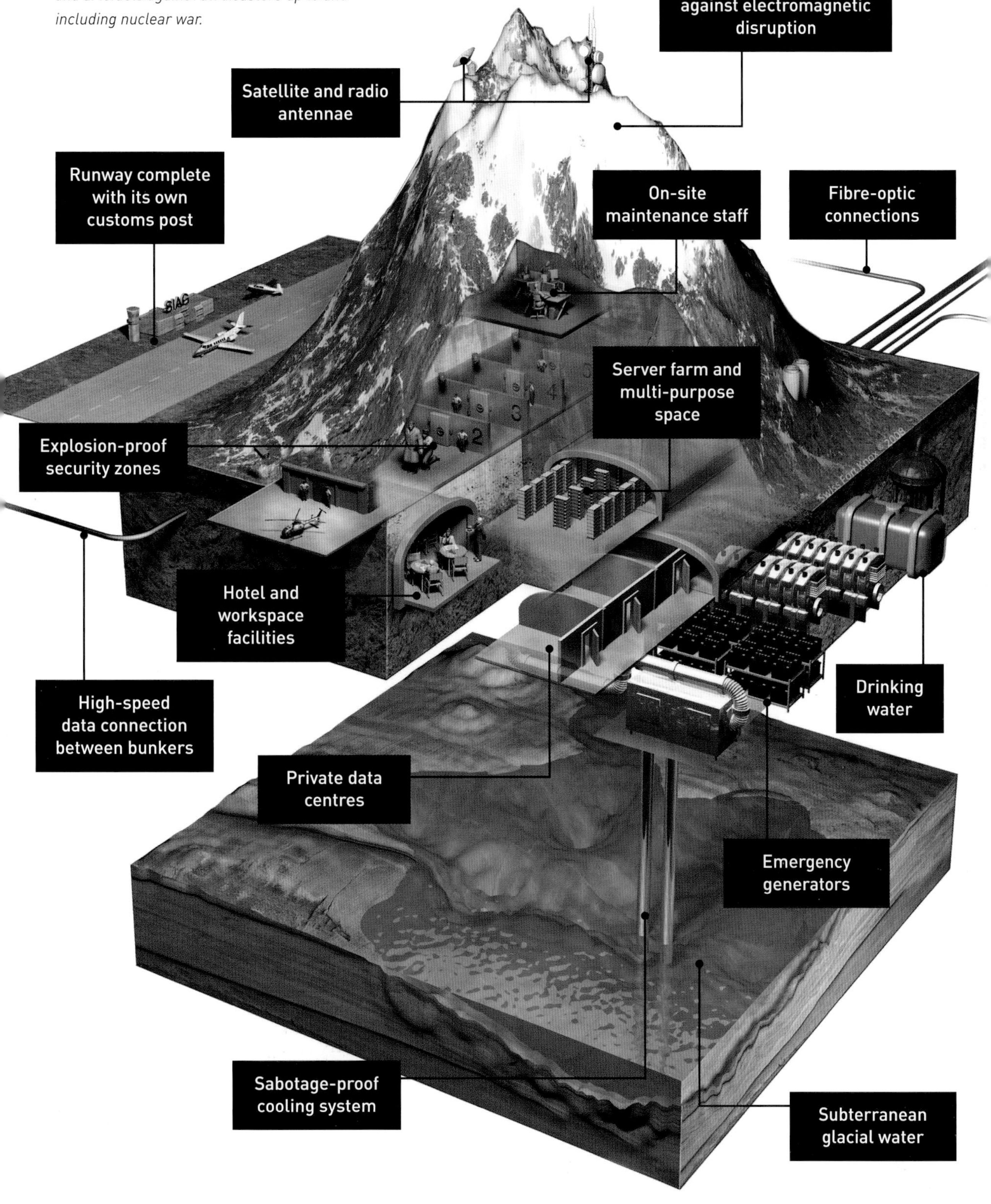

Mountain rocks protect against electromagnetic disruption

Satellite and radio antennae

Runway complete with its own customs post

On-site maintenance staff

Fibre-optic connections

Server farm and multi-purpose space

Explosion-proof security zones

Hotel and workspace facilities

Drinking water

High-speed data connection between bunkers

Private data centres

Emergency generators

Sabotage-proof cooling system

Subterranean glacial water

55 Bavarian *Erdställe*

LOCATION Bavaria, Germany

NEAREST POPULATION HUB Munich

SECRECY OVERVIEW Site of historic mystery: an ancient complex of mysterious underground tunnels.

Southern Germany is home to a labyrinth of over 700 subterranean passages and chambers, known as *Erdställe* and believed to date from between the 10th and 13th centuries. Entrances into the network have been found in disparate locations, within churches, graveyards and private houses, as well as among woodland. However, answers to the questions of who built them and why remain as elusive as ever.

Similar underground networks are evident elsewhere in Europe, notably in Austria, Hungary, Ireland and Spain. A priest by the name of Lambert Karner was the first to extensively explore the Bavarian tunnels in the late 19th and early 20th centuries.

The passages vary greatly in size – some are so small that they can only be entered on hands and knees while others are relatively spacious and stretch in excess of 100 metres (330 ft). In Germany, the passages have also traditionally been referred to as 'goblin holes' (*Schrazelloch*), reflecting a once widely held belief that they were supernatural in nature.

Others have speculated that they were built for religious purposes, perhaps by druids or to serve as places of healing. Yet further theories suggest they were used as routes to escape marauding raiders, or as dungeons, hiding places for treasure or winter quarters for itinerant tribes or groups of monks.

Curiously, the historical record makes no reference to the construction of any such subterranean networks. A few caverns show evidence of doorways and rudimentary building materials, while a ploughshare and millstones have also been recovered. However, barely any chambers are large enough to have realistically hosted people for any length of time. There is also a notable lack of evidence of food remains, faeces (human or animal) or sources of light and heat.

So the mystery endures. It is probable that at some stages of their history, the passages were used for storage, but all the clues suggest that this underground world was not designed to support human existence to any great extent or for very long. A group of academics have come together as the Working Group for Erdstall Research to probe the tunnels further, and perhaps one day they will come up with an explanation as to their origins. In the meantime, we are left to ponder whether the folk who spoke of goblin holes in times past knew what they were talking about after all.

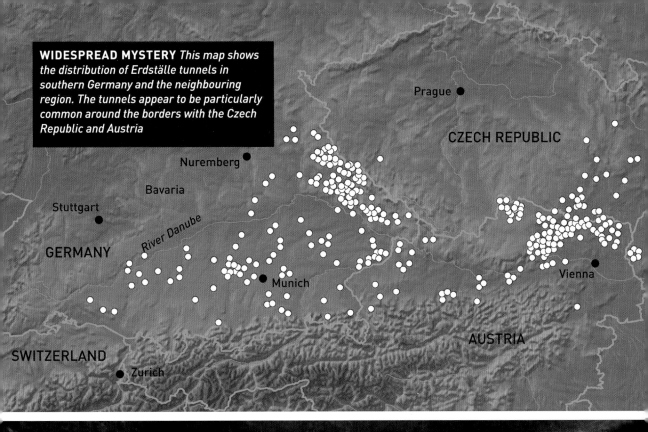

WIDESPREAD MYSTERY *This map shows the distribution of Erdställe tunnels in southern Germany and the neighbouring region. The tunnels appear to be particularly common around the borders with the Czech Republic and Austria*

Prague

CZECH REPUBLIC

Nuremberg

Bavaria

Stuttgart

River Danube

GERMANY

Munich

Vienna

AUSTRIA

SWITZERLAND

Zurich

HIDDEN ENTRANCES *Erdställe are frequently accessed through church crypts and other subterranean spaces. The people of the region have a long history of using underground vaults for shelter and storage.*

The Amber Room

LOCATION Purportedly in an underground cavern on the German-Czech border
NEAREST POPULATION HUB Chemnitz, Germany
SECRECY OVERVIEW Site of historic mystery: an ornate room seized by the Nazis and later lost.

Sometimes described as the 'eighth wonder of the world', the Amber Room was constructed using 6 tonnes of amber backed with gold leaf. Once given by Prussia to Russia as a symbol of peace, it was stolen from the USSR by Nazi forces during the Second World War. In the chaos that accompanied Germany's defeat in 1945, the location of the room was lost, sparking an enduring quest to recover it.

A woman of unerringly expensive tastes, Queen Sophia Charlotte of Hanover persuaded her husband, Friedrich I of Prussia, to commission the Amber Room for Charlottenburg Palace in Berlin. Designed in the baroque style by Andreas Schlüter, it was crafted under the supervision of a Dane, Gottfried Wolfram, between 1701 and 1709.

By the time it was finished, Sophia Charlotte had been dead for four years, and Friedrich would die, too, in 1713. He was succeeded by his son, Friedrich Wilhelm I. Keen to consolidate good relations with Peter the Great of Russia, Friedrich Wilhelm made him a gift of the room in 1716. It was packed into 18 large crates and sent to St Petersburg, where it was installed in the Winter Palace. In 1755 the Tsarina Elizabeth had it moved once more, this time to the Catherine Palace in Tsarkoye Selo (now part of Pushkin, a suburb of St Petersburg).

An Italian designer called Bartolemeo Francesco Rastrelli oversaw a redesign for this new space, importing yet more amber from Berlin for the job. After subsequent renovations, the room covered 55 square metres (590 sq ft) and is estimated to have been worth something approaching US$150 million in today's money.

The room remained at Tsarkoye Selo until 1941, when Hitler launched Operation Barbarossa, sending 3 million German troops into what was now the Soviet Union. Among the many crimes committed at this time, looting of art treasures was widespread. Officials at the Catherine Palace hurriedly set about dismantling the Amber Room to put into safe storage, but as they began their work, they found the antique amber crumbled. They decided instead to cover the room in conventional wallpaper, in the hope that the Germans would fail to realize what lay behind it, but the plan was an utter failure.

Within 36 hours of the arrival of German troops at the Palace, they had taken the room apart and stored it in 27 boxes that were soon transferred to

FIT FOR A TSAR

The Winter Palace in St Petersburg became the official residence of Russia's rulers from 1732. The Amber Room's journey from Berlin in 1716 took six arduous weeks, and the panels are believed to have been left unassembled in a palace wing for several years.

Königsberg (now Kaliningrad) on the Baltic coast. Here, it was put back together again in the city's castle museum. When the tide of the war turned against Germany after 1943, the museum director was charged with once again disassembling the room and moving it to a safe place. However, in 1944 Königsberg was bombed by British forces and much of the city, including its museum, burned. The fate of the Amber Room is unknown.

Over the subsequent years, theories have abounded. Some believe that it perished in the fires or was destroyed by a direct hit. Others say it was burnt by Russian soldiers who captured the city in 1945, while another theory suggests that the room was dismantled and put to sea on a German ship that was then torpedoed and sunk. It has even been suggested (though not very credibly) that after his suicide Hitler's body was not burned in Berlin, but was buried in this legendary room.

But for many, the paths lead inextricably to the town of Deutschneudorf, near the border of Saxony and the Czech Republic. In 1997, a single panel from the original room was found during a raid by German police. It belonged to the family of a soldier who was allegedly present when the room was dismantled during the war. In 2008, a team of excavators claimed that they had found a man-made chamber 20 metres (66 ft) below ground near Deutschneudorf and that, after conducting electromagnetic tests on the site, they were convinced it contained some 2 tonnes of Nazi gold. The mayor of Deutschneudorf, Heinz-Peter Haustein, said that the area is home to a vast network of underground storage rooms from the period, and that he was '90 per cent sure' that the Amber Room lies somewhere within the complex. Indeed, the area is honeycombed by old silver, tin and copper mines, so there is no shortage of hiding places. But to date, the Amber Room's location remains a mystery.

In the meantime, a reconstruction of the room may now be seen at Tsarskoye Selo in the Catherine Palace. It opened in 2003, having taken 24 years to complete. Much of the US$11 million funding for the project was donated by German companies – perhaps one day it will be possible to compare it with the original.

The Führerbunker

LOCATION Beneath
Berlin, Germany
NEAREST POPULATION HUB
Berlin
SECRECY OVERVIEW
Location uncertain:
Hitler's underground
hideaway in the last days
of the Second World War.

Adolf Hitler spent his final days and hours in an underground bunker beneath the very buildings he had hoped would serve as the command centre for his Thousand Year Reich. Instead, the Führerbunker witnessed some of the most tawdry scenes in the story of history's most tawdry regime. After the war, the remains of the bunker festered beneath Berlin, sealed from the public and left to fade in the memory.

The Führerbunker was situated beneath the formidable Old Chancellery buildings (located at 77 Wilhelmstraße, close to the New Reich Chancellery that he had his favourite architect, Albert Speer, build for him on one of Wilhelmstraße's offshoots, Voßstraße). An entrance to the bunker led from the Chancellery gardens. The subterranean complex was built in two distinct phases, the first beginning in 1936 and the second in 1943. It was originally intended as a fairly standard air raid shelter, but as the tide of the war turned, Hitler envisaged it as an alternative command centre.

In terms of architecture, the complex was built on a split-level connected by a staircase. Each section had a steel door and a bulkhead so that they could be closed off from each other if necessary. Hitler's quarters were on the lower level, at a depth of about 15 metres (50 ft).

The bunker lay beneath a curtain of reinforced concrete, and was divided into around 18 rooms along a central corridor. Hitler and his lover (and, ultimately, wife), Eva Braun, shared a suite of six rooms decorated with furniture brought from the Chancellery. There was also a map room, a communications room and several guardrooms, as well as space for Martin Bormann (Hitler's private secretary), the family of Propaganda Minister Josef Goebbels and assorted other cohorts, all of whom lived out the last days of the war there.

The Battle for Berlin began in mid-April 1945, by which time Hitler had moved into the bunker. Overcome with paranoia and quite delusional, he clung to the hope that the city might be saved, but there was no realistic chance of escape. Hitler made his final trip to the world above on 20 April to award Iron Crosses to members of the Hitler Youth. Nine days later, he married Eva Braun in the map room before dictating his last will and testament. The following day the newlyweds killed themselves in the bunker, and were cremated in a shell hole in front of one of its emergency exits. The following day, Goebbels and

TYRANT'S END *A view of the Reich Chancellery gardens, with an entrance to the Führerbunker visible on the left. It was here, in a crater, that Hitler and his new bride, Eva Braun, were cremated after they had committed suicide in April 1945.*

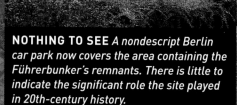

NOTHING TO SEE *A nondescript Berlin car park now covers the area containing the Führerbunker's remnants. There is little to indicate the significant role the site played in 20th-century history.*

River Spree

Central Berlin

Wannsee

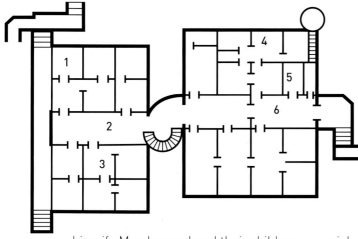

BUNKER PLANS *An overhead view of the Führerbunker as it would have looked in operation. The oldest part was the upper section (Vorbunker), completed in 1936 beneath a reception hall at the Reich Chancellery. The complex was extended by the HOCHTIEF construction company as the Second World War approached its final stages.*
Key: 1. Kitchen area, 2. Dining area, 3. Goebbels' family apartments, 4. Hitler's private rooms, 5. Map room, 6. Conference room.

his wife Magda murdered their children and then committed suicide.

By that point, the city was flooding with Soviet forces intent on wreaking revenge on their most bitter of enemies. When Red Army troops uncovered the bunker on 2 May, they discovered at least a dozen bodies within its confines. Though they would subsequently raze both the Old and New Chancellery buildings to the ground, the Führerbunker remained largely unharmed except for some flooding.

It was a long-held aim of post-war German governments to ensure the bunker did not become a pilgrimage site for neo-Nazis. In 1947, the Soviets attempted to blow it up completely, but only the separation walls suffered real damage. Much of the bunker lay in land that came under East German governance in the post-war era. Under Moscow's influence, East Germany did a characteristically effective job of erasing the site from the historical record. Although an attempt to blow up the remaining parts of the bunker ended in failure in 1959, the area became neglected and largely forgotten.

Building works in the locality in the 1980s led to further destruction of the Führerbunker's concrete canopy,

a job undertaken efficiently and without publicity. A further section was discovered during preparations for a 1990 concert celebrating German reunification by Roger Waters of Pink Floyd. However, it was promptly sealed up by the city authorities. Subsequent road and building projects (including the construction of housing for regional administrators) further hid whatever still remains beneath the ground. Even the Info Box, one of Berlin's leading tourist attractions in the 1990s, failed to mention the location of the site, although the attraction itself was within view of it.

As time passes, the argument grows that to recognize what is left of the bunker is not to glorify its chief builder. Other important locations from the war, such as Auschwitz-Birkenau or the Topography of Terror Museum on the site of the former SS and Gestapo headquarters, have proved valuable in teaching new generations about the horrors of the period. What is left of the Führerbunker is uncertain, but it is likely that some sections remain in place, should it ever be decided to open them up for historical study. In the meantime, since 2006 the location has been marked by a simple information board erected in the middle of a drab car park, some 200 metres (660 ft) from the city's Holocaust Memorial.

58

Vatican Secret Archives

LOCATION Vatican City
NEAREST POPULATION HUB Rome, Italy
SECRECY OVERVIEW Access restricted: the historical archives of the Roman Catholic Church.

The only entry in this book so hush-hush that it includes the word 'Secret' in its name, the Vatican Secret Archives is the repository for many of the most important documents related to the history of the papacy and the Roman Catholic Church. Although open to accredited researchers, much of the Archive's contents remains off-limits: critics suggest it hides evidence of numerous dark episodes from the past.

In reality, the word *Secretum* in the Archive's Latin name *Archivum Secretum Vaticanum* has more of a sense of 'privacy' than 'secrecy' – that is to say, the Archive is the papacy's private possession. Today it contains somewhere in the region of 85 kilometres (53 miles) of shelving, holding materials that date back to the eighth century.

It was Pope Paul V, in 1611, who commanded the construction of what became the Secret Archives, now located next to the Vatican Museums. The Archives opened on 31 January 1612, with Baldassarre Ansidei as their first custodian. In 1810, Napoleon Bonaparte transferred many of the contents to Paris, but most were returned by 1817 following Napoleon's fall from power. In 1881, Pope Leo XIII took the momentous step of opening up the Archives for scholarly research. Documentation has subsequently been released on a pontificate-by-pontificate basis – at present, access is available to materials dating to the end of Pope Pius XI's reign in 1939.

In 1980, Pope John Paul II inaugurated an extension to the Archives, a two-storey underground bunker beneath the Vatican Museums' Cortile della Pigna. Providing 31,000 cubic metres (330,000 cu ft) of climate-controlled storage in a reinforced, fire-resistant concrete structure fitted with the latest security features, it is now home to some of the Church's most valuable documents.

Among the Archive's treasure are documents relating to the bloody period of the Inquisition. It also houses King Henry VIII of England's petitions for divorce from Catherine of Aragon, the rejection of which led to the foundation of the Church of England beyond papal jurisdiction. (Pope Clement VII may have received as many as 80 petitions on the issue, all bound in red ribbons that some believe are the origin of the phrase 'red tape' to indicate excessive bureaucracy).

There is also literature relating to the trial of Galileo in 1633 on charges of heresy (the papacy not being overly keen on his insistence that the Earth was not

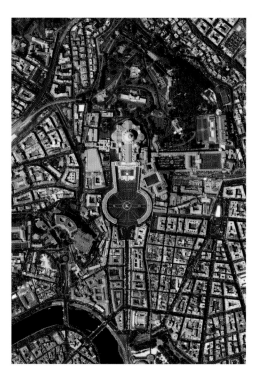

at the centre of the Universe), as well as a letter from Michelangelo complaining about late payment for his painting and decorating work.

However, some outside of the Church accuse the Archives of being too reticent about sharing its history. For instance, many questions have been posed about the Catholic Church's actions during the Second World War. In 2005, the US-based Coalition for Jewish Concerns even threatened to sue the Vatican unless it produced materials that could identify Jewish children baptized as Catholics to save them from Nazi persecution.

The Church, on the other hand, points to the fact that it is quite normal for deposits in other archives to remain unopened for decades and even centuries in the hope that the passage of time will protect them from the threat of political manipulation. Furthermore, it has sanctioned some early releases, as in 2004 when it opened files relating to the Vatican's relations with Germany from 1922 up to the outbreak of the war. Pope John Paul II also granted early access to files concerning prisoners of war in the 1939–45 period.

Yet access even to those parts of the Archive that are open is no simple business. All researchers must have a university degree or equivalent, and members of the clergy need a licentiate degree or PhD. Before access is granted, a formal application must be made, accompanied by a letter from a recognized institute or qualified individual in the field of historical research. If there is already someone

researching in your particular area of interest, you've probably had it.

One group that can command early access to documentation are postulators of sainthood (i.e. those putting forward a candidate for sainthood). This, it must be presumed, is to ensure that the Church's saints have no nasty skeletons lurking in the cupboard. But even postulators must be granted special access from the Vatican's secretary of state, and are duty-bound not to divulge any information that they may turn up.

In 2012, an exhibition featuring a hundred documents from the Archives was held in Rome's Capitoline Museums. It was the first time any of them had been allowed outside of the Vatican. While it was a further step along the road to transparency, the suspicion lingers that the Archives are rather like a giant iceberg – the bits you can see are fascinating, but the really amazing stuff is hidden underneath the surface.

59

Radio Liberty Building

LOCATION Hagibor, Prague, Czech Republic
NEAREST POPULATION HUB Prague
SECRECY OVERVIEW High-security location: home of Radio Free Europe/Radio Liberty.

Now into its seventh decade of providing uncensored news to regions where it is in short supply, Radio Free Europe/Radio Liberty (RFE/RL) has regularly attracted the opprobrium of governments and, increasingly, militant organizations. Because of this, it has been forced to construct one of the world's most secure buildings to serve as its headquarters.

Radio Free Europe was established in 1950, at the start of the Cold War. Its original aim was to maintain a supply of uncensored news to audiences in the Soviet sphere of influence, including the citizens of Bulgaria, Czechoslovakia, Hungary, Poland and Romania. Radio Liberty emerged three years later to broadcast to the USSR. For many years both stations were primarily funded by the CIA, and in 1976 they were merged.

RFE/RL soon became a prime target for governments behind the Iron Curtain. In 1978, for instance, the Bulgarian dissident and RFE contributor Georgi Markov was assassinated in London by Bulgarian secret police, who infamously used a poisoned umbrella to kill him. Three years later, RFE/RL's Munich headquarters were bombed by the Romanian secret services.

After the collapse of communism around 1990, RFE/RL stopped broadcasting to many of its former territories, but began operations in several new regions, including the states of the former Yugoslavia, Iran, Iraq, Afghanistan and Pakistan. Today, it broadcasts in 28 different languages across 20 countries, to a weekly audience of 25 million.

Having struggled to continue financing its Munich headquarters, RFE/RL moved to Prague in 1995 at the invitation of Czech President Vaclav Havel. Somewhat ironically, the station worked out of headquarters that were once home to the country's communist party.

However, in 2009 RFE/RL moved again, this time to new, purpose-built premises in the Hagibor district of the city. Designed by Jakub Cigler and Vincent Marani, the five-storey headquarters houses 500 employees. It is one of the most heavily protected buildings in the world – a necessity given the station's on-going status as a terrorist target. Security provisions include strengthened steel doors and barriers, and under-vehicle surveillance at entrance points. Door codes are even required to gain access between floors. Freedom and liberty, it seems, come at a price.

Svalbard Global Seed Vault

60

LOCATION Spitsbergen, Svalbard, Norway
NEAREST POPULATION HUB Longyearbyen, Svalbard
SECRECY OVERVIEW High-security location: an underground vault for the storage of plant seeds from around the world.

With the world constantly on the brink of disaster, many countries have taken the precaution of putting seed samples from plants (especially food crops) into secure storage. If a species is unexpectedly wiped out, it can be recreated from deposits held in such seed banks. The Svalbard Vault is essentially 'the banker's bank', home to backup seed samples from other seed banks scattered across the globe.

While many nations have established seed banks within their own boundaries, they face the eternal question of what happens if whatever destroys a species in the first place also takes out the seed bank. Nuclear weapons or tsunamis are, after all, indiscriminate. The Global Seed Vault, sited some 1,300 kilometres (800 miles) from the North Pole is, in effect, a vast insurance policy against global catastrophe and the loss of diversity.

Located on Spitsbergen, the largest island of the Svalbard archipelago (a possession of Norway), the Vault consists of three main chambers, some 120 metres (390 ft) within a sandstone mountain. This location was chosen in part for it remoteness – any would-be intruders would face quite a task to even get to Svalbard, let alone enter the Vault itself. Just as importantly, however, the region is among the most peaceful and politically stable in the world (no doubt because of the relatively small numbers of people). In addition, the area lies 130 metres (430 ft) above sea level, so would likely escape unscathed even in the event of the polar ice caps melting. It also experiences little disruptive tectonic activity and has a permafrost ideal for maintaining the optimum climatic conditions to preserve the seeds.

Opened in 2008, the Vault cost just short of US$10 million to build and is run according to an agreement signed by the government of Norway, the Nordic Genetic Resource Centre and the Global Crop Diversity Trust. It receives funding from assorted national governments and international non-governmental organizations. As with other types of safe deposit banks, deposits remain the exclusive property of the depositor and neither the Vault's management nor the Norwegian government have any claim upon them. However, if a country were no longer to exist for any reason, it is unclear who would then own that nation's particular deposit.

The Vault was designed with a lifespan of some 1,000 years. Access to its chambers is via a 98-metre (320-ft) tunnel, which has a brushed-steel

Main chambers, each 20 metres (66 ft) long

SUSPENDED ANIMATION

The Svalbard Global Seed Vault stores back-up samples of seeds from around the world at subzero temperatures deep beneath the Arctic permafrost. Access to the storage chambers is secured by a 98-metre (320-ft) tunnel divided into three locked sections.

Access doors requiring multiple keys

Control room and refrigeration plant maintaining temperature around -18°C (0°F)

Reinforced 'sleeve' protecting access tunnel from erosion

Entrance building

SOWING THE SEEDS

Samples are securely stored in plastic containers kept on metal shelves in one of three climate-controlled main storage chambers. There is no charge to make a deposit, with costs covered by a mixture of charitable and governmental contributions.

entrance portal. The tunnel itself is divided into three separate locked sections, each section progressively colder and icier. A thick concrete wall and a large metal door blocks the way to the chambers. Each chamber – some 20 metres (66 ft) deep, 10 metres (33 ft) across and 6 metres (20 ft) high – is kept at a steady -18°C (0°F). Any uninvited guests will soon feel the effects of this low temperature and the low oxygen levels necessary to delay seed ageing. There is enough room in the Vault to store 4.5 million seed samples.

Each deposit goes into an extra-thick, heat-sealed padded envelope that excludes any possibility of the contents being exposed to the elements. Deposits are X-rayed upon arrival on the island, to ensure they contain nothing harmful or dangerous.

The Vault is opened, on average, twice a year to make new deposits, but entry is strictly limited. It is said that the Vault doors can be opened by one of only four individual keys. Rumour has it that on an official visit, not even the Norwegian royal family were allowed into the main

chambers themselves, and while it is possible to arrange visits to the general site, you will need to thoroughly prove your credentials and undergo extensive security checks. The limited roll call evidenced by the Vault's guest book includes UN Secretary-General Ban Ki-moon and former US President and Nobel Peace Prize winner, Jimmy Carter. Considering that the contents of the seed Vault might one day just save the planet from extinction, one can hardly complain about this exclusivity.

It should also be noted that an extra layer of security is offered around Spitsbergen by the population of native polar bears, among the most dangerous species on the planet and far more able to operate in the Arctic conditions than any human.

However, should you find yourself in the area, you may wish to treat yourself to dinner at Huset in Longyearbyen, the administrative capital of the archipelago. This is the world's most northerly restaurant to boast a Michelin star – and fortunately, the menu is not overly reliant on local produce.

61

Pionen White Mountains

LOCATION Vita Berg Park, Stockholm, Sweden
NEAREST POPULATION HUB Stockholm
SECRECY OVERVIEW High-security location: a secure data centre best known for hosting the servers of WikiLeaks.

A spectacular underground facility drilled into the granite beneath Vita Berg Park (White Mountain Park) in the Södermalm district of Stockholm, Pionen White Mountains is one of the world's most advanced computer centres. It hosts the servers of numerous companies, including, since the end of 2010, the controversial WikiLeaks organization.

Within a year of launching its website in 2007, WikiLeaks boasted a database of almost 1.25 million secret and confidential documents, often deposited by anonymous whistle-blowers from around the world.

Led by an enigmatic Australian called Julian Assange, the organization quickly became a major thorn in the side of authorities on every continent. It won particular notoriety when it released extensive material relating to the wars in Iraq and Afghanistan, prompting serious examination of Allied conduct during those conflicts.

In 2010, WikiLeaks also released vast numbers of confidential US diplomatic cables, causing Washington severe embarrassment since many prominent public figures were described in less-than-flattering terms. Originally, the documents were published with certain key information excluded to protect the identity of individuals, but this precaution was later lifted by Assange (who had by then been indicted for sex offences in

Sweden). His decision drew widespread opprobrium from critics, who claimed he was putting the safety of named individuals at risk for his own idealistic belief in 'openness'. Some called his actions treasonous, and WikiLeaks became the focus of renewed attention from governments across the globe.

The hosting of the expanding WikiLeaks database had already moved several times, and was then thrown off Amazon's servers, apparently for breaching its terms of service. In late 2010, the organization relocated its hosting to Bahnhof, one of Sweden's oldest internet companies (founded by Oscar Swartz in 1994) and the owners of the Pionen White Mountains.

The Vita Berg facility was originally built during the Second World War and was later converted to be able to withstand a Soviet nuclear attack. It lies under 30 metres (100 ft) of bedrock beneath the city, protected by armour-plated metal doors almost half a metre (20 in) thick. Accessible by a single entrance,

BRAINSTORMING

Even if you're only reviewing the latest quarterly profit figures, Pionen offers a range of ultramodern conference facilities fit for a Bond villain – guaranteed to make you feel like global domination is only a breath away.

SNOWY MOUNTAIN

The main entrance to the Bahnhof server rooms is embedded in the side of the Vita Bergen hill in Stockholm's Södermalm district. In winter, hot exhaust from the air-conditioning envelopes the entrance in mist.

FINLAND

NORWAY

ESTONIA

SWEDEN

LATVIA

LITHUANIA

DENMARK

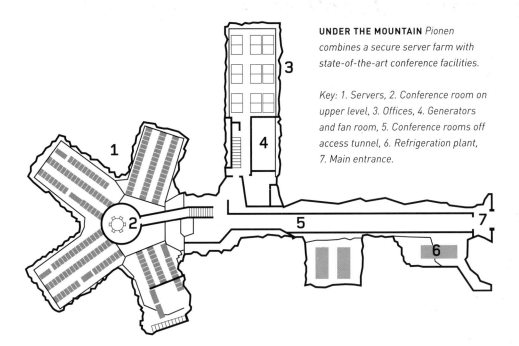

the bunker has 24-hour surveillance cameras in operation to ensure that no visitors go unrecorded.

This distinctly unglamorous Cold War-era space had long been out of operation when, in 2007-08, Albert France-Lanord Architects completely overhauled and significantly expanded it for Bahnhof. It now covers 1,200 square metres (13,000 sq ft), and is often likened to the lair of a James Bond villain, with good reason. The space is filled with exotic jungle-like foliage, artificial waterfalls and solar lighting, while the floors are designed to resemble space-scapes. There is a futuristic 'floating' conference room, suspended glass corridors and even two German V12 diesel submarine engines providing a back-up power supply. It is about as sexy as cutting-edge internet technology can hope to get.

The relationship between Bahnhof and Assange seems well matched. Assange is undoubtedly fond of the dramatic gesture and no doubt the spectacular design of Pionen White Mountains appeals to that side of him. Perhaps more significantly, Sweden has particularly strong legislation protecting journalistic sources. Assange has confirmed that he set out to nurture a relationship with the country (along with others such as Switzerland and Iceland) 'specifically because those nations offer legal protection to the disclosures made on the site'.

In other words, the servers at Pionen White Mountains, which no doubt contain yet more information to make life difficult for powerful figures across the planet, have statutory legal protection to go along with the extensive security systems guarding this subterranean Hollywood set.

Meanwhile, Bahnhof is clear that WikiLeaks is treated with the same discretion and respect as any of the other clients who rent its hosting services. As Jon Karlung, Bahnhof's head (and unsurprisingly, an avowed fan of the Bond movies) told *Forbes* magazine in 2010: 'The internet should be an open source for freedom of speech, and the role of an ISP [Internet Service Provider] is to be a neutral technological tool of access, not an instrument for collecting information from customers.'

Varosha

LOCATION Eastern Cyprus
NEAREST POPULATION HUB
Famagusta, Cyprus
SECRECY OVERVIEW Access
restricted: a fenced-off
ghost town since the
Turkish invasion of
Cyprus in 1974.

In its heyday, the sun-soaked Mediterranean beaches of Varosha made it one of the world's most popular holiday destinations. Filled with luxurious high-rise hotels, it was beloved by the Hollywood jet set, with visitors ranging from Elizabeth Taylor and Richard Burton to Brigitte Bardot. But in 1974, politics intervened and life as it was known in this tourist playground came to a grinding halt.

The Varosha area is a neighbourhood (if it can now be called that) of Famagusta, a city lying just north of the Atilla Line that today divides Cyprus between the Greek south and the Turkish north. The impressive John F Kennedy Avenue that runs boldly through the middle of Varosha was once the focal point of its tourist industry, the resort a veritable byword for Mediterranean glamour.

Then in 1974 a Greek-backed coup was launched against Makarios III. Makarios was the Cypriot Orthodox archbishop who had served as President since Cyprus gained independence in 1960. His rule, though, was a divisive one and UN forces were required to keep the peace between the resident Turkish and Greek populations. The 1974 Athens-inspired coup prompted an invasion by Turkish forces and saw the island split between the Greek-run south and the Turkish Republic of Northern Cyprus, a situation that continues to this day.

Famagusta fell under the control of the Turkish authorities, and the population

of Varosha – almost all of whom were Greek-Cypriot – fled their beach paradise on 15 August 1974, in fear of the fighting then raging less than a mile away between Greek and Turkish troops.

Varosha now resembles a modern-day Pompeii, capturing a lost moment of time. Breakfasts sit half-eaten on tables beneath light bulbs that burned for years, no one having turned them off in the exodus. Car dealerships sit silent, their forecourts filled with what were the latest models back in 1974. Similarly, boutiques are stocked with the dubious fashions of the mid-1970s.

Meanwhile, buildings uncared for and unloved for almost four decades, slowly deteriorate as nature inexorably reclaims her territory. The roots of untended plants and trees are gradually undermining the structural safety of once grand edifices, as untreated roads crack under season after season of raging sunshine. Beaches once populated by sun-seekers are now home to colonies of sea turtles.

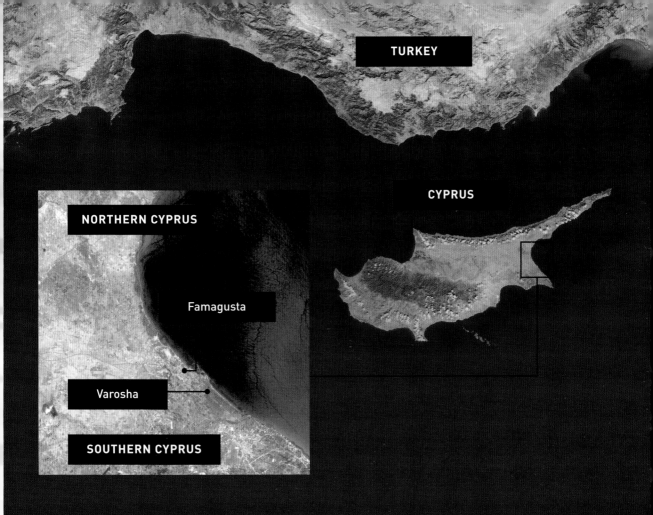

TURKEY

CYPRUS

NORTHERN CYPRUS

Famagusta

Varosha

SOUTHERN CYPRUS

VACANCIES *A row of luxury hotels and apartment blocks stares blankly across the sands of Varosha beach, towards the Mediterranean. Nearby beach umbrellas seem to await the return of long-vanished sunbathers.*

cattle. Doves, widely kept as pets, are another popular import.

Dug to a depth of between 3 and 20 metres (10–66 ft), with most lying at about 15 metres (50 ft), the tunnels can stretch as far as 800 metres (half a mile). Their size varies enormously, but most are little more than shoulder-width. On the Gazan side they are often accessed from basements beneath private properties (and on occasion from secluded olive groves), using ladders down brick shafts. They tend to be private enterprises, offering significant profits to the individuals or groups who fund them. With everyone from the owners and smugglers to Hamas inspectors getting a cut, it can be big business

Construction costs for a typical tunnel approach US$100,000, and management costs are also significant. Some projects incorporate electric power, communications systems and advanced ventilation. However, in 2009 there were reports that many natives of Gaza had lost their life-savings to dishonest

entrepreneurs in tunnel investment schemes. Anywhere between US$100 million and US$500 million of capital was believed to have disappeared in this manner. Estimates made in 2010 suggest that there are more than 1,000 tunnels in existence, employing a workforce of some 7,000. Life in the tunnels can be dangerous and collapses are not unknown, with fatalities often the result.

Attempts have been made over the years to stifle the illicit trading. The international community, including leading NATO members, has vowed to work to bring an end to this unregulated and dangerous subterranean world. Israel has destroyed several hundred tunnels in airstrikes, and developed electro-optic technology for the specific purpose of identifying the location of tunnels through soil displacements that are invisible to the human eye. In 2009, Egypt began construction of an underground barrier to block existing tunnels and hinder the creation of new ones. Yet perhaps the death knell for the tunnels will only come when official imports into the territory are regularized.

Mossad Headquarters

LOCATION Herzliya, Tel Aviv, Israel
NEAREST POPULATION HUB Tel Aviv
SECRECY OVERVIEW Location uncertain: headquarters of the Israeli secret intelligence agency.

Israel's Institute for Intelligence and Special Operations – better known as Mossad – is one of the world's most feared security services. Its stated role is to 'collect information, analyze intelligence and perform special covert operations beyond its borders'. The organization's headquarters are in Tel Aviv, though their exact location is not in the public domain.

The modern state of Israel was founded in 1948, situated amid Arab nations that were at best apathetic to its creation, and with the Holocaust a recent memory. The nation's first prime minister, David Ben-Gurion, made it a priority to establish an intelligence service to ensure national security, commenting: 'For our state which since its creation has been under siege by its enemies, intelligence constitutes the first line of defence.'

In late 1949, the Central Institute for Coordination was set up under the directorship of Reuven Shiloah. Shortly afterwards, it was redesignated as the Central Institute for Intelligence and Security, before a further restructure resulted in the creation of Mossad in 1951. Directly answerable to the Prime Minister, its subsequent operational focus has been on intelligence-gathering, counter-terrorism and covert action. Today it is estimated to have somewhere between 1,000 and 2,000 personnel.

Mossad's name became famous through high-profile operations such as the 1960 capture in Argentina of Adolf Eichmann, one of the chief architects of Hitler's Holocaust. However, other operations – especially the activities of its Special Operations Division – have sometimes led to run-ins with other nations. For instance, the 1986 kidnap of nuclear programme whistle-blower Mordechai Vanunu from Italy (see page 166) was particularly controversial. As recently as 2010, the UK expelled Mossad's London station chief after Israeli operatives used cloned British passports in a mission to assassinate a leading Hamas member in Dubai.

Despite recent attempts to bring a little transparency to the service (it even has a website these days), the precise location of its Tel Aviv headquarters is kept out of the public sphere. Some have speculated that it is in Herzliya, the diplomatic quarter in the west of the city. German magazine *Der Spiegel*, meanwhile, has alluded to an 'inconspicuous block of houses located among eucalyptus trees'. It is not, one suspects, an office notably keen on surprise visits.

SECRET SERVICE *While the location of the Mossad headquarters is a closely guarded secret, many believe it is situated somewhere in Herzliya, a coastal town on the outskirts of Tel Aviv. Its Herzliya Pituah neighbourhood is among the most affluent in the country, and home to many foreign diplomats.*

DEFENDING ISRAEL
Mossad operatives are thought to be posted at many Israeli embassies around the world, but evidence suggests that some of its most controversial activities have been carried out by agents masquerading as foreign nationals using faked passports.

65 Negev Nuclear Research Centre

LOCATION Negev Desert, southern Israel
NEAREST POPULATION HUB Dimona
SECRECY OVERVIEW Operations classified: centre of Israel's nuclear weapons development programme.

While the government in Tel Aviv acknowledges the existence of an installation in the Negev Desert, it maintains silence on its exact purpose. Nonetheless, there is widespread speculation that this is the heart of Israel's nuclear project – an initiative that has prompted the International Atomic Energy Agency (IAEA) to express concerns about nuclear proliferation in the Middle East.

Israel itself operates a policy of 'nuclear ambiguity', whereby the question of whether the country has nuclear weapons is never officially confirmed or denied. Instead, since 1965 the country has stated that it will 'not be the first' country to introduce weapons to the Middle East – a line that is open to disparate interpretations. It is one of four nations (along with India, North Korea and Pakistan) believed or known to have nuclear capabilities but who are not signatories to the Nuclear Non-Proliferation Treaty.

According to the Israel Atomic Energy Commission, the work undertaken at Negev is to 'broaden basic knowledge in nuclear sciences and adjacent fields and to provide the foundation of the practical and economic utilization of nuclear energy'. Construction of the research centre began in secret in 1958, with French assistance. As many as 1,500 Israelis were employed in building it at any one time, and it is alleged that an Office of Science Liaisons was established in Israel specifically to provide the enterprise with security and intelligence. The facility became operational at the end of 1963.

However, the West became aware of Negev as early as 1960 in a series of opaque and then gradually more explicit newspaper revelations. The news prompted Israeli Prime Minister David Ben-Gurion to claim that Negev was a facility dedicated to 'peaceful purposes'. However, the chairman of the Israel Atomic Energy Commission was later quoted as saying: 'There is no distinction between nuclear energy for peaceful purposes or warlike ones.'

US inspectors made several visits to Negev over the course of the 1960s, although the Israeli authorities demanded prior warning of their arrival. While these inspections failed to uncover evidence of weapons-related activity (which some have alleged was as a result of Israeli obstruction), other intelligence had led the US to conclude by the end of the decade that Israel might well be in possession of the bomb.

Haifa

NUCLEAR AMBIGUITY *A ground-level view of the complex near Dimona, taken around 2000. While Tel Aviv continues its policy of neither confirming nor denying possessing the bomb, fears grow that Iran may join Israel as a regional nuclear power.*

Tel Aviv

Dead Sea

ISRAEL

JORDAN

Dimona

DESERT STORM
An overhead view of the controversial complex at Negev, taken by an American strategic reconnaissance satellite – Corona KH-4 – in November 1968. Such images left Washington to conclude that Tel Aviv was indeed in possession of the bomb.

EGYPT

INCENDIARY IMAGES

This photograph was taken in 1985 by Mordechai Vanunu, allegedly showing components to be used in Israel's nuclear weapons programme. Vanunu came to the West to blow the whistle on what he had seen at Negev, turning his own life upside-down in the process.

Confirmation of these rumours apparently came in 1986, when a former Negev nuclear engineer named Mordechai Vanunu defected from Israel and travelled to the UK. Vanunu had worked at Negev since 1977 but harboured severe doubts about several aspects of Israeli foreign policy. He lost his job at Negev in 1985, whereupon he undertook a period of travel, during which he met a journalist who acted as his agent in a deal with the *Sunday Times* newspaper. Vanunu revealed what he knew about Negev, backed up with photographs he had secretly taken. His evidence, considered credible by numerous experts, led to an estimate that the Israeli arsenal consisted of over 100 weapons.

What followed was a storyline worthy of any movie. Mossad, Israel's secret service (see page 162), employed a female agent to pose as an American and befriend Vanunu, who was rumoured to be lonely away from his homeland. The agent persuaded Vanunu to accompany her on a holiday to Rome. Once settled in the Eternal City, three more Mossad agents arrived on the scene, drugged their quarry and smuggled him back to Israel. There, he was tried for treason and espionage and sentenced to 18 years in prison. In 2004

Vanunu would make entirely unproven claims that Israel had been complicit in the assassination of President John F. Kennedy as a result of Washington's demands for information on Negev.

Most of Negev's facilities are built underground, purportedly to a depth of six floors. The airspace above the base is closed to aircraft, with Israeli Air Force jets on standby to scramble in the event of a breach. It is also rumoured that a battery of anti-aircraft missile launchers are in operation around the site. Existing security measures on the ground (including fences and a heavy presence of guards) were supplemented with additional cutting-edge cameras and surveillance equipment following a security review in late 2011.

Mystery continues to surround Negev, with varying estimates as to the quantity of plutonium that it is capable of producing. This has led to wildly differing guesses as to how many nuclear weapons now comprise Israel's arsenal. In early 2012, it was reported in the Western media that Negev may close as Israel seeks to safeguard its assets in the event of an Iranian air strike. The story, however, was denied by an Israeli official.

Camp 1391

LOCATION Northern Israel
NEAREST POPULATION HUB
Tel Aviv
SECRECY OVERVIEW
Existence unacknowledged:
controversial prison camp
for 'high-risk' prisoners,
previously unacknowledged
by Israel.

Unknown to the wider world until 2003, Camp 1391 is located about an hour's drive from Tel Aviv, though its exact position has never been confirmed. Described by some commentators as 'Israel's Guantánamo', it has been accused of breaches of the United Nations Convention Against Torture. Petitions to inspect the camp by the UN Committee Against Torture have repeatedly been rejected.

Camp 1391 came to light by chance, as a result of a small footnote in an academic journal. The article's author was a historian called Gad Krozier. While inspecting maps of police compounds dating back to the British rule of the 1930s and 1940s, he noticed discrepancies with modern maps over one site in particular. After the article and its footnote were published, the military censor demanded to know why the piece had not been sent for prior inspection. The site, apparently erased from Israeli history books, turned out to be Camp 1391, run by Israel's security service since the early 1980s.

Official information about the prison is virtually nonexistent, and most details in the public sphere come from sources who claim to have been held there. Israel's courts have consistently rejected appeals to reveal its precise location. However, it has been suggested that it is based in a single-storey building, designed by Sir Charles Tegart in the 1930s and now part of a larger military compound. 'Tegart forts' were built in their dozens by the British in Palestine, being robust if basic reinforced-concrete structures designed to be all but impregnable. It has been reported that the site of Camp 1391 also lies within a double fence, complete with watchtowers and regular guard-dog patrols.

Cells are described as about 2 metres (6.6 ft) square and lacking any natural light. It is alleged that prisoners are kept in solitary confinement for long spells, sometimes naked and hooded. Former inmates claim they were forced to endure a constant buzzing drone and insanitary conditions, as well as inhumane and degrading treatment.

Some prisoners allege they were given no indication of their true whereabouts, or were told that they were being held abroad. Many say they were not allowed contact with family or lawyers, or even visits from the Red Cross. The Israeli authorities argue that meetings with lawyers and the Red Cross are, in fact, permitted at an off-site location, though this has been questioned by the UN.

Al Kibar

LOCATION
Northeastern Syria
NEAREST POPULATION HUB
Dayr az Zawr
SECRECY OVERVIEW
Operations classified:
site of a suspected
nuclear facility bombed
by Israel in 2007.

On 6 September 2007, it is widely accepted that a squadron of Israeli jet fighters flew across Syria and razed a major complex at Al Kibar to rubble in a mission known as Operation Orchard. Later, Israel would deny that such an incident took place, while Syria protested the violation of their airspace but denied that there had been significant damage. So what exactly was going on in the Syrian desert?

Within hours of the attack, the Syrian news agency reported an incident in which air defence units had confronted Israeli planes and 'forced them to leave after they dropped some ammunition in deserted areas without causing any human or material damage'. An Israeli spokesman was reported as saying that 'This incident never occurred', while US officials spoke of 'second-hand reports' that contradicted each other.

The rumour mill inevitably went into overdrive, with claims that Al Kibar was actually a nuclear complex built with the assistance of North Korea. Syrian scientists at the plant, it was said, were on the verge of building a viable nuclear bomb. It is now thought that work on the complex got underway around 2002, and in 2004 US intelligence picked up on an unusually high volume of contact between Al Kibar and Pyongyang. The US would later release photographs showing what seemed to be reactor components at the site, and others showing the construction of buildings apparently designed to disguise what lay within.

Al Kibar remains strictly off-limits to visitors, a fact attested to by residents of Dayr az Zawr, the last major outpost of civilization before the vast stretch of desert in which Al Kibar lies. Anyone who dares to cross the inhospitable landscape will soon find themselves subject to impassable roadblocks, while locals are warned that access is forbidden on security grounds.

Under international pressure, the Syrian government eventually claimed that the site had been a conventional weapons facility, and categorically denied any involvement by international partners. In 2008, Damascus finally allowed experts from the International Atomic Energy Agency (IAEA) to inspect Al Kibar. They found a site that had been hurriedly cleared of debris and concreted over – suggesting the Syrians had something to hide. Sure enough, despite the absence of a 'smoking gun', the IAEA concluded in 2011 that Al Kibar almost certainly had been a nuclear facility – one that for a long time none of the key regional players have wanted to admit existed.

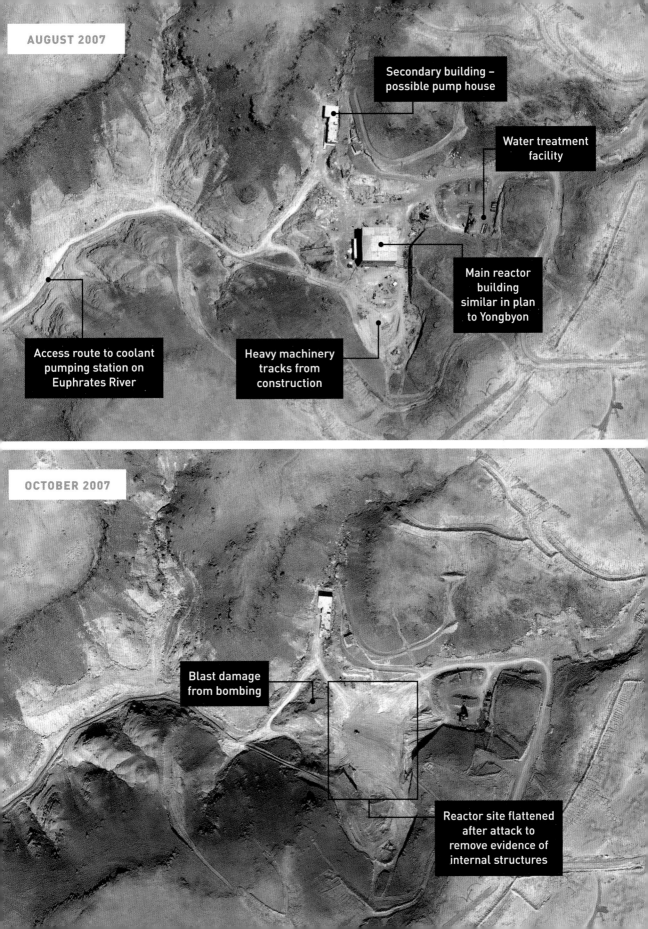

AUGUST 2007

Secondary building –
possible pump house

Water treatment
facility

Main reactor
building
similar in plan
to Yongbyon

Access route to coolant
pumping station on
Euphrates River

Heavy machinery
tracks from
construction

OCTOBER 2007

Blast damage
from bombing

Reactor site flattened
after attack to
remove evidence of
internal structures

The Ararat anomaly

LOCATION Mount Ararat, Turkey

NEAREST POPULATION HUB Dogubayazıt

SECRECY OVERVIEW Site of historic mystery: an unexplained object seen on satellite photos that some claim is Noah's Ark.

In 1949, a US Air Force surveillance plane took pictures above Mount Ararat where, according to the Book of Genesis, Noah's Ark came to rest after the retreat of the biblical flood. When the images were inspected, some claimed they revealed a partially buried object on the northwest corner of the mountain's Western Plateau. Was it, some have asked, the remains of the Ark?

Mount Ararat, situated close to the sensitive border of Turkey, Iran and what was then the Soviet Union, understandably became a site of great interest to the US government in the early years of the Cold War. The 1949 images, taken during a reconnaissance flight authorized by Headquarters US Air Force Europe – reveal a strange anomaly about 4,700 metres (15,500 ft) up the mountain, which has a summit of some 5,100 metres (16,700 ft). The pictures were immediately classified as secret, and a file was opened which would go on to include numerous other images of the anomaly taken from a variety of aircraft and satellites over the ensuing decades.

Expeditions have been attempting to track down the remains of the Ark on Ararat since at least the 19th century, and rumours insisted that the various reconnaissance flights and other missions had seen something. However, it was only in 1995, thanks to the persistence of University of Richmond Professor Porcher Taylor, that stills

from the 1949 footage were finally declassified. Other images still remain secret even today.

What exactly is depicted is a source of heated debate. In the opinion of the US Defense Intelligence Agency, the images show nothing more than 'linear façades in the glacial ice underlying more recently accumulated ice and snow'. Meanwhile, Dino Brugioni, the founder of the CIA's National Photographic Interpretation Center, concluded that: 'Oh, it looked like a bow of a ship stuck in the mountain. But it did not conform with the Bible dimensions. It was much too large.' Others have claimed that they can make out a number of carved wooden beams.

Of course, the chances of a wooden boat surviving several thousand years up a mountain are remote. Furthermore, no one has yet brought back physical evidence from the site of the anomaly. But if it's all just a trick of the light, why does so much official secrecy still surround the images?

QUICKBIRD CLOSE-UP

The DigitalGlobe QuickBird satellite made this image of the Ararat Anomaly in 2003, revealing that its surface is apparently quite smooth in relation to the rougher rocks around it (though not as smooth as the overlying snowcap).

GEORGIA

ARMENIA

AZERBAIJAN

TURKEY

IRAN

BIBLICAL PEAK *While Mount Ararat itself has become associated with the Ark in the Western imagination, the biblical text actually says that the ship came to rest in the Mountains of Ararat – a far larger region straddling the borders of Turkey. The Armenian monastery at Khor Virap (above) commands spectacular views of the mountain.*

Chernobyl Exclusion Zone

69

LOCATION Kiev Oblast, Ukraine
NEAREST POPULATION HUB Kiev
SECRECY OVERVIEW Access restricted: the now-deserted scene of the world's worst nuclear accident.

In 1986, Chernobyl in the Ukraine was the scene of the most devastating nuclear disaster in history. An Exclusion Zone around the site of the reactor that exploded, sometimes known as the Zone of Alienation, extends for 30 kilometres (19 miles) and remains a largely no-go area for all but a small community of researchers tracking the continuing impact of the tragedy.

Construction of the Chernobyl Nuclear Power Plant, situated close to the border of the Ukraine and Belarus, began in 1970. At that time, the Ukraine was one of the constituent states of the Soviet Union, and the plant was officially called the V.I. Lenin Nuclear Power Station. An entire city, Pripyat, was built at the same time to provide homes for the plant's workers and their families. The first reactor went into service in 1977, and three more were running by 1983. Two more reactors were under construction when disaster struck on 26 April 1986.

By that stage, Chernobyl's four reactors were producing about 10 per cent of the Ukraine's electricity. However, the plant already had a somewhat calamitous history – in 1982, Reactor No. 1 suffered a partial meltdown that was covered up by the communist regime in Moscow. But this incident paled in comparison to what happened to Reactor 4 on that April Saturday. A power surge led to a series of explosions within the reactor, exposing its graphite moderator, which then caught fire. Vast clouds of radioactive smoke rose into the skies over Europe, with the highest proportion of fallout landing on Belarus. Large-scale releases of radionuclides continued for ten days after the accident, and it is estimated that some 200,000 square kilometres (80,000 square miles) of Europe suffered at least some contamination.

The immediate priority for the government in Moscow was crisis containment. The 53,000 inhabitants of Pripyat were not evacuated until the following day, and news of the disaster was not broadcast until the following Monday, and then only as a television announcement lasting less than 30 seconds. The longer-term impact of events at Chernobyl is hard to calculate – Soviet figures attributed just 31 deaths to the disaster, but other health experts suggest that tens of thousands might eventually die of cancers related to the effects of the fallout.

The Soviet government incurred massive expense in attempting a clean-up and relocating more than 350,000 people

Pripyat River

SCATTERED DEBRIS *More than 1,000 square kilometres (380 sq miles) of land directly around Chernobyl were blanketed with dangerous heavy elements following the explosion. Lighter radioactive isotopes were scattered across much of Europe, affecting agriculture for years.*

Town of Pripyat

Cooling pond

Reactor No. 4

Electricity pylons

Water conduit to reactors

Reactors under construction in 1986

ABANDONED DREAMS
A deserted classroom stands eerie and silent witness to the devastation wrought by the Chernobyl disaster. The entire area was hurriedly evacuated and those who dare venture back today can expect to find an unsettling world reminiscent of a modern-day Marie Celeste.

FINAL RESTING PLACE *Shortly after the initial disaster in 1986, a metal and concrete sarcophagus was hastily erected over Reactor 4 to lock in some 250,000 tonnes of radioactive materials. Amid concerns about its structural integrity, there are now plans to build a replacement 'New Safe Confinement' structure.*

costing US$1.4 billion would be built by 2013. Amazingly, Chernobyl continued to operate for many years after the disaster. In 1991 another fire broke out (this time in Reactor 2), and it was only in 2000 that the plant was finally closed down by the now-independent Ukrainian government. Nonetheless, decommissioning is expected to last for many more years.

As for the citizens of Pripyat, they were commanded to abandon their previous lives with virtually no notice. Most were unceremoniously forced on to buses by armed soldiers in an afternoon. Many left assuming they would soon return. They never have, and today Pripyat stands abandoned. A rusty, lonely-looking Ferris wheel that once brought pleasure to the town's visitors is now one of the more potent symbols of what happened at Chernobyl. Many of its inhabitants have subsequently complained of health problems, both physical and psychological. Indeed, the Chernobyl Forum (an initiative of the International Atomic Energy Agency) reported that 'the mental health impact of Chernobyl is the largest public health problem unleashed by the accident to date'.

The area covered by the Exclusion Zone has been subject to minor alterations over the years, and pollution levels within its boundaries are highly variable. It remains, though, predominantly uninhabited, save for a few returned ex-residents and some squatters, all of whom live there without official permission but are broadly tolerated by the authorities. Spread across the zone are at least 800 'burial grounds' for abandoned, contaminated vehicles. The perimeter is constantly patrolled by police and military, with visitors forced to present their documentation at check-points. Most who enter are carrying out scientific research work or are employed in the lengthy decommissioning process.

from areas in peril. Agriculture and forestry in the area around Chernobyl was devastated, with the loss of 800,000 hectares (2 million acres) of farmland and 700,000 hectares (1.7 million acres) of forest from productive use. Some have suggested that the disaster cost the economy hundreds of millions of dollars over the years that followed, and hastened the USSR's economic collapse.

Reactor 4 itself was hastily encased in a concrete and steel 'sarcophagus'. Doubts as to its long-term safety were expressed by some in the scientific community, and in 2007 it was reported that a new steel containment structure

70

UVB-76 transmitter

LOCATION Northwestern Russia
NEAREST POPULATION HUB Pskov
SECRECY OVERVIEW Location uncertain: transmitter broadcasting a mysterious shortwave radio station.

UVB-76, known to radio hams as 'the Buzzer', is not everybody's idea of the perfect radio station. Broadcasting almost continuously since 1982, its output consists not of lively chat or the latest hit music, but of a buzzing sound repeated on average 25 times per minute, every minute of every hour of every day. But for some it holds an unyielding fascination – who is behind its broadcasts, and what is it all about?

Even the bosses of UVB-76 know that variety is the spice of life. In the early 1990s, the beeping noise that had been in operation for ten years changed to the buzz that we have today. Then there is an attention-grabbing double buzz on the hour and, irregularly but every few weeks or so, a male voice reciting a short refrain of numbers or words – often a string of Russian names – all transmitted on an AM frequency of 4625 kilohertz. Background noises including unintelligible conversations suggest that these bizarre broadcasts are sent from a microphone that is constantly left open.

It is believed by some that the site of the transmitter responsible for UVB-76 moved in 2010. Around this time, a voice was heard on the station apparently giving it a new call sign of MDZhB (though fans, who monitor the stations' activities and produce eyecatching plots of its signal like the one shown here, tend to stick with the UVB-76 moniker). Until this time, the transmitter was thought to lie close to Povarovo, a town near Moscow that once had a strong military presence, but is now largely deserted. It has been conjectured that today the transmitter resides somewhere near Pskov in the northwest of the country. Such a move may have been associated with a wider reorganization of Russia's defence forces.

What it all means, no one seems to know. Neither the Russian government nor the country's broadcast authorities have ever explained what purpose the station serves. Some have suggested that its occasional verbal messages are a means of testing whether receiving stations are maintaining a suitable level of alertness.

Others say that UVB-76 is transmitting information to a network of international spies: it may be a so-called 'numbers station', designed to send encrypted messages to listeners in possession of a code key. More prosaically, many observers suspect that it may simply be a hangover from the Soviet era, its true purpose now lost amid a Cold War bureaucracy that is fast being forgotten.

71 FSB Headquarters

LOCATION Lubyanka
Square, Moscow, Russia
NEAREST POPULATION HUB
Moscow
SECRECY OVERVIEW
Operations classified:
home to Russia's security
service and once the feared
headquarters of the KGB.

The building once inhabited by the KGB and now by part of the
FSB security service in downtown Moscow's Lubyanka Square was
designed by Aleksandr V. Ivanov at the end of the 19th century as the
headquarters of an insurance company. After the Bolshevik Revolution,
it was converted to its more famous use, and it retains its role as the
focal point of Russia's secret services.

Today, the Lubyanka encompasses three
buildings, with the FSB largely inhabiting
a grey block to the left of the iconic
central yellow building. This yellow neo-
baroque structure housed the operations
of the Rossiya insurance company from
1898 until the Bolsheviks took it over 20
years later. It was then turned over to the
Cheka, the forerunner organization of
the KGB. The building was significantly
expanded in the 1940s on the designs of
Alexsey Shchusev.

From its formation in 1954, the KGB
was responsible for internal security,
intelligence gathering and the secret
police in the Soviet Union. In short, it
bred the climate of fear and paranoia
that sullied the USSR for the greater
part of the 20th century. The Lubyanka
building with its accompanying prison
was a potent symbol of that terror.
Anyone unfortunate enough to be taken
there against their wishes knew that the
future was bleak. Indeed, a bitter old
Russian joke described it as the tallest
building in the city, since you could see
Siberia from its basement.

Since the collapse of the USSR, much
has been done to make Lubyanka Square
seem a friendlier place. Not least, the
statue of Felix Dzerzhinsky (founder of
the Cheka) has been taken down, while a
monument to those who suffered in the
Gulag has been erected.

Yet, while perhaps not having quite the
reputation of its Soviet predecessor,
the FSB remains a feared and closed
organization. Established in its current
guise in 1995, the FSB is involved in
border control, counter-intelligence and
counter-terrorism, with a reputation
for 'targeted killings'. When Alexander
Litvinenko was murdered with
radioactive polonium in London in
2006, there were those who pointed
to his past as an FSB agent and his
subsequent criticisms of the Russian
secret services (though any links
remain unproven in a court of law).

The Soviet era may be an ever more
distant memory, but it is safe to assume
that the Lubyanka building still holds
many secrets.

HOUSE OF FEAR *The imposing Lubyanka Building was built in 1898 on the designs of Aleksandr V. Ivanov and significantly added to by Aleksey Shchusev some five decades later. Many of those who found their way inside its walls were never heard from again.*

POWER BASE *A bird's-eye view of Lubyanka Square. From 1926 to 1990 it was known as Dzerzhinsky Square, after Felix Dzerzhinsky, founder of the feared Cheka and godfather of the Soviet secret police in all its various guises.*

Moscow Metro-2

LOCATION Beneath Moscow, Russia
NEAREST POPULATION HUB Moscow
SECRECY OVERVIEW Existence unacknowledged: a secret underground metro system created in the Soviet era.

The Cold War was littered with tales of ingenious subterfuges and outrageous hoodwinking, but few stories can better that which tells of an entire underground secret transport system for use by government officials, built beneath the streets of Moscow and entirely separate from the official Metro. The Kremlin and FSB (Russia's security service) refuse to confirm or deny its existence to this day.

It is often claimed that the Metro-2 project was instigated during the rule of Josef Stalin, during the early Cold War era characterized by paranoia on all sides. A variety of dates for the beginning of its construction have been suggested, the earliest of which is 1947, when a narrow-gauge line was supposedly built to connect the Kremlin and one of Stalin's dachas (a second home in the countryside near Moscow).

The name Metro-2 gained common coinage after it was featured in a novel, *The Nether World*, written by Vladimir Gonik and published in 1992. According to Gonik, he had been researching the possibility of a secret underground system connecting government bunkers since the 1970s. The system, he suggested, was put in place so that the Soviet hierarchy would be able to continue to exert their command in the event of war. The KGB is alleged to have given the system the codename D-6.

Advocates of Metro-2 contend that it has up to four lines, the longest stretching

for some 60 kilometres (37 miles), at a depth of between 50 and 200 metres (165 and 660 ft) below the city. The tunnels are said to be virtually the same size as the official Metro, but there is no third rail, suggesting that its trains were diesel powered. Rails are recessed into concrete, perhaps to allow the possibility of other vehicles (cars, trucks or tanks, for instance) using the tunnels.

Metro-2 is said to connect a number of important locations including the Kremlin, the headquarters of the FSB (see page 176) and Vnukovo airport, southwest of the city. Some sources have also claimed that it runs to Ramenki, the supposed site of a vast underground bunker capable of housing 15,000 or more people for up to 30 years in the event of a nuclear strike. Indeed, for some the word bunker does not begin to describe Ramenki, and it is actually an entire underground town that could serve as a command post in an emergency.

Of course, there are plenty of cynics ready to pour cold water on the idea

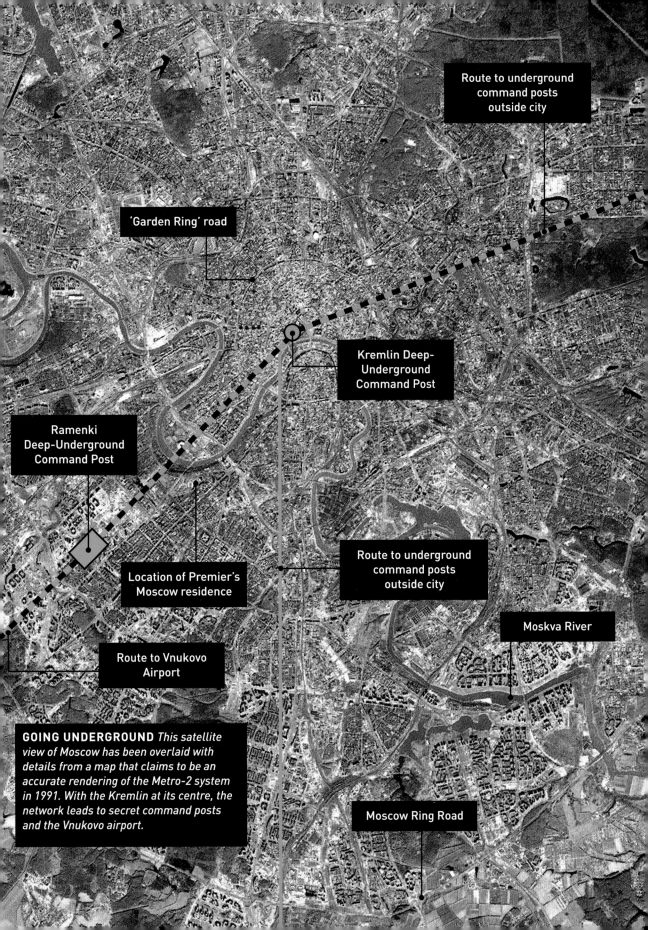

Route to underground command posts outside city

'Garden Ring' road

Kremlin Deep-Underground Command Post

Ramenki Deep-Underground Command Post

Location of Premier's Moscow residence

Route to underground command posts outside city

Moskva River

Route to Vnukovo Airport

GOING UNDERGROUND *This satellite view of Moscow has been overlaid with details from a map that claims to be an accurate rendering of the Metro-2 system in 1991. With the Kremlin at its centre, the network leads to secret command posts and the Vnukovo airport.*

Moscow Ring Road

MYSTERY TRAIN *Moscow's Metro system is famous for its elaborate stations – but did a clandestine second network once run alongside the public one, and might some of its trains still run today?*

of such an elaborate network. Firstly, they argue, the creation of such a system would require huge amounts of manpower and the excavation of unimaginable amounts of rubble – so where did all the rubble go, never to be spotted by a passing spy satellite? Then there is the question of heat – the deeper you dig, the hotter it gets, and if Metro-2 lies at the higher end of the depth estimates, it is difficult to imagine how dangerous overheating could not be a problem for passengers. Moscow also has a shallow water table, with groundwater an ongoing problem for the official Metro lines, let alone the even deeper Metro-2. Furthermore, it is claimed that ventilation shafts in the tunnels are relatively few and far between. If it is accepted that the system used diesel trains, then the lack of ventilation would not only render the air unpleasant but potentially noxious.

However, there is significant evidence to suggest that a second underground system was indeed built, and still exists in some form. For instance, in 1991 the

US Department of Defense published a report on the changing global political climate that concluded: 'The Soviets have constructed deep-underground both in urban Moscow and outside the city. These facilities are interconnected by a network of deep interconnected subway lines that provide a quick and secure means of evacuation for the leadership.' In addition, in recent years several former Soviet officials have all but confirmed the existence of something resembling Metro-2. Many, though, have pointed out that if the system does actually exist, it is likely to need significant repairs and upgrading to turn it into a practically useful system today.

Ultimately, the odds seem in favour of a secret underground system of some sort, though its exact composition remains open to debate. And that is perhaps how the Soviets would have wanted it, for what is the use of building a secret underground world if not to occupy the minds of your enemy as to just what is down there?

Mount Yamantau

LOCATION Southern Urals, Bashkortostan, Russia
NEAREST POPULATION HUB Magnitogorsk, Chelyabinsk Oblast
SECRECY OVERVIEW Operations classified: underground complex near a 'closed' city.

Mount Yamantau in the Southern Urals has an elevation of some 1,640 metres (5,380 ft), and the military complex it contains is believed to be located around 1,000 metres (3,300 ft) below the summit. It first came to the attention of the wider world thanks to US spy photographs released in the 1990s, but the international community remains in the dark as to its intended purpose.

Yamantau lies within an area sprinkled with Russian defence establishments. Nearby, for instance, is the town of Mezhgorye, a closed military settlement founded around 1995 from two former garrisons, Beloretsk 15 and 16, which had hosted military populations since the late 1970s. While there is scant official data concerning Mezhgorye, it is believed to have a population of up to 30,000.

Work on Yamantau is generally thought to have begun during the tenure of communist supremo Leonid Brezhnev (1964–82). Some observers suggest that the entire facility may cover 1,000 square kilometres (385 sq miles). It has been speculated that there is sufficient room to house a population of 60,000 for a period of several months, and that the vast bunker is capable of resisting virtually any form of modern attack, whether nuclear, chemical or biological.

Building was still going on throughout the 1990s, and possibly into the new century. Billions were pumped into the project at a time when post-communist

Russia was receiving international aid to support its nuclear decommissioning programme. There was understandable consternation in Washington when Russia acknowledged that Yamantau was under the jurisdiction of the Ministry of Defence in Moscow. The Kremlin has so far refused to make further disclosures about its purpose, though it has stressed it offers no threat to the US.

Well served by road and rail links, it has been variously described as the centre of a mining operation, a vault for state treasures, a repository for emergency food and clothing stocks, and a nuclear bunker. Other defence observers have suggested that it serves instead as a nuclear weapons storage area and alternative command centre. Some have even speculated that it forms part of Russia's fabled 'Dead Hand' system, capable of automatically triggering a retaliatory nuclear attack. With journalists and international observers banned entirely from the area, positive confirmation of any of these theories remains far off.

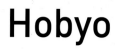

Hobyo

74

LOCATION Galmudug region, central Somalia
NEAREST POPULATION HUB Galkayo
SECRECY OVERVIEW Access restricted: a pirate-controlled enclave in war-torn Somalia.

A small coastal town on Somalia's east coast, in recent years Hobyo has become synonymous with the endemic piracy problem around the Horn of Africa. As well as being home to a large number of the pirates themselves, it has been used as a dock in which to harbour hijacked vessels. Civil war has rendered the surrounding region lawless, leaving Hobyo essentially off-limits to outsiders.

Situated in Somalia's semi-autonomous Galmudug region, Hobyo was once capital of a prosperous Sultanate, but went into decline after it came under the jurisdiction of Italian East Africa in 1936. Today, it boasts a population of around 12,000. The small town has a scattering of run-down buildings, fighting an everlasting battle against the sands of the receding coastline. Its water supply is compromised, there are no hospitals or schools in operation, agriculture has all but died and tourism is out of the question. For some, piracy seems the only answer (though few locals seem to reap the benefits from the vast revenues it raises). Some estimates suggest the illicit business employs 10 per cent of the population.

Instances of piracy in Somali waters and beyond have rocketed in the 21st century as Somalia's civil war left the country stripped of stable government and unable to develop its economy. Many pirates are former fishermen, with several organizations highlighting the impact of international fishing and waste dumping on their traditional means of earning a living. The economic impact of the pirates on global trade has been measured in billions of dollars, with targeted vessels ranging from small private yachts to huge tankers.

Hobyo's pirates are not so much Jack Sparrows as modern militiamen, though most claim an interest only in money, not in harming their victims. That, however, is scant consolation for those who have suffered at their hands. It has also been suggested that the pirates serve as a sort of defence against encroachment by the feared militant Islamists of the Al-Shabaab group. Whatever the motivation, Hobyo's streets are often patrolled by Kalashnikov-wielding children as young as ten.

Many international navies now send vessels to patrol the waters around Somalia and keep them safe for commercial ships. This has had some impact on the pirates' ability to hijack vessels, but piracy remains the only viable trade for many.

ALL AT SEA *These suspected pirates were apprehended by the USS Vella Gulf in the Gulf of Aden in 2009. Vella Gulf is part of an international fleet charged with countering the pirates and maintaining order across a vast swathe of ocean.*

ARABIAN PENINSULA

Gulf of Aden

ARABIAN SEA

SOMALIA

ETHIOPIA

TREASURE ISLAND *Somalia's pirates have been responsible for hundreds of attacks on international shipping in recent years. Hobyo is just one of several coastal towns living in fear not only of these modern-day buccaneers but also of potential military action by frustrated foreign powers.*

Reported pirate attacks

KENYA

INDIAN OCEAN

75

Chapel of the Ark of the Covenant

LOCATION
Northern Ethiopia
NEAREST POPULATION HUB
Axum
SECRECY OVERVIEW
Access restricted: the purported home of the Ark of the Covenant.

The Ark of the Covenant is described in the biblical Book of Exodus as the chest that contained the tablets of stone inscribed with the Ten Commandments which Moses brought down from Mount Sinai. The Ark disappeared from Jerusalem long ago under mysterious circumstances and believers claim it came to Axum in Ethiopia during the reign of Menelik I in the mid-tenth century BC.

The Ark is of immense symbolic value, documented not only in the Bible but featuring also in Judaic and Islamic scripture. While its fate has long been argued over, Ethiopia's authorities say it has resided at Axum for centuries, and now lies in a specially built treasury next to the Church of St Mary of Zion. The treasury is kept under heavy guard and surrounded by fencing, all under the watchful eye of a High Priest who is the only man permitted to enter the chapel.

This virtuous elderly monk is given the post for life, and is expected to name a successor on his deathbed. The Ark used to be released for a public procession once a year, but in more recent times the unstable geopolitical climate (not least Ethiopia's strained relations with neighbouring Eritrea) has seen it locked permanently in its shrine, which contains other treasures including Ethiopia's royal crowns.

The Book of Exodus tells how the Ark was built in accordance with instructions from God. Measuring a little over 1 metre

(40 in) long and 70 centimetres (28 in) wide and high, it was constructed from acacia wood and covered with gold. Two long rods of acacia and gold were used to carry it, and two sculptures of winged cherubim surmounted on the lid were said to keep guard over it.

According to the Bible, the Ark was carried (covered in skins and cloths so that no one could set eyes on it) out of Egypt during the exodus of the Israelites. The Book of Joshua also describes its key role in the fall of Jericho. It was later said to have been captured by the Philistines (who returned it to the Israelites after being smitten with a series of plagues), while Solomon worshipped in front of it after he had his dream in which God promised him wisdom.

The royal chronicles of Ethiopia, which were written in the 13th century and undoubtedly served as propaganda for the reigning dynasty of that time, hold that the Ark came to Ethiopia with Menelik, said to be the son of King

RED SEA

HOLY RELIC *This illustration from the 1728* Figures de la Bible *(published by P. de Hondt of The Hague), shows the Ark of the Covenant in a depiction of the erection of the Tabernacle and the Sacred Vessels, as described in the biblical Book of Exodus.*

SUDAN

DJIBOUTI

ETHIOPIA

SACRED HOME
A deacon of the Axumite church holds a sistrum (a type of musical instrument) in front of the treasury said to contain the Ark of the Covenant. The treasury is attached to the Church of St Mary of Zion, believed to have been established in the fourth century.

ANCIENT CITY *An aerial view of Axum, a commercial powerhouse from the fourth century BC to the tenth century AD. Steeped in history, it is dotted with areas of archaeological interest and is particularly famed for its huge obelisks known as stelae.*

the mid-second century BC to the tenth century AD. To this day, huge granite obelisks, the tallest single pieces of stone quarried and raised in the ancient world, tell of just how important the area was. If the Ark really was in Ethiopia at this point, Axum would have certainly made a suitable home.

The Axumite king Ezana converted to Christianity in AD 331, and had the first Church of St Mary built some 40 years later. According to tradition, the Ark remained at Axum until the 16th century, when it was hidden after the city came under Muslim attack. It was returned in the following century, and in 1965 Ethiopian leader Haile Selassie (reputedly a descendant of Menelik) had the current treasury built to house it. Of course, there are plenty of people who do not believe that the treasure at Axum is the real Ark at all. Alternative theories about its location abound. These include a cave in Mount Nebo in Jordan, Chartres Cathedral or the village of Rennes-le-Château in France, Temple Herdewyke in England, the Basilica of St John Lateran in Rome and the Dumghe Mountains of South Africa. The Indiana Jones movie *Raiders of the Lost Ark*, meanwhile, proposes that the Ark found its way to Egypt.

We will probably never know for certain whether Axum is home to the true Ark of the Covenant. What is more certain is that the contents of the treasury are considered sacred by vast numbers of people, and no one has yet provided conclusive proof that it is *not* the true Ark. But your chances of gaining access to the treasury to check for yourself are negligible, even if your name is Indiana Jones. The best we can hope is that one day Ethiopia's fraught political climate will have stabilized to a point where the treasure can again be released for occasional public processions.

Solomon and the Queen of Sheba. The story tells that a forgery of the Ark was left back in Solomon's Temple in Jerusalem, where it was presumed destroyed after the Babylonian sack of Jerusalem in 586 BC.

Meanwhile, the city of Axum became the focal point of the Kingdom of Axum, which was a leading regional power from

76 Fordo uranium enrichment plant

LOCATION Qom Province, northern Iran
NEAREST POPULATION HUB Qom
SECRECY OVERVIEW Operations classified: uranium-processing facility at the centre of international concern.

The nuclear facility at Fordo is built into a mountainside, not far from the sacred city of Qom. Iran only admitted to the facility's existence in September 2009, insisting that it was purely for civilian uses. The international community's fears that its purpose was not necessarily peaceful were seemingly confirmed by the International Atomic Energy Agency (IAEA) in January 2012.

That month, the IAEA announced that the plant had begun production of uranium enriched up to 20 per cent, which is regarded as a milestone on the journey towards weapons-grade enrichment. Iran, meanwhile, holds that its enrichment programme is guided not by the quest for nuclear weapons (a US intelligence report in 2007 concluded that its previous nuclear armaments programme ceased in 2003) but that enriched uranium is needed for fuel in research reactors and in the production of cancer-fighting isotopes.

Western intelligence agencies had first identified the Fordo facility in September 2009, at which point Tehran admitted that its construction had been underway since 2007 (though the IAEA subsequently suggested a more likely date of 2006). To fulfil its duties to the IAEA, Tehran should have volunteered details much earlier than it did.

Carved into a mountain (thus reducing the possibility of damaging air strikes), the facility is heavily fortified and located close to military installations armed with anti-aircraft defences and weapons silos. Iran claims these are necessary precautions to protect a legitimate project from US or Israeli attacks.

The nearby settlement of Fordo is claimed by some to have lost a greater percentage of its population than any other village during the war with Iraq that raged from 1980 to 1988. Quite what its inhabitants make of being at the centre of a new dispute with such militaristic undertones can only be imagined. Fordo lies about 30 kilometres (19 miles) north of Qom, itself about 150 kilometres (90 miles) southwest of Tehran and one of the principal places of learning for Shi'a Muslims, as well as an important site of pilgrimage.

Iran's nuclear programme has been used alternately as a threat and a bargaining chip in the long-running war of words between Tehran and the West. While the government of President Mahmoud Ahmadinejad had previously told IAEA inspectors that Fordo was intended

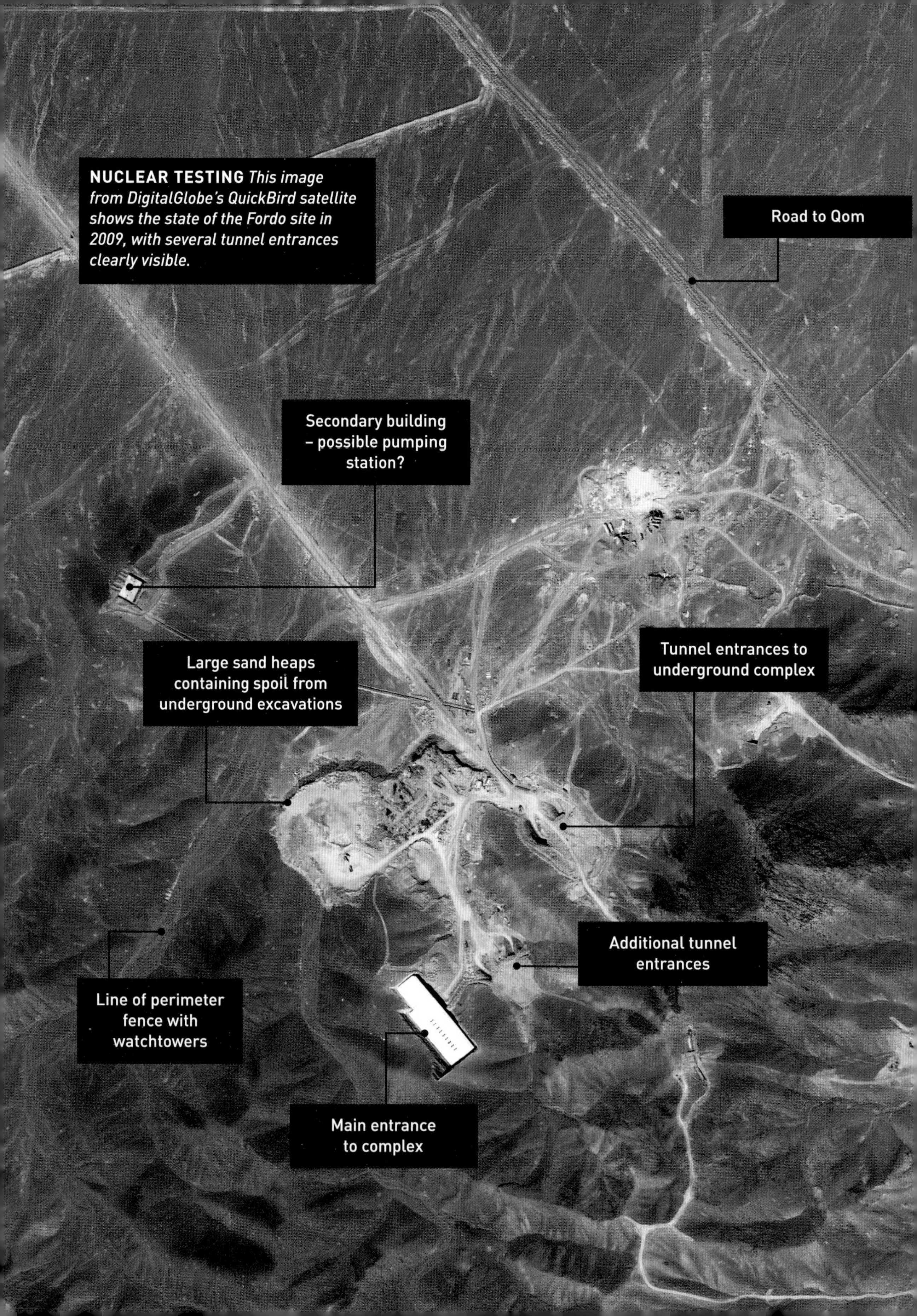

NUCLEAR TESTING *This image from DigitalGlobe's QuickBird satellite shows the state of the Fordo site in 2009, with several tunnel entrances clearly visible.*

Road to Qom

Secondary building – possible pumping station?

Tunnel entrances to underground complex

Large sand heaps containing spoil from underground excavations

Additional tunnel entrances

Line of perimeter fence with watchtowers

Main entrance to complex

HIGH STAKES *Iran's President Mahmoud Ahmadinejad (third from right) received a tour of the nuclear power plant at Bushehr in 2006. Since coming to power in 2005, Ahmadinejad has fiercely defended Iran's right to run a peaceful nuclear power programme.*

to produce uranium enriched to 5 per cent (a level commonly used in nuclear power production), it announced in June 2011 that it was working on 20 per cent enrichment, taking over enrichment previously undertaken at the Natanz plant in Isfahan Province.

Fordo is one of a number of sites within the country causing concern to the wider world. Others include the Bushehr power station (begun in 1974 as a joint project with West Germany, abandoned after the Islamic revolution of 1979, but revived in the 1990s with Russian assistance), a heavy water plant at Arak (scheduled to operate from 2013), a uranium mine at Gachin (opened in 2004) and, perhaps most ominously, an area of the Parchin munitions centre identified as a possible nuclear weapons development lab.

Suspicions over Iran's nuclear intentions have been heightened by the country's reluctance to cooperate with the IAEA's programme of inspections, to which it is obliged to submit as a signatory of the Nuclear Non-Proliferation Treaty. In November 2011, the IAEA reported that Iran had undertaken work 'relevant to the development of a nuclear explosive

device', though it stopped short of confirming whether or when the country would be capable of producing a working bomb. As a result of its refusal to comply with IAEA rules, Tehran has been hit by a variety of sanctions imposed by the UN, the US and the EU.

Intermittently, Iran has claimed no interest in developing nuclear weapons capabilities, insisting that it is merely exercising its legal right to develop a nuclear programme for civilian use. Ahmadinejad, never one to shy away from a scuffle with the West, has been quoted as saying: 'We do not need an atomic bomb. The Iranian nation is wise. It won't build two atomic bombs while you [the US] have 20,000 warheads.' Elsewhere, Iran's spiritual head and Supreme Leader, Ayatollah Ali Khamenei, has reportedly issued a *fatwa* against nuclear weapons.

But like North Korea, Iran has realized that retaining some mystery about its nuclear capabilities can serve as a useful bargaining chip at the international negotiating table. And what better way to retain that air of mystery than by hiding key facilities inside mountains?

Tora Bora cave complex

LOCATION Nangarhar Province, Afghanistan
NEAREST POPULATION HUB Jalalabad
SECRECY OVERVIEW Access restricted: fabled cave network used by Osama bin Laden.

The caves of Tora Bora shot to the attention of the world in 2001, when they became the focus of US attacks against Afghanistan's ruling Taliban and Osama bin Laden's Al-Qaeda. After a ferocious battle, bin Laden somehow evaded the grasp of US forces and dodged capture for a further ten years. Tora Bora itself became the subject of rumour, myth and confusion, often serving to disguise the truth.

The Tora Bora caves were formed naturally by water running through the limestone of the White Mountains in eastern Afghanistan. The range rises to over 4,000 metres (13,100 ft), its terrain often steep and its peaks snow-capped. In the 1980s the caves, which lie within easy reach of the Pakistani border, served as a labyrinthine base for the *mujahideen* insurgents fighting against the Soviet occupation of the country, which had begun in 1979. The rebels extended the complex using money supplied by the CIA, and it was during this time that bin Laden first became familiar with them. It was said that he later used some of his own vast personal wealth (as well as his expertise as a civil engineering graduate) to have them enlarged and upgraded beyond recognition.

After the 11 September terrorist attacks on America made a massive retaliation inevitable, bin Laden withdrew into this secret complex, apparently with a sizable army of Taliban and Al-Qaeda fighters. In early December 2001, two months after

the beginning of the Allied air campaign, a force of Afghan Northern Alliance fighters backed by small numbers of US troops began a ground assault on the caves. By that time, Tora Bora had already been subject to several weeks of bombardment and aerial attack. The fighting was hard, and dragged on for several more weeks before bin Laden's men were dislodged. He is believed to have left the scene some time around 16 December. In 2009, a US Senate Foreign Relations Committee concluded that the Battle of Tora Bora represented a prime opportunity to capture bin Laden, and that if the assault on the caves had been better coordinated, he might not have remained free until 2011 (see page 196).

At the height of the battle, the Western media made some extraordinary claims about Tora Bora, which was frequently described as 'impregnable'. London's reputable *Times* newspaper, for instance, produced a schematic of a veritable mountain fortress. The blueprints showed a base worthy of a James Bond villain, replete with a hydroelectric

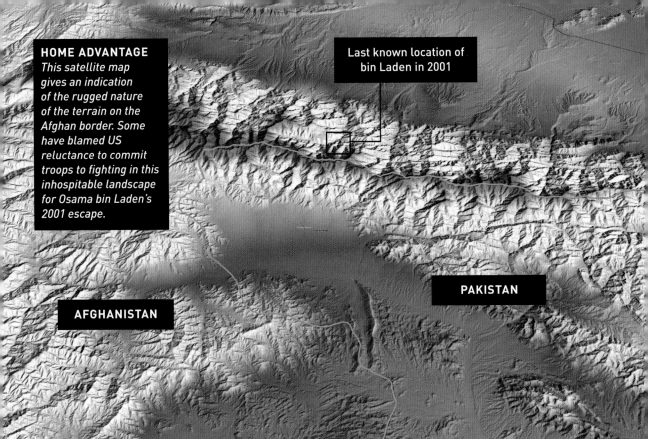

HOME ADVANTAGE
This satellite map gives an indication of the rugged nature of the terrain on the Afghan border. Some have blamed US reluctance to commit troops to fighting in this inhospitable landscape for Osama bin Laden's 2001 escape.

Last known location of bin Laden in 2001

PAKISTAN

AFGHANISTAN

CHASING SHADOWS
A glimpse inside Tora Bora during 2004. When Western forces searched the complex in the aftermath of the Battle of Tora Bora, they found little evidence of the futuristic underground complex that some speculated bin Laden had constructed there.

SHOCK AND AWE *A phalanx of Afghan anti-Taliban fighters look on as plumes of smoke rise during US bombing raids on Tora Bora in December 2001. The US assault made use of devastating BLU-82 'daisy cutter' bombs, but despite the intensity of the attacks, Osama bin Laden was able to escape capture.*

power station, wiring for lights, power and ventilation, offices, bedrooms and communal rooms, underground armouries and secret exits guarded by booby-trapped steel doors. In other publications, there were descriptions of tunnels large enough to drive tanks through. On sober reflection, it seems as though news editors had given their journalists and graphics departments free range to exercise their imaginations, just as long as they came up with something engaging to print alongside the images of war.

What the US–Northern Alliance forces eventually found inside the caves seemed to bear little resemblance to the media flights of fancy. This was no slick underground lair – instead there were bunkers hewn roughly out of the mountain, sometimes propped up with bits of wood and often barely big enough for a man to stand upright. The floors were covered in mud and rubble (and there were none of the smooth plastered-walls some had suggested). Remnants of ammunition (some live, some spent) were strewn about here and there.

How many fighters had been encamped inside Tora Bora was not obvious, but it seemed unlikely to have been the thousands of well-armed warriors that had been speculated about. There was no mass capture of Al-Qaeda belligerents, and some observers began to whisper that perhaps the whole concept of an Al-Qaeda organization in the traditional sense was misjudged. When Donald Rumsfeld, the US Secretary of State for Defense, was presented with the imagined plans of Tora Bora during the battle, he had commented: 'There's not one of those, there are many of those.' It turned out that only his first clause was correct.

As of 2010, NATO troops were still fighting insurgent forces within Tora Bora but this time they were not under the illusion that there was a 21st-century fortress inside. It remains something of a mystery as to how the world's media could have got things quite so wrong in 2001: it could be argued that it was an early symptom of a War on Terror which, like the Cold War that preceded it, was often characterized by supposition, paranoia and myth.

78 Diego Garcia

LOCATION Chagos Archipelago, Indian Ocean
NEAREST POPULATION HUB Malé, the Maldives
SECRECY OVERVIEW Access restricted: island home of extensive US military operations in the Indian Ocean.

Officially a British Indian Ocean Territory, Diego Garcia has served as a strategically-important base for US military operations since the early 1970s. Although the island now operates as a *de facto* US territory, the Chagossians who inhabited it until the arrival of the Americans continue to fight for their right to return. In the meantime, no one except for approved military and support personnel is permitted entry.

Lying in the Indian Ocean south of the Maldives, Diego Garcia is an atoll – a coral island enclosing a lagoon – with a total area of 174 square kilometres (67 sq miles). It is named after Diego Garcia de Moguer, a Spanish sailor believed to have sighted the island in the 1550s. However, it remained uninhabited until the French established a settlement here in the late 18th century. It briefly fell under the jurisdiction of the British East India Company before the French claimed it back, using it as a leper colony until 1793, when the first coconut plantation came into operation.

Following the defeat of Napoleon, the 1814 Treaty of Paris granted the island to Britain, which administered it from Mauritius. A resident population of plantation workers expanded over the subsequent centuries, and for a brief period between 1942 and 1946, there was a British Flying Boat Base on the east coast of the island.

Twenty years later, with the US keen to gain a military foothold in the Indian

Ocean to expand its Cold War sphere of influence, London and Washington reached an agreement in 1966 that the US could make long-term use of British territory in the region. The deal suited both parties – the British were happy to reduce their military commitments and save money (they also received a US$14 million sweetener discount on their purchase of the Polaris missile system) while the US made strategic gains for relatively little expense or trouble.

Diego Garcia seemed the perfect island, blessed as it is with a large natural harbour as well as enough room for an airstrip. Washington did make one stipulation, however: they wanted an island that was uninhabited – there was to be no trouble with the natives. Alas, on Diego Garcia there was a permanent population of several hundred Chagossians (sometimes also known as Îlois), descended from generations of plantation workers. Some had family roots going back to the 18th century. Under international law, the interests of any permanent population

STAR GAZING
The island is home to one of America's three operational facilities for the Ground-Based Electro-Optical Deep Space Surveillance (GEODSS) system. GEODSS is used to track man-made objects as they orbit the Earth up to 32,000 kilometres (20,000 miles) away.

WAR AND PEACE *US Air Force B-1 Lancer bombers on Diego Garcia's runway 13, preparing to fly into action over Afghanistan in late 2001. A once quiet backwater in the Indian Ocean has become a key element in the United States' regional strategy.*

on the island should have been of paramount importance.

To avoid this problem, a legal sleight of hand was used: Diego Garcia's inhabitants were classified as 'transient workers', robbing them of the usual safeguards, and they were informed by the British that they were residing illegally unless they could produce non-existent documentation proving their right to remain. The British then began the process of moving them out, some claim forcibly. The plantations were dismantled, and food and medical stocks were run down and not replaced. In 1971, most of the residents were relocated to other islands in the archipelago, or to Mauritius or the Seychelles, where they faced uncertain futures.

The US now had the unpeopled island it desired, and put it to immediate use. By 1977, a naval support facility had been built, port facilities for fleet vessels were developed and a military airbase established, along with state-of-the-art communications and tracking facilities. All of this came at a cost of several billion dollars, and it was clear the Americans were here for the long-run. Secrecy on the island has reigned ever since. It was a key base for American bombers during both the Afghan and Iraqi wars in the early 2000s and, most controversially, was used as a stopping-off point for US rendition flights transferring prisoners to Guantánamo Bay (see page 94) and elsewhere. No journalist has ever received permission to visit the island.

Today, there is a resident population of between 3,000 and 5,000 US military personnel and civilian support staff, and Washington is less keen than ever to reduce its presence in the region. Yet, against these vast odds, the Chagossian nation continues to fight for its right to return. Its cause received a huge boost in 2000, when the British High Court ruled that their expulsion had been illegal.

DEADLY PAYLOAD *A Northrop Grumman B-2 Spirit drops its missiles during a training mission. Diego Garcia is home to specially designed hangars that house these state-of-the-art stealth bombers. The B-2 Spirit has been active in American military operations since the late 1990s.*

Subsequent rulings by other courts seemed to overturn that decision, but the legal process goes on to this day, with the European Court of Human Rights considering the case. In 2010, a WikiLeaks release of diplomatic cables seemed to suggest that the British government was considering an attempt to have the British Indian Ocean Territory designated as a marine reserve, thus effectively removing the chance of resettlement on environmental grounds. Until a final decision is reached, the island that was once a palm-fringed ocean paradise serves as a secretive military enclave, key to America's foreign policy strategy.

Osama bin Laden's compound, Abbottabad

LOCATION Khyber Pakhtunkhwa, Pakistan
NEAREST POPULATION HUB Islamabad
SECRECY OVERVIEW High-security location: the long-hidden home of Osama bin Laden and, in 2011, scene of his death.

On 2 May 2011, American president Barack Obama announced to the world that US Navy Seals had finally tracked down and killed Osama bin Laden, the world's most wanted man for the past decade. It would subsequently emerge that bin Laden had spent many of the years since his flight from Afghanistan living apparently unnoticed in a middle-class Pakistani town, just down the road from a military base.

The thriving town of Abbottabad lies in the Orash Valley of northern Pakistan. A popular stop on the tourist trail, it is surrounded on all sides by sweeping hills, and offers a gateway to the Karakoram Highway, following the route of the ancient Silk Road.

This moderate-sized town is named after a British army officer, Major James Abbott, who founded it in 1853. For many years, it has served as home to the Pakistan Military Academy, the training school for the nation's army officers, and has a prominent population of retired military. All in all, its residents would tell you, Abbottabad is a pleasant and secure place in which to live.

Yet it was here that the man responsible for a number of atrocities, including the 11 September 2001 terrorist attacks on the USA, lived unhindered for at least five years. How that could have been is a mystery yet to be solved, and one that severely strained the bonds of trust between Washington and Islamabad.

BEHIND CLOSED DOORS *This view of the Abbottabad complex shows just how well protected and concealed its inhabitants were. Nonetheless, many in the international intelligence community have cast doubt on bin Laden's ability to stay so long in hiding without the assistance of powerful figures within Pakistan.*

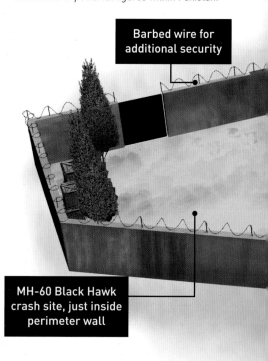

Barbed wire for additional security

MH-60 Black Hawk crash site, just inside perimeter wall

Construction on what would become the bin Laden compound is believed to have been completed in 2005, and the owner was allegedly one Abu Ahmed al-Kuwaiti. Built within less than a mile of the Military Academy, the main building consists of three storeys with at least eight bedrooms, and has a footprint of some 3,500 square metres (37,500 sq ft). It is surrounded by a concrete perimeter wall that rises between 4 and 6 metres (13 and 20 ft) in height, and is topped with barbed wire. There are relatively few windows, and the third floor (where bin Laden resided) is surrounded by a

2-metre (6.6-ft) high 'privacy wall' of its own. Entry was via heavy security gates and there were numerous surveillance cameras in operation, though no provision existed for internet or telephone connections.

Intelligence sources indicate that bin Laden probably moved to the premises on 6 January 2006. Its official address is House No. 3, Street No. 8-A, Garga Road, Thanda Chowa, Hashmi Colony, Abbottabad. However, it was given the nickname of Waziristan *Haveli* by locals. *Haveli* is the local word for a mansion,

Bin Laden's private quarters on 3rd storey

2-metre (6.6–ft) 'privacy wall' shielding bin Laden's apartment.

Main gate leads to narrow defensive alleyway

Corner of the garden area used for secure burning of trash

Highest sections of wall, up to 6 m (20 ft) tall

Secondary gate providing additional security

Several additional houses contained within compound

DEMOLITION JOB *Two security officials and a group of Abbottabad locals watch the destruction of the now-deserted bin Laden compound in February 2012. Once the site had been picked clean for evidence of Al-Qaeda operations, Pakistani officials were understandably eager to remove all trace of this embarrassing landmark.*

while Waziristan, ironically, is a region of Pakistan in which many commentators believed bin Laden had been sheltered for years.

Although the building's structure was somewhat atypical, it did not immediately set alarm bells ringing. The locals noticed that the inhabitants kept themselves to themselves, and the house was not kept in the best state of repair. If local children were playing cricket nearby and batted a ball into the compound, the occupants gave them generous financial recompense for their loss, but the balls were never returned. This, it may be assumed, was as a security precaution. Nor did they ever dispose of their rubbish in the normal way – instead, waste was assiduously burned in an outside area. But all of this could perhaps be put down to eccentricity rather than anything more sinister.

Eventually, American intelligence forces began tracking al-Kuwaiti, whom they had identified as a bin Laden courier. After establishing that he resided in Abbottabad, it became clear that his home there had all the characteristics of a hide-away, and prolonged surveillance led to the conclusion that bin Laden could be the object of its protection. On 2 May 2011, in a raid codenamed Neptune Spear, 24 commandos arrived in Abbottabad from Afghanistan on two Black Hawk helicopters (one of which crashed and had to be abandoned), and took down the outer wall with explosives. They then raided the building within, engaging several other residents of the compound in fire fights before shooting bin Laden dead at around 1 a.m. After confirming his identity, they left with the body, which was later buried at sea.

Today, the compound is under the protection of the Pakistani police force. Sightseers, while allowed to approach the remaining parts of the external wall, are not permitted entry. It is believed that the Pakistani security services intend to destroy the building so that it does not become a shrine for jihadists. But before then it will be minutely scrutinized to discover just how it managed to hide its notorious occupant for so long.

80 Line of Control

LOCATION Kashmir,
Indian Subcontinent
NEAREST POPULATION HUB
Islamabad, Pakistan/
Srinagar, India
SECRECY OVERVIEW Access
restricted: UN-regulated
dividing line between India
and Pakistan.

When the British gave up control of India in 1947, the country was divided into two independent states along broadly religious lines: Hindu India and Muslim Pakistan. As a result of the vagaries of politics, Kashmir became the focus of a bitter border dispute that has rumbled on for almost seven decades with little prospect of resolution. In the meantime, the area is a virtual no-go area for outsiders.

With the end of British rule over India in the aftermath of the Second World War, each state within India was given the choice of becoming part of the new India or acceding to Pakistan. With a predominantly Muslim population, it was widely assumed that Jammu and Kashmir would choose the latter option. However, when the state's Hindu Maharajah, Hari Singh, hesitated, the territory was subject to incursions from Pakistan. The Maharajah appealed to the British for military assistance, which was granted in return for a promise to accede to India. Jammu and Kashmir thus became the only Indian state with a Muslim majority, making a bitter armed struggle all but inevitable.

The United Nations oversaw a ceasefire between the two sides and demanded a plebiscite on the state's future, but this was never carried out. The stage was set for a prolonged tug-of-war between India and Pakistan, culminating in further all-out military offensives in 1965, 1971 and 1999, with many more minor outbreaks of violence in between.

India has maintained control of southern Kashmir, which it rules as the state of Jammu and Kashmir and which contains two-thirds of the population (about 9 million people). Pakistan, meanwhile, administers the northern part of the territory as the Gilgit-Baltistan and Azad Kashmir provinces, with a combined population of about 3 million. Neither side recognizes the other's jurisdiction. To complicate matters further, China lays claim to Aksai Chin and the Trans-Karakoram Tract in the northeast of the region. India and China clashed over this area in 1962.

Today, the Line of Control stretches for 734 kilometres (456 miles) through dense forests, over imposing mountains and across other rugged terrain. Though not an internationally recognized border, it serves as the *de facto* frontier between India and Pakistan, and its origins go back to the Ceasefire Line established by the United Nations after the fighting of 1947–8 (though slightly tweaked under the terms of the 1972 Simla Agreement that ended renewed hostilities).

AFGHANISTAN

CHINA

Northern Areas
(Pakistani controlled)

Srinagar

Jammu and Kashmir
(Indian controlled)

PAKISTAN

INDIA

UNEASY PEACE
*An Indian soldier
surveys the scene
along the Line of
Control at Baraf Post,
some 165 kilometres
(100 miles) north
of Srinagar. Even in
quiet times, an uneasy
tension prevails along
the disputed border,
heightened by the
knowledge that both
India and Pakistan
have nuclear arsenals.*

The Line of Control was set up in the hope that it would be respected until a long-term solution could be found. While the UN maintains an observer presence along the Line, India does not recognize its jurisdiction, although it does tolerate its presence. One of the few areas of agreement between India and Pakistan is that any long-term resolution must be a bilateral settlement, achieved without further international intervention.

Despite the negotiations that went on when the Line was originally drawn up, differences in interpretation continue to lead to skirmishes. When tensions were at their highest, up to 80,000 troops amassed along its course, sometimes encamped on mountainsides less than 100 metres (330 ft) apart. An already delicate situation has grown yet more complex with the emergence of an armed separatist movement among Muslims on the Indian side, who want to be part of neither state.

In the 1990s, India began construction of a barrier on its side of the Line, designed, it said, to stem the flow of arms to militants on the Indian side and to prevent incursions from the Pakistani side. Completed in 2004, the barrier consists of two rows of heavily alarmed barbed-wire fencing, varying in height from 2.5 to 4 metres (8–13 ft), with the land in between laced with mines. Pakistan argues that the barrier breaches various bilateral and international agreements, and that the border should remain undemarcated. Islamabad also claims that mines have maimed and killed a large number of civilians going about legitimate daily business. India, meanwhile, says that Pakistani incursions were reduced by 80 per cent within a year of the barrier's completion.

The result of this ongoing stalemate is an area that is effectively closed off to the outside world and kept in stasis. The economy is wretched, and has little prospect of securing significant investment while Indian, Pakistani and separatist forces continue to slug it out. It has been estimated that in the worst periods of fighting, the territory has suffered as many as 400,000 rounds of shelling in a month. Indo-Pakistani relations in the new century have hardly been warm and, with both nations boasting nuclear arsenals, the stakes surrounding Kashmir have never been higher. As with the majority of modern wars, it is the civilian population that pays the heaviest price, forced to live in a virtual no-man's-land.

HAIR TRIGGER *A band of armed militants at a base on the Pakistani side of the Line of Control in 1999. The dispute is not simply between those wanting to be part of India or Pakistan, but includes other groups demanding autonomy and the further complication of Chinese interests in the region.*

81

Temple Vaults
Sree Padmanabhaswamy

LOCATION
Thiruvananthapuram
District, Kerala, India
NEAREST POPULATION HUB
Thiruvananthapuram
SECRECY OVERVIEW High-
security location: sight of
a treasure horde worth
billions.

Southern India's Sree Padmanabhaswamy Temple was built in the 18th century. When in 2011 its vaults were opened for the first time in over a century, they were found to contain gold, silver and jewels with an estimated value of over US$15 billion. Perhaps unsurprisingly, a portion of this new-found wealth was immediately spent on improving the temple's security.

The enormous Thiruvananthapuram temple, dedicated to the Hindu god Lord Vishnu, was built by the rulers of the Travancore kingdom (which joined with Cochin in the 20th century to become modern-day Kerala). Its construction included six large, granite vaults into which offerings to Vishnu were deposited over the course of several hundred years.

After Indian independence in 1947, the temple remained under the control of a trust administered by descendants of the Travancore dynasty. However, concerns over their capability to protect the temple and its contents saw the Supreme Court appoint an independent panel to audit its wealth and make suitable security arrangements in 2011. It is believed that several of the underground chambers had been sealed for at least 130 years.

Some of the vaults offered up more treasure than others, but few had expected the amount and extent of valuables that would be revealed. The trove included solid gold idols, a gold chain said to weigh more than 3 kilograms (6.5 lb), antique diamonds by the handful and even two coconut shells covered in beaten gold and adorned with rubies and emeralds.

Overnight, the temple became the wealthiest in the state, prompting a review of its hitherto low-key security. Where previously the temple had a force of some 50 guards to ensure its safe day-to-day running and oversee crowd control, it now has an additional 250 police officers patrolling the area on the lookout for intruders. Moves have been made towards installing state-of-the-art locking systems in the vaults, while windows and doors have been fitted with toughened glass and steel bars. In addition, hidden surveillance cameras have been installed, along with metal detectors, X-ray scanners and vibration-sensitive alarm systems.

Perhaps inevitably, though, the discovery of these riches prompted an immediate dispute as to who owned the wealth, with some proclaiming that it should be used for the public good.

82

North Sentinel Island

LOCATION Andaman Islands, Bay of Bengal
NEAREST POPULATION HUB Port Blair, Great Andaman
SECRECY OVERVIEW Access restricted: a remote island whose people reject contact with the outside world.

North Sentinel Island, which covers only 72 square kilometres (28 sq miles), has an indigenous population of somewhere between 50 and 400 Sentinelese, a dark-skinned and short-statured people and one of the last groups on earth to have resisted contact with the modern world. Jealously protective of their isolation, any attempt by outsiders to land on the island is likely to result in a hail of arrows.

North Sentinel lies to the west of the southern tip of South Andaman Island and is one of 572 islands in an 800-kilometre (500-mile) arc. Here, the Sentinelese live as hunter-gatherers and do not seem to have developed any forms of agriculture. Their diet includes fruits, nuts, tubers, fish, wild pigs, honey and the eggs of seagulls and turtles. Their language is significantly different to any of the other tongues spoken in the island group, leading academics to conclude that they have avoided contact even with relatively near neighbours for several millennia. The island lacks any natural harbours and is surrounded by uncharted coral reefs that have largely kept out visitors as well as keeping in the Sentinelese, whose own rudimentary boats are suited only to calm lagoons.

In 1880, Maurice Portman, an administrator in the British Raj, led the first known expedition to North Sentinel. After a few days of exploration, Portman and his team captured six natives (two adults and four children), whom they took back to Port Blair, the administrative capital of the Andamans. However, the enterprise ended in disaster when the adults died from illness. The orphaned children were dispatched home loaded with presents – scant compensation for their loss.

Tentative attempts from the 1960s to make contact with the Sentinelese met with limited success. Incidents such as the one in 1974 when a visiting documentary crew was attacked and the director suffered an arrow to the thigh were not uncommon. After many years of regular landings and gift offerings, the first recorded friendly contact was made in 1991.

However, similar schemes with other native peoples of the islands (including the Great Andamanese and the Jarawa) had ended disastrously when those populations were decimated by exposure to common but unfamiliar diseases. Under pressure from groups arguing that the Sentinelese should not be forced into contact, the government gave up on its contact programme in 1996.

BURMA
(MYANMAR)

INDIA

BAY OF BENGAL

Andaman and
Nicobar Islands

UNWELCOME VISIT *A tribesman greets an approaching helicopter with traditional Sentinelese hospitality in 2004. The aircraft, belonging to the Indian Coast Guard, flew over the island to gauge conditions following the devastating Indian Ocean tsunami. North Sentinel emerged in miraculously good health.*

Naypyidaw

LOCATION Between the Bago Yoma and Shan Yoma mountain ranges, Burma
NEAREST POPULATION HUB Pyinmana
SECRECY OVERVIEW Access restricted: recently-established capital of the Burmese government.

In 2006, Naypyidaw, which roughly translates as 'abode of the kings', was declared the new capital city of Burma (also known as Myanmar). The decision by the insular Burmese administration to shift the capital to a dusty and isolated backwater some 320 km (200 miles) from its predecessor, Yangon (Rangoon), remains one shrouded in mystery.

The new capital, which consists of eight distinct townships, covers an area of approximately 7,000 square kilometres (2,700 sq miles) and now boasts a population approaching 1 million. Building started in earnest in 2002, and the process of moving the country's main administrative institutions from Yangon to the site began in late 2005.

In fact, it began specifically at 6.37 a.m. on the 6 November, a moment that had been designated as one of particular astrological importance by advisers to the country's *de facto* military leader, General Than Shwe. It had been hoped that the move would largely be finished by the early months of 2006, but such was the lack of infrastructure in Naypyidaw that many government officials and civil servants chose not to relocate their families, hence delaying the overall process.

It is a city designed so that everybody within it knows their place. There is a special zone for commercial vendors, and an entire district (off-limits to casual civilians) given over to the military. Apartments are designated on the basis of seniority and marital status. Even the roofs are colour-coded, indicating the government department in which the occupants work. It is also alleged that government employees are not permitted private telephone lines, but must instead use public phones. A select band of senior officials are put up in mansions and there is a presidential palace. There are also unconfirmed reports of a warren of underground tunnels and bunkers.

The city's first significant public display came on 27 March 2006 – Armed Forces Day commemorating Burma's stand in 1945 against its Japanese occupation. After a spectacular military display involving 12,000 personnel, it was on this day that the city had its naming ceremony and was formally recognized as the country's capital. Tellingly, footage of the metropolis was restricted to what was on show at the parade ground.

Why the government opted for a change in capital is subject to much debate. The

SHOW OF STRENGTH

The annual military parade in the capital each 27 March – Armed Forces Day – is a chance for Burma's ruling regime to put on a display of might for the domestic and international audience.

This picture was taken in 2007, a year to the day after Naypyidaw's naming ceremony.

LONE RIDER

A policeman cruises down Naypyidaw's vast Yazahdani Road. After some early hiccups, the city now boasts an impressive infrastructure yet remains oddly devoid of the atmosphere usually associated with a capital city claiming a population of a million.

official line is that Yangon was simply too overcrowded and congested for a government planning future expansion. In addition, Naypyidaw has a central location and might become a stabilizing influence on one of the country's more turbulent regions.

It is also true that Burma has something of a history when it comes to changing its seat of government. The capital moved from Amarapura to Mandalay (another purpose-built capital) in 1859, and then on again to Yangon (or Rangoon, as it was then better known) after the British conquest in 1885. It may well be that Nyapyidaw represented a chance for the country's autocratic leader, Than Shwe, to leave his great legacy.

Others believe the move is symbolic of a government that has longed looked inward. Yangon, situated on the coast, is by no means an impenetrable fortress. With the Burmese administration having eschewed closer relations with the outside world, it has been speculated

that Naypyidaw offers better hope of defence against any external attack. Crucially, it also seems to lessen the chance of an internal uprising. Where Yangon is a thriving city that saw the government side-by-side with its people, it is far harder to imagine a revolution in the sanitized and almost other-worldly atmosphere of Naypyidaw, Some observers, though, believe the government may have overplayed its hand, and by distancing itself physically (as well as psychologically) from the population it dominates, it has actually increased the prospect of a civil uprising in the future. In a country where the leading pro-democracy leader, Aung San Suu Kyi, has spent much of her adult life in prison or under house arrest, only time will tell.

What is certain is that the rulers of Burma have long operated away from the scrutiny of the international community. Now they have a new capital where foreigners require permission even to visit, and to which travel agents are nervous even to sell train tickets.

Bang Kwang Central Prison

LOCATION On the Chao Phraya River, Nonthaburi Province, Thailand
NEAREST POPULATION HUB Bangkok
SECRECY OVERVIEW High-security location: one of the most notorious prisons in the world.

Located a few miles north of downtown Bangkok, the Bang Kwang Central Prison is known ironically as 'the Bangkok Hilton'. Built in the 1930s, it is a maximum security facility that has regularly attracted concern from international observers. Its inmates are all men facing death sentences or serving long spells of incarceration (typically at least 25 years).

Many of the prison's inmates have been convicted of drugs offences, and there is a small but significant population of foreigners. Punishments for drugs crimes are notably harsh in Thailand, which has taken a hard line to fight the illegal drug trade that blights Asia's 'Golden Triangle' (of which the country is a part along with Burma, Laos and Vietnam). Those on death row are generally given only two hours' notice before being executed by lethal injection.

The prison is chronically overcrowded (there are in excess of 8,000 inmates, several thousand more than it was designed for) and understaffed, with an inmate-to-guard ratio approaching 50 to 1. Up to 30 prisoners may share a single cell, sleeping on cold floors without bedding. A bare bulb shines all night, and there is an open toilet in the corner of each cell. Sustenance comes via a daily bowl of rice in a grim (and usually protein-free) broth.

Prisoners are said to be required to wear leg irons for at least the first few months after arriving at the institution, although Bang Kwang officials have denied this in the past. Meanwhile, prisoners who have the misfortune to end up in the infirmary (and serious illness as a result of poor hygiene and malnutrition is common) are shackled to their beds. At visiting time, prisoners sit on long benches facing their visitors, but separated by two fences 1 metre (40 in) apart so that normal communication is virtually impossible. International prison watchdogs regularly highlight the attendant risks to inmates' psychological well-being.

Gobi Desert unidentified structures

LOCATION Borders of Gansu Province and Xinjiang Autonomous Region, China
NEAREST POPULATION HUB Dunhuang, Gansu Province
SECRECY OVERVIEW Operations classified: mysterious features found in satellite images.

During the course of 2011, satellite imaging across a remote stretch of the Gobi desert lying near the centre of a network of Chinese research facilities, revealed a curious array of objects and structures. Several theories as to their true nature and purpose have rapidly emerged, some of which are more plausible than others – but a conclusive explanation has yet to be found.

The Gobi desert stretches across northern China and southern Mongolia, covering more than 1.25 million square kilometres (500,000 sq miles). It is, in short, a perfect location if you require a lot of space and privacy, and as such, it has become something of a hub for several Chinese defence and space programmes.

In 2011, the curiosity of the international community was piqued by a series of aerial photos showing several curious and vast structures that had sprung up in the desert. The images show:
- A series of reflective rectangles with sides up to a mile in length
- A network of intersecting white lines in a seemingly random pattern
- A set of concentric circles, at the centre of which sat three jet planes
- A circle of bright orange blocks, each the size of a shipping container
- A grid system extending 29 kilometres (18 miles) in length
- Metallic squares covered in unidentified debris
- A large man-made body of water.

There are no major permanent settlements or obvious military facilities particularly close to the affected area, but some observers have noted that the Ding Xin military airbase (with a reputation for secret development programmes) and the salt lakes of Lop Nur (site of many nuclear tests until the mid-1990s) both lie within 600 kilometres (370 miles) of the site. Meanwhile, the Jiuquan Satellite Launch Centre, a major base for the burgeoning Chinese space programme (see page 212) is less than 150 kilometres (90 miles) away.

Some have suggested that the structures are designed to simulate street grids, perhaps acting as targets for missile tests. Others have pondered the possibility of a huge water purification plant or solar energy facility. But the truth is that no one outside China really knows. What is left is a truly modern-day mystery, though it is appealing to speculate that the whole thing may turn out to be a mischievous practical joke dreamed up in Beijing to occupy the international intelligence community.

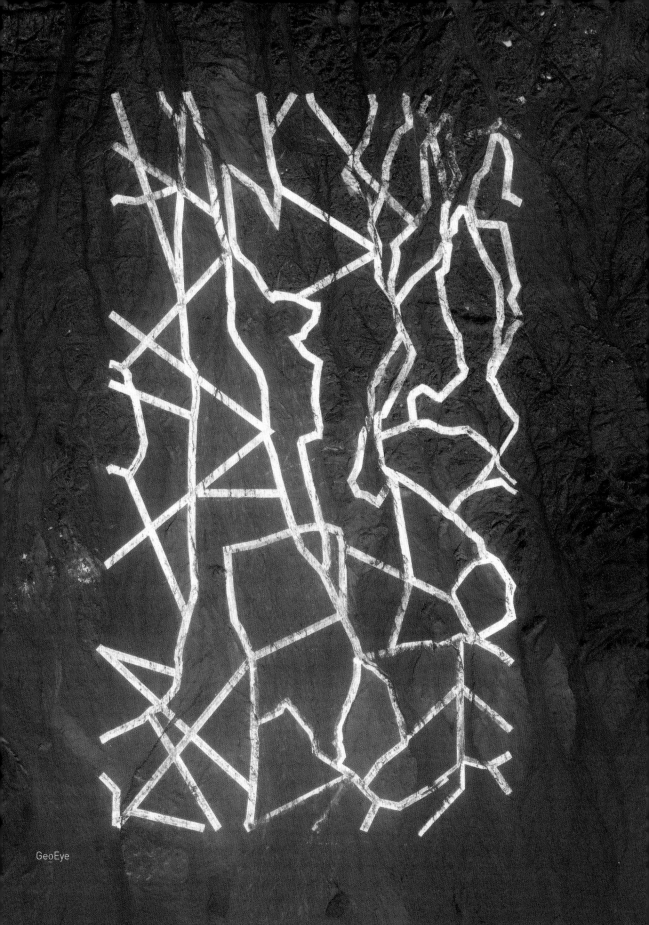

GeoEye

86 Jiuquan Satellite Launch Centre

LOCATION Borders of
Gansu Province and
Inner Mongolia, China
NEAREST POPULATION HUB
Jiuquan
SECRECY OVERVIEW
Operations classified:
secretive centre of China's
space programme.

In 2003, Yang Liwei became the first man launched into orbit by China. When he took off from the Jiuquan Launch Centre, China became only the third country to manage the feat. Largely hidden from the glare of attention in its isolated desert location, the Centre's South launch site is the focus of the nation's space programme. However, much of the huge complex remains off-bounds to outside observers.

Construction of a rocket facility at Jiuquan began in 1958, with assistance from the Soviet Union. In its early years, Jiuquan's principal purpose was to test launch surface-to-surface and surface-to-air missiles, a fact that greatly disturbed Washington when it became aware of the facility in 1963. Originally known as Base 20, it was China's chief site for missile development and testing until at least 1980. This work was largely carried out at what is known as the North Launch Site, a facility that was officially decommissioned in 1996.

The South Launch Site, with its 105-metre (344-ft) launch tower, sprouted from the sands of the Gobi Desert in the 1990s to serve as the headquarters of China's expanding space programme. The region's weather conditions ensure that launches are possible for around 80 per cent of the year, while the isolated location reduces the risk of failed rockets falling back to Earth over populated areas. Jiuquan saw its first launch at the end

of the decade, and in 2003 came Yang Liwei's momentous mission, designated Shenzhou 5. After orbiting the planet 14 times, the first 'taikonaut' returned to terra firma to find himself a popular hero and Jiuquan firmly fixed in the national consciousness.

Just as the space race had been for the Cold War superpowers of the USA and the USSR in the second half of the 20th century, space exploration for booming 21st-century China is not simply about pushing back the boundaries of science. Perhaps just as important is the role a space programme can have in establishing China's credentials as a new superpower (particularly when its only rival to such a status, the US, has recently struggled to find the dollars to fund its own missions).

Such ambitions have been fermenting for a long time. For instance, Deng Xiaopeng, the country's *de facto* leader from 1978–92, is reported to have remarked: 'If China had not developed a nuclear bomb and had not launched a

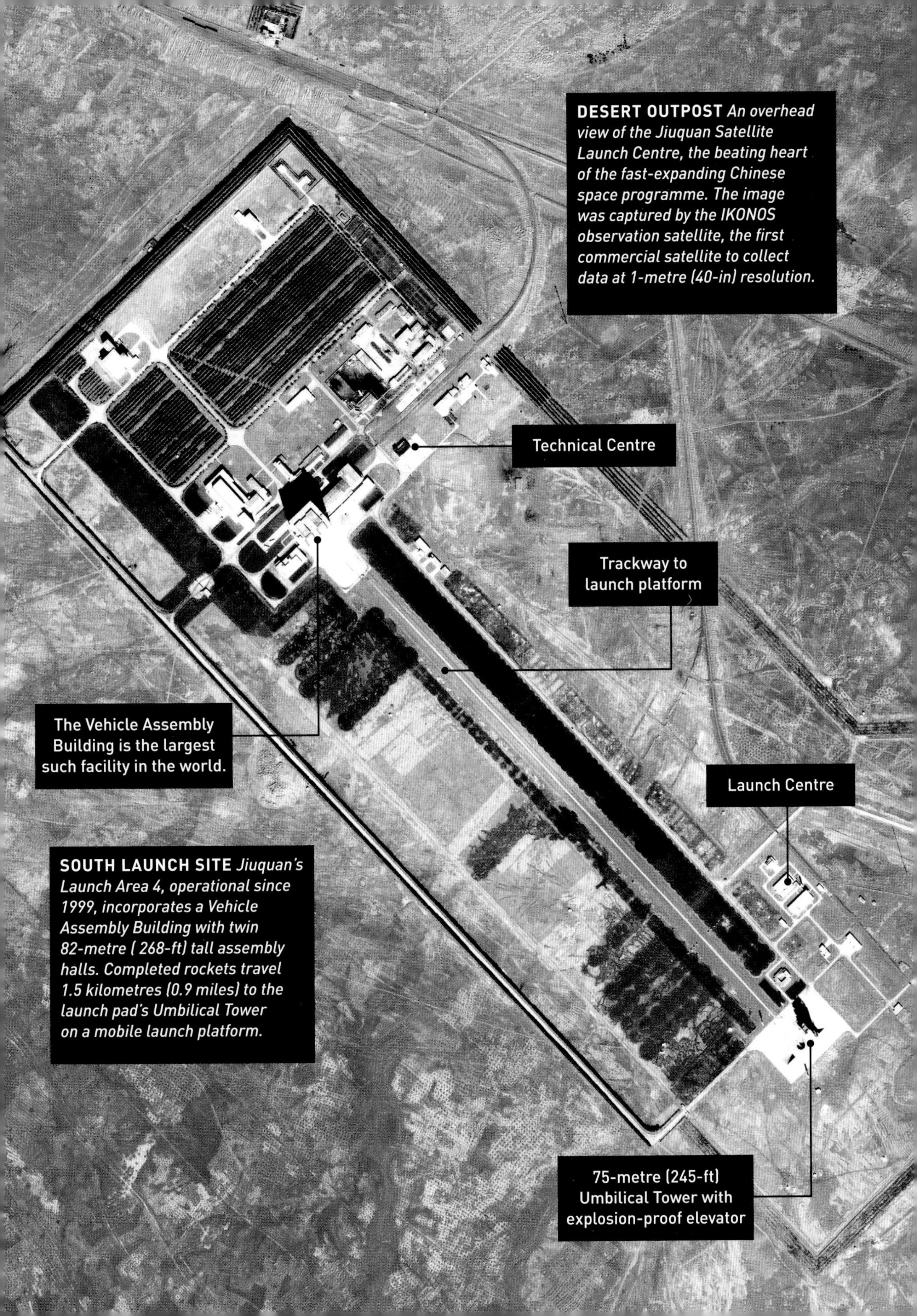

DESERT OUTPOST *An overhead view of the Jiuquan Satellite Launch Centre, the beating heart of the fast-expanding Chinese space programme. The image was captured by the IKONOS observation satellite, the first commercial satellite to collect data at 1-metre (40-in) resolution.*

Technical Centre

Trackway to launch platform

The Vehicle Assembly Building is the largest such facility in the world.

Launch Centre

SOUTH LAUNCH SITE *Jiuquan's Launch Area 4, operational since 1999, incorporates a Vehicle Assembly Building with twin 82-metre (268-ft) tall assembly halls. Completed rockets travel 1.5 kilometres (0.9 miles) to the launch pad's Umbilical Tower on a mobile launch platform.*

75-metre (245-ft) Umbilical Tower with explosion-proof elevator

BLAST OFF *A Long-March II-F carrier rocket launches from Jiuquan on 25 September 2008, carrying the Shenzhou 7 spacecraft. This was China's third manned space mission, sending a crew of three into orbit. Controversy ensued when Shenzhou passed within just 45 km (28 miles) of the International Space Station.*

satellite, then China would not be able to call itself a great power.'

A second manned mission, Shenzhou 6, was launched from Jiuquan in 2005, this time sending up two taikonauts. Shenzhou 7 followed in 2008, and took the project another step by incorporating extra-vehicular activity (a space-walk, in layman's terms). While the American and Soviet pioneers of the space race tested each new stage of development with frequent multiple missions, the Chinese approach is more sporadic, but each new mission, when it comes, involves another giant leap forward. Ultimately, China makes no secret of its ambitions to put a permanent manned station into orbit, to establish a base on the Moon, and perhaps even to send a manned mission to Mars.

In gestures largely uncharacteristic of Beijing, international journalists have been occasionally invited to share in the state-of-the art work going on at Jiuquan – or at least, they have been invited to see certain specified areas such as the South Launch Site and Donfeng Space City, which is home to several tens of thousands of employees (both military and scientific) and their families. With modern facilities including schools, cinemas, beauty parlours and fast-food joints, one could almost be forgiven for thinking that the entire project is some sort of elaborate space theme park, and indeed, even tightly controlled tourist groups have been welcomed into certain corners of Jiuquan. The Chinese space programme, it seems, operates with unusual openness.

Yet the fear remains that there is more going on at Jiuquan than simply space exploration. The Centre is a vast operation, with a footprint of some 2,800 square kilometres (1,100 square miles) and its own railway that links to the national network. While the South Site serves to highlight mankind's continuing determination to become masters of the universe, what goes on elsewhere at the Centre is rather more mysterious. Much of it is closed to visitors, with military personnel patrolling to ensure that its exclusion zones are not breached. Those parts where prying eyes are not welcome are said to include an airbase, radar tracking stations and missile testing ranges still in operation. As the US and the Soviet Union discovered, space technology throws up a lot of 'transferable' science, and many observers believe that Jiuquan's role in China's military endeavours may well turn out to be as important as its more widely heralded space projects.

The Tomb of Qin Shi Huang

LOCATION Shaanxi
Province, China
NEAREST POPULATION HUB
Xi'an
SECRECY OVERVIEW
Site of historic mystery:
the legendary tomb of
China's first emperor.

From 221 BC, Qin Shi Huang ruled over a vast empire of once-disunited states, laying the platform for the modern Chinese state. Keen to build a suitable monument to himself for after his death, he ordered the construction of one of history's most spectacular mausoleums. While parts of the complex – including the incredible Terracotta Army – have been revealed in recent decades, much of it still lies buried.

Qin Shi Huang came to the throne of the Chinese state of Qin in 246 BC when he was only 13 years old. A figure of vast ego and ambition, he spent a good deal of his life planning for his legacy, and building of his mausoleum began soon after he ascended to the throne. He somehow also found time to unite a disparate group of previously warring kingdoms, imposing order in the form of vast infrastructure projects (including a forerunner of the Great Wall of China), as well as sweeping economic and political reforms, including the standardization of currency, weights and measures. For this, he is generally acknowledged as the First Emperor of China.

The more successful he became as a leader, the more ambitious his plans for his afterlife seem to have become. It has also been speculated that, in a bid to discover the elixir of life, he consumed all manner of substances that slowly drove him insane. Regardless, on the advice of his trusted geomancers (who offered spiritual guidance by interpreting geographical features), he hit upon Li

Mountain as a particularly auspicious site. Today it is roughly equivalent in size to the Great Pyramid at Giza, but it was considerably larger in Qin Shi Huang's time. It is located about 35 kilometres (22 miles) east of Xi'an, between the Lishan Mountains and the River Wei. The Emperor decreed that an area several kilometres wide around the mountain was to be given over to his grand project. The mausoleum complex was designed to echo the plans of his great dynastic capital, Xianyang, with his 'palace' at the centre and the 'city walls' enclosed by outer walls. We have a relatively contemporary account of the tomb's construction in the form of Sima Qian's *Records of the Grand Historian*, written about a hundred years after the Emperor's death. In it, Sima Qian reports that 700,000 workers were tasked with building the tomb. Some experts have concluded that this must be an exaggeration, but it nonetheless gives an idea of the scale of the work.

Sima Qian also tells of how three rivers were burrowed through and filled with

ULTIMATE MYSTERY *Reconstructions of the tomb's interior must rely on a handful of historic sources that often contradict one another, and sometimes fail to agree on basic features such as the mound's height. However, all are agreed that the mound was never breached, even by ancient tomb raiders.*

Original mound may have been up to 115 metres (377 ft) high

Surrounding temple complexes (now lost)

Stepped pyramid with four processional stairways

'Middle Gate' chamber contains the Emperor's coffin

Burial pits of Terracotta Army are scattered through surrounding countryside

Outer chamber modelled on a map of the known world

Entrances into the tomb are sealed and now lost. Ancient booby traps such as automatic crossbows may still be active

NEVER FORGOTTEN *Today, the Mausoleum of Qin Shi Huang still forms an imposing mound some 43 metres (141 ft) high. External structures have long since vanished, and the ancient pyramid is overgrown with trees. But while the tomb and its surroundings now draw hordes of tourists, attempts at amateur archaeology are strictly forbidden.*

bronze. A map of the entire Qin empire was carved into the floor, while the roof was encrusted with precious gems to resemble the night sky. Rivers of mercury flowed through mountains and hills of bronze. To add a bitter aftertaste to the story, it is said that in a bid to preserve secrecy, the Emperor had every one of the labourers who worked upon it executed, many by burial within the mound itself. It all sounds somewhat implausible, yet more than 4,000 soil samples have shown notably high levels of mercury vapour, suggesting that the tales could be rooted in fact after all.

The general public's first inkling of what might be contained in the tomb came in 1974 with the serendipitous discovery of a pit by a party of well diggers. They had uncovered the first evidence of the terracotta warriors, a life-sized sculpted imperial honour guard. This remarkable army – with some troops on foot and others in horse-drawn chariots – is estimated to total 8,000 figures. Further pits have since been found containing figures of actors, dancers, musicians, acrobats and civil servants – all the staff you might need in the Next World. Subsequent archaeological investigation has revealed around 180 different sites of interest within the tomb complex, from towers and gardens to offices.

New rooms, pits and other features are regularly added to the list. The tomb itself is believed to be encased in copper, residing within a purpose-built, treasure-filled chamber. To deter intruders, the Emperor had the mausoleum extensively booby-trapped. A network of crossbows is said to be rigged to fire at anyone who manages to break in.

Somewhat remarkably, non-invasive ground surveys indicate that the main vaults are indeed largely undisturbed – quite a feat in a country where grave-robbing is a lucrative and organized business. In 2010, for instance, it was found that the grave of Zhuang Xiang, father of Qin Shi Huang, had been broken into. The Tomb of the First Emperor may well be one of the world's most important archaeological treasures, on a par with (if not surpassing) the tomb of Tutankhamun. As such, the site has been put under the highest security and it would take a skilled or reckless robber to attempt to breach it today.

Requests by academic teams to excavate the main tomb area have so far been resisted by the Chinese authorities, not least because earlier attempts at excavating imperial tombs ended badly as a result of poor working methods. For the foreseeable future at least, it seems the Emperor can rest in peace.

Hainan submarine base

LOCATION Hainan Province, Southern China
NEAREST POPULATION HUB Haikou
SECRECY OVERVIEW Operations classified: site of an underground submarine base.

Despite rumours circulating since 2002, it was only in 2008 that satellite images confirmed that the People's Liberation Army Navy was constructing a base on Hainan Island. Hainan lies off the south coast of the Chinese mainland, offering a gateway to the South China Sea, and it is widely believed that the base is being built as a home for a large part of China's nuclear submarine fleet.

China undertook the construction of its naval base at Hainan away from the glare of publicity, despite the fact that it lies just a few miles from the popular tourist city of Sanya. Beijing has so far refused to elaborate on what purpose its base will serve but the respected *Janes Intelligence Review*, which first confirmed the base's existence, concluded that it could be used for 'expeditionary as well as defensive operations'.

The complex includes a harbour large enough to accommodate nuclear-armed submarines as well as aircraft carriers, with piers extending almost 1,000 metres (3,300 ft). Even more intriguingly, as many as 11 tunnels are built into the surrounding hillsides, with entrances around 20 metres (66 ft) high. It has been suggested that these tunnels could provide space to house up to 20 nuclear submarines out of view of passing spy satellites. Furthermore, waters are as deep as 5,000 metres (16,500 ft) within a few miles of Hainan, allowing vessels to dive quickly to depths where they would be virtually impossible to detect.

The Hainan facility, it seems, will give China a strategic base from which it can wield greater influence over the South China Sea shipping lanes, which are crucial for the oil and mineral imports that drive the Chinese economy. It could also provide China with increased opportunity to build its military presence around the disputed Spratly and Paracel Island groups, with the added incentive to Beijing of serving to unnerve Taiwan.

The Spratly and Paracel archipelagos have been at the centre of disputes over sovereignty for centuries, but the competition to secure influence has heated up in recent decades, involving not only China and Taiwan but Vietnam, Malaysia and the Philippines too. The disputes are less concerned with the islands themselves and more with their territorial waters, which are believed to contain vast reserves of oil and natural gas. Some commentators have also suggested that Hainan could quite feasibly support Chinese plans for a 'blue-water' naval presence stretching far beyond the South China Sea.

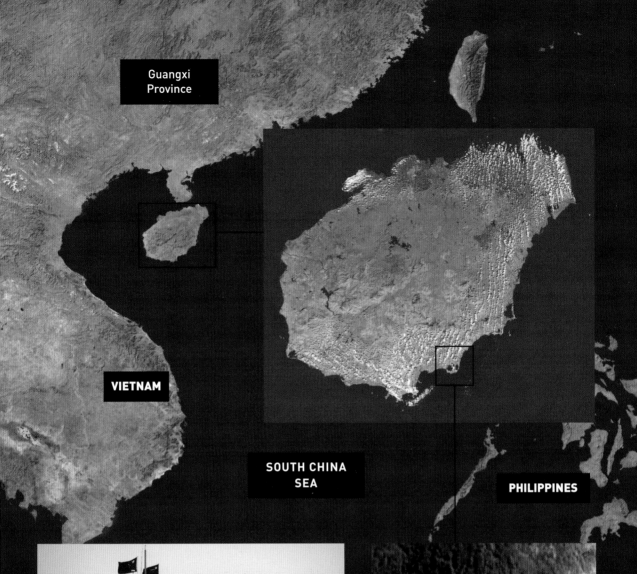

Guangxi
Province

VIETNAM

SOUTH CHINA
SEA

PHILIPPINES

MONSTER OF THE DEEP *A nuclear-powered submarine of the People's Liberation Army Navy, pictured in 2009. The potential riches in the waters around Asia have led to a massive expansion of the continent's submarine fleets as nations vie to establish their sovereignty over the sea.*

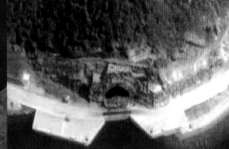

HARBOURING AMBITIONS *An aerial view of the impressive architecture on display at the Hainan base. It has clearly been built to accommodate serious naval hardware and has attracted the concerned attention of several of China's regional competitors.*

The Tomb of Genghis Khan

LOCATION Assumed to be in the Khentii Province of eastern Mongolia
NEAREST POPULATION HUB Ulan Bator
SECRECY OVERVIEW Location uncertain: last resting place of the legendary Mongol leader.

Given the name Temujin at birth, Genghis Khan went on to unite disparate nomadic tribes to establish the Mongol Empire, winning himself a reputation as one of history's most feared warriors in the process. In accordance with his wishes, he was buried in the utmost secrecy: the location of his tomb remains one of history's enduring conundrums, despite numerous attempts to find it.

Temujin was in his mid-40s by the time he became leader of the Mongols in the early 13th century. During his reign, he laid the foundations for a vast empire that would eventually stretch from China to Hungary, taking a title, Genghis Khan, that struck fear into the hearts of both subjects and rivals. But he was more than a bloodthirsty tyrant, introducing a written language system and doing much to bring the cultures of East and West together.

He died in 1227, aged around 65. The exact cause of his death is disputed, with explanations ranging from a riding accident to illness to sexual misadventure. Regardless, it was his wish to be buried in secret in accordance with tribal custom, his resting place to remain unmarked. To this end, extraordinary and infamous precautions were undertaken. Legend has it that members of his funeral escort slaughtered any person unfortunate enough to stray across their path. The slaves who built the tomb were murdered once it was completed so that they could not divulge its location, and the soldiers who killed them were in turn dispatched. It is said that the ground was then trampled by horses, planted with trees and even had a river diverted over it to hide the tomb entrance.

Debate rages as to the location of the emperor's body. Many believe that it is probably in Mongolia's Khentii Province, perhaps close to the sacred Burkhan Kaldun mountain where Temujin was born. In 2004, an archaeological team claimed to have found his long-lost palace in this region, which many experts assume would have been close to his final resting place. In another recent project, Dr Albert Yu-Min Lin of the University of California at San Diego has attempted to harness the power of an army of internet enthusiasts, to analyze satellite images of Khentii.

Yet the grave remains elusive and that is no doubt what Genghis Khan would want. According to Mongolian tradition, as long as his tomb is left undisturbed his soul will be kept protected.

RUSSIA

Lake Baikal

Mongolian Steppe

Burkhan Kaldun, birthplace of Temujin

OUT THERE SOMEWHERE *The expansive plains of Mongolia offer tomb-seekers plenty of opportunity for speculative searching. Serious researchers, though, are increasingly utilizing high-tech imaging technology and the goodwill of internet archaeologists in a bid to narrow down the search area.*

MONGOLIA

Ulan Bator

FEARED LEADER *This 14th-century portrait of Genghis Khan hangs in Taiwan's National Palace Museum in Taipei. Scientific studies have concluded that as many as 2.5 per cent of all the men alive today can trace their lineage back to the prolific warrior.*

Gobi Desert

CHINA

Chinese Information Security Base

LOCATION Beijing, China
NEAREST POPULATION HUB Beijing
SECRECY OVERVIEW Operations classified: China's front line in the age of cyber warfare.

Ever since the rise of the internet, futurologists have predicted that where wars were once fought on battlefields and won with gunfire, they will one day be fought in the cyberworld against a backdrop of mouse clicks. In 2010, China seemed to signal the approach of this new age when it announced the establishment of a government-run cyber defence base.

There are those who argue convincingly that we are already living in a world of cyber wars, where lapses in electronic security are exploited for commercial, political or even military advantage. For instance, it has been widely speculated that the Stuxnet virus that infiltrated Iran's nuclear facilities in 2010 originated in Israel. India has also claimed that some of its government networks have been hit from Chinese bases. But it has so far been impossible to prove whether such attacks stemmed from the concerted efforts of government agencies, or from groups or individuals with their own agendas. The maverick actions of hacker collectives such as Anonymous and Lulzsec has further clouded the issue.

However, in 2009 the US-China Economic and Security Review Commission concluded that 'there has been a marked increase in cyber intrusions originating in China and targeting US government and defense-related systems'. In turn, China has accused the White House of waging its own cyber attacks, a claim vehemently denied in Washington.

In truth, many of the world's most powerful nations are developing cyber warfare divisions within their armed services. Washington established its US Cyber Command unit in 2009 to counteract online criminal and espionage activity. But the announcement by the Chinese People's Liberation Army a year later that it had set up an Information Security Base, under the jurisdiction of the powerful General Staff headquarters in Beijing, ramped up the sense of tension.

The announcement's lack of even the most basic details about the base and its operations did little to steady nerves, though a Chinese spokesman insisted that 'it is a "defensive" base for information security, not an offensive headquarters for cyber war'. Just don't expect to be able to take a tour around its headquarters to decide for yourself any time soon.

Room 39

LOCATION Pyongyang, North Korea
NEAREST POPULATION HUB Pyongyang
SECRECY OVERVIEW Operations classified: the secretive financial hub responsible for maintaining North Korea's ruling elite.

Sometimes also referred to as Bureau 39, North Korea's Room 39 has been described by journalist Kelly Olsen as 'one of the most secret organizations in arguably the world's most secretive state'. Analysts believe it raises funds for the governing regime through a mixture of legal and illegal enterprises. Much of the money it produces is allegedly used to buy the ongoing support of senior officials.

Established sometime in the late 1970s, Room 39 is believed to be housed in the ruling Workers' Party Building in the Central Committee precinct, located in downtown Pyongyang. From here, a central staff of around 130 people coordinates international operations. Their activities have been likened to those of an international investment bank – although much of the work 'on the ground' is left to local and relatively small-scale criminal gangs. The principal aim of Room 39 is to provide a stash of hard currency for the personal use of senior government figures. Until his death in 2011, it was essentially the personal slush fund of North Korean leader Kim Jong-il.

It is estimated that Room 39 generates between half a billion and a billion dollars each year through various illegal enterprises. Among the illegitimate businesses it is supposedly involved in are the counterfeiting of bank notes, money laundering, exporting fake cigarettes and pharmaceuticals, and smuggling narcotics (especially heroin

and crystal methamphetamine). Other areas of its business are ostensibly legitimate (ranging from overseas restaurant chains to mining and agricultural operations) though few are untainted by the claims of money laundering. Room 39 keeps a lot of fingers in a lot of pies, with interests in at least a hundred overseas trading companies. Pyongyang, however, denies that it is party to any irregular activities.

Kim Jong-il was said to have used the cash generated by Room 39 to lavish gifts upon key figures within his cabinet, the ruling Workers' Party and the military. It is alleged that he spent millions each year on high-end consumer goods including cognac, luxury cars and the latest electronic items in order to secure his power base. Other money, it has been suggested, was used to prop up his spending on nuclear weapons and ballistic missiles programmes.

One of Room 39's most successful scams has been the counterfeiting

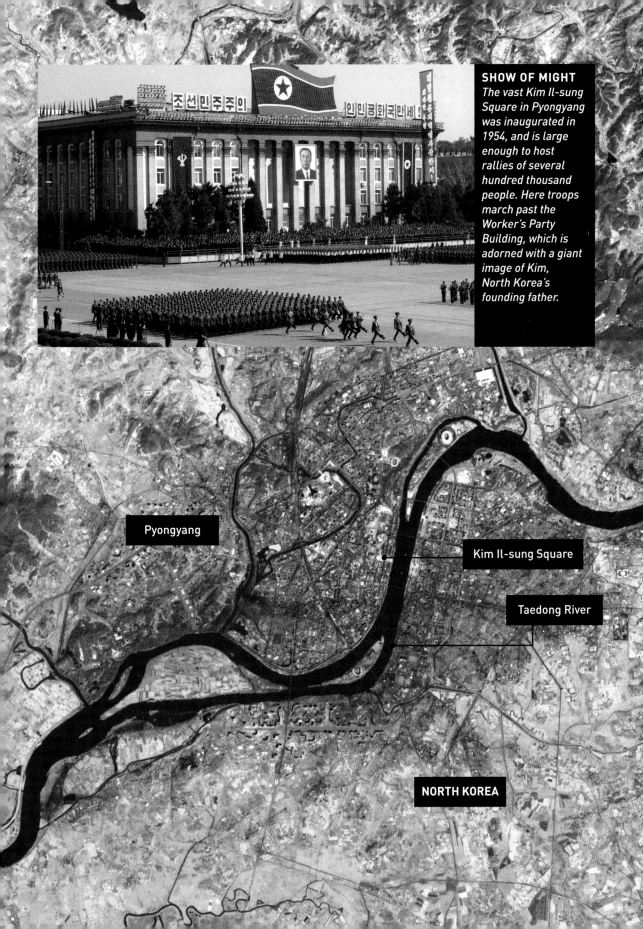

SHOW OF MIGHT
The vast Kim Il-sung Square in Pyongyang was inaugurated in 1954, and is large enough to host rallies of several hundred thousand people. Here troops march past the Worker's Party Building, which is adorned with a giant image of Kim, North Korea's founding father.

Pyongyang

Kim Il-sung Square

Taedong River

NORTH KOREA

FAKE BENJAMINS *The 'superdollar' (counterfeit hundred-dollar bill) was in worldwide circulation by the late 1980s. Expertly produced, these forgeries replicate many of the security features employed by genuine currency. While the finger of blame has pointed in several directions, North Korea's Room 39 is thought mostly likely to be behind the scheme.*

The international community, and the United States in particular, has long grappled to confront the threat from Room 39. For instance, in 2004 Austria – under pressure from Washington – closed down the North Korean-owned Golden Star Bank in Vienna, which was suspected of participating in laundering. Even more significantly, a year later the Banco Delta Asia in Macao (a Chinese dependency) was labelled by the US Treasury as a 'primary money-laundering concern' and US$25 million of assets linked to Kim were frozen.

Another important money-making scheme was large-scale insurance fraud, which came to prominence after the international community moved to undermine Pyongyang's counterfeiting operations. According to evidence from North Korean defectors, the state-owned Korean National Insurance Company (KNIC) was highly active in selling on its insurance liabilities to companies in other parts of the world. It is then alleged that, under the guidance of Room 39, major accidents were faked. One cited example was a helicopter crashing into a government warehouse in the capital city. Ferry and rail disasters are also alleged to have been set up. KNIC would then pick up multi-million dollar pay-outs from foreign companies that had bought its liabilities. It is believed that this scam has brought in US$50–60 million per year.

of US currency. For many years, the US government has been aware of the widespread circulation of so-called 'superdollars' – fake US$100 bills of such high quality that only sophisticated laboratory testing can expose them. These notes are smuggled across international boundaries to be laundered, leaving the North Korean regime with huge volumes of genuine currency. Estimates of the value of Room 39-created superdollars vary from around US$45 million to several hundred million dollars.

In a country that consistently runs massive trade deficits, Room 39 went a long way to making the Kim clan's largesse possible and maintaining its 'court economy', a system that protects government funding despite the failure of North Korea's traditional economy. Just how the 2011 death of Kim Jong-il and the succession of his son Kim Jong-un will affect the future of Room 39 remains to be seen.

92

Yongbyon Nuclear Scientific Research Centre

LOCATION North Pyongan Province, North Korea
NEAREST POPULATION HUB Kaechon
SECRECY OVERVIEW Operations classified: the heart of North Korea's controversial nuclear programme.

The Yongbyon Nuclear Scientific Research Centre has been a source of friction between North Korea and the international community ever since it began operating in the 1980s. North Korea's refusal to submit to inspections by the International Atomic Energy Agency (IAEA) has led to several stand-offs with the wider world, which is keen to establish Pyongyang's nuclear capabilities.

While North Korea is quite within its legal rights to foster a nuclear programme for civilian purposes, the international community (and most of all South Korea, with whom North Korea has never signed a formal peace treaty to end the war of 1950–53) fear that the real focus of such a programme is inevitably on manufacturing weapons.

Yongbyon lies within a mountain clearing in North Pyongan province, about 100 kilometres (60 miles) north of Pyongyang. The centre includes a five-megawatt reactor and a fuel reprocessing facility, where weapons-grade plutonium can be extracted from spent fuel rods. Yongbyon's history has closely followed the changing fortunes of the international talks designed to steer Pyongyang away from a nuclear weapons programme.

The complex was built in the early 1980s, but its existence was not declared to the international community as it was required to be. By 1990, US intelligence had evidence that it included facilities for producing weapons-grade fuel. In 1991, North Korea signed a Joint Declaration with South Korea on denuclearization of the Korean Peninsula, and the following year agreed to IAEA inspections (as it should have done back in 1985 when it signed the Nuclear Non-Proliferation Treaty). However, in 1993 Pyongyang objected to certain IAEA demands, spurring renewed concerns about its nuclear intentions.

The North promptly threatened to leave the treaty altogether, raising tensions with both South Korea and the US. New hope came in 1994, however, with an Agreed Framework between Washington and Pyongyang. Yongbyon was to be dismantled in return for an easing of sanctions and the provision of alternative energy supplies.

However, the situation took a turn for the worse in 2002, with North Korea acknowledging its nuclear weapons programme for the first time and US President George W. Bush labelling the country as part of an 'axis of evil'.

CHINA

NORTH KOREA

Pyongyang

Seoul

SOUTH KOREA

SITE OF CONCERN *Satellite imagery of the nuclear reactor at Yongbyon, taken in 2005. The North Korean regime has consistently refused to play ball with the international community over access to the facility, using it instead as a pawn in its international relations.*

TEST REACTOR *A detailed view reveals the tower of the 5MW experimental reactor at Yongbyon, source of much of the radioactive material used in North Korea's nuclear tests. The cooling tower dismantled in 2008 can be seen at upper right – a new reactor is now under construction in its place.*

Pyongyang announced in February 2003 that Yongbyon had been reactivated and that North Korea was indeed withdrawing from the Nuclear Non-Proliferation Treaty.

However, by late 2005, six-party talks involving North and South Korea, China, Japan, Russia and the USA seemed to have established a new settlement, with North Korea again agreeing to abandon its nuclear ambitions in return for much-needed financial aid and certain political concessions. However, when talks became deadlocked, North Korea conducted its first nuclear weapons test. The following year, Pyongyang eased its position again, allowing IAEA inspectors to visit Yongbyon and promising to shut down the reactor in return for being removed from Washington's list of state sponsors of terrorism. The dismantling process began in June 2008 with the spectacular destruction of the main cooling tower at Yongbyon.

Yet doubts remained as to how honest North Korea was being about its nuclear facilities, and relations soon took another downward turn. North Korea banned further IAEA inspections, withdrew from talks in 2009 and conducted another nuclear test. In 2010, Pyongyang was blamed for the sinking of a South Korean naval vessel and for shelling a South Korean-held island, further raising the stakes.

In November 2010, satellite imagery confirmed that Kim Jong-il's regime was in the process of building a new reactor at Yongbyon, on the site of the former cooling tower. More satellite photos in 2011 backed up assertions from Pyongyang that building was 'progressing apace'. Experts concluded that while it is designed for civilian purposes, it could be easily adapted for the production of weapons-grade uranium. During 2010, Pyongyang had used a military parade to showcase a new class of intermediate-range ballistic missiles capable of bearing a nuclear payload. Whether the North has yet developed a warhead to fit the missile is not known.

For several decades, the ruling regime in North Korea has been characterized by paranoia about its standing in the world. In that light, its nuclear programme has proved a useful tool in drawing concessions on various issues. Nonetheless, by keeping independent observers away from Yongbyon for prolonged periods, Pyongyang has entered into a risky game of brinkmanship, in which no one can be sure of the outcome. But, ever more isolated on the international stage and with its economy crippled by a lack of international trade, the country may have few other cards left to play.

KEEPING COOL *The cooling tower at Yongbyon was blown up by the North Korean authorities in 2008 in an apparent gesture of rapprochement with the West. However, hopes of more cordial relations were soon dashed as Pyongyang ordered a new nuclear test.*

Mount Baekdu hideout

93

LOCATION Ryanggang
Province, North Korea
NEAREST POPULATION HUB
Hyesan
SECRECY OVERVIEW
Existence unacknowledged:
secret mountain lair of
the former North Korean
leader, Kim Jong-il.

Kim Jong-il, reputedly a great fan of the James Bond movies, all but completed his transformation into the perfect Bond villain by ordering construction of a secret military command centre inside his country's most sacred mountain, Mount Baekdu. Uncovered by foreign defence analysts in 2010, the complex is believed to have been many years in the building.

Mount Baekdu (which translates as 'the white-headed mountain') rises to over 2,700 metres (8,850 ft) on North Korea's border with China. It is a spectacular stratovolcano with a habit of erupting about once a century on average (the next eruption is currently overdue). According to Korea's foundation story, its first kingdom emerged here in the third millennium BC, and as such, the mountain is a highly venerated site.

North Korea's founding father, Kim Il-sung, is said to have led Korea's resistance against Japanese occupation from the dense forests around the mountain until 1945. It then became an important base for communist forces during the Korean War. North Korea's official history claims that Kim Jong-il was born on the mountain beneath a double rainbow, though most evidence points to his birthplace as a small village near Khabarovsk in Russia.

The secret base, revealed by the Hong Kong bureau of the Kanwa Information

Centre in 2010, was said to have been built into the mountainside to serve as a command post should North Korea ever suffer an invasion from one or both of South Korea and the USA, or in the event that the Kim dynasty was threatened by an internal coup. Built close to one of the 'Dear Leader' Kim Jong-il's palaces, the complex has storage space for helicopters and fighter jets, with an airfield located conveniently close by. Evidence for the lair's existence was garnered from a combination of satellite photos and the testimony of defectors.

If the world was hoping for a change in North Korea's political approach after Kim Jong-il's death in late 2011, a proclamation attributed to the National Defence Commission suggested otherwise: 'We declare solemnly and confidently that foolish politicians around the world, including the puppet forces in South Korea, that they should not expect any change from us.' As long as the isolated state retains this ferocious attitude, the Mount Baekdu base will surely remain on standby.

CHINA

Lake Chon

NORTH KOREA

FABLED MOUNTAIN
An official North Korean photograph shows Kim Jong-il, the nation's leader from 1994 until his death in 2011, casually posing at the top of Mount Baekdu. Official claims that he was born at this revered site are likely nothing more than myth.

SOUTH KOREA

94 Korean Demilitarized Zone

LOCATION A strip of land along the 38th Parallel
NEAREST POPULATION HUB Kaesong, North Korea/ Uijeongbu, South Korea
SECRECY OVERVIEW Access restricted: the world's most heavily militarized border.

Reportedly described by then US President Bill Clinton as 'the scariest place on earth' during a visit in 1993, the Korean Demilitarized Zone (commonly abbreviated as the DMZ) is the buffer zone that divides North and South Korea. Widely accepted as the most heavily armed border in the world, the DMZ is a virtual no-go area along most of its 248-kilometre (154-mile) length.

The DMZ runs along the 38th parallel, the line of latitude that was used to demarcate the newly established nations of North and South Korea in 1948. Stretching from the mouth of the River Han on the Peninsula's west coast all the way over to the east coast, it is an average of 4 km (2.5 miles) wide, with as many as a million troops stationed on the North's side and well over half a million in the South (including a US contingent of several tens of thousands). The territory covered by the DMZ is defaced with razor wire, heavy weaponry, countless watch towers and concealed tank-traps and landmines.

When North Korea attacked across the 38th parallel in 1950, it sparked a bitter three-year war that claimed the lives of 2 million people. Fighting came to an end in July 1953 with the signing of a ceasefire armistice, though no permanent peace was ever concluded. The DMZ was set up under the terms of the internationally brokered armistice, with a Military Demarcation Line running along its centre. Either side may patrol within the DMZ up to the Demarcation Line, but must not set foot over it.

The DMZ remains a swathe of land in which danger is ever present. Indeed, were the North to encroach on the territory of the South, the US would be drawn to South Korea's defence under the terms of a 1954 agreement. And were that to happen, we would very likely find ourselves in the middle of a Third World War.

Six decades after the Korean War ostensibly ended, relations between the North and South remain strained, sometimes to breaking point. Border skirmishes have been a regular feature throughout the DMZ's history, often with little provocation. Furthermore, from the 1970s South Korea discovered a series of tunnels crossing the DMZ from the North, arousing suspicions that the North still harboured plans for invasion.

For its part, the North has accused the South of building a huge wall the length of the DMZ, constructed from concrete

NEIGHBOURHOOD WATCH *Two North Korean troops survey the South Korean portion of the Joint Security Area (popularly known as Truce Village). Despite the presence of international observers to ensure that the peace is kept, there have been sporadic skirmishes.*

THE GOOD LIFE *Gijeong-dong is North Korea's 'Propaganda Village', visible from the South's sector of the DMZ. According to Pyongyang, 200 families enjoy an enviable quality of life on a collective farm, though others claim that the settlement is nothing but an elaborate ruse.*

Pyongyang

NORTH KOREA

Demilitarized Zone

Seoul

SOUTH KOREA

COLD WAR *South Korean infantry soldiers in winter uniform patrol a barbed-wire-topped fence that runs parallel to the Military Demarcation Line, dividing North and South Korea along the 38th parallel.*

negotiations between the two sides, it was at Panmunjom that over a thousand sessions of talks were held ahead of the 1953 armistice. Today, Swedish and Swiss representatives from the Neutral Nations Supervisory Commission keep a permanent presence here to ensure that the DMZ continues to be observed.

Yet even Panmunjom has not been free from incident. For example, in 1976 several South Korean and US personnel were killed by axe blows when an attempt to prune a bush provoked a clash with troops from the North. While this is the only place in the DMZ where visitors are allowed, it should be noted that only approved tour groups are accepted, and visitors must sign a waiver that begins: 'The visit to the Joint Security Area at Panmunjeon will entail entry into a hostile area and the possibility of injury or death.'

UNITED FRONT *This Reunification Memorial sits by a North Korean entrance to the DMZ. The slogan translates as: 'Let us pass to the next generation a united country.' It is a sentiment that seems destined to go unfulfilled, with relations between the two neighbours rarely more than strained at best.*

and adorned with assorted military posts. Pyongyang has claimed the wall offers the South a bridgehead into the North's territory. The South and the US both deny the existence of any such construction, though they do admit that sections of anti-tank barriers have been erected.

Panmunjom, towards the western end of the DMZ, is a rare enclave of normality (though that is a relative term). It is home to the Joint Security Area, sometimes known as the Truce Village. Neither the North nor South can claim dominion over it, but both contribute to its policing. Host to countless rounds of

Not far from Panmunjom is Daeseong-dong (which translates as Freedom Village), the only South Korean-run settlement in the DMZ. The town of Gijeong-dong, 2 kilometres (1.2 miles) from Daeseong-dong on the North's side, is the only other village in the DMZ. Supposedly a model town with a school, hospital and collective farm as well as high-quality housing, it was designed to prove that the North's way was the best way (for a while it even laid claim to the world's tallest flagpole, upon which is suspended a huge North Korean flag). However, it is widely suspected that there is no permanent population there save for a few military personnel.

Curiously and ironically, while the DMZ remains a place of great danger for humans, the absence of mankind's influence has turned it into an unlikely nature reserve – today it plays home to numerous rare species, including cranes and even big cats.

95 Camp 22

LOCATION Northeastern North Korea

NEAREST POPULATION HUB Hoeryong

SECRECY OVERVIEW Existence unacknowledged: a prison camp holding 50,000 people, mostly for criticizing the government.

A detention centre for political prisoners and their families, Camp 22 lies in a mountainous setting close to North Korea's borders with Russia and China. Though the secretive North Korean government denies its existence and it does not appear on any maps, several former inmates and members of staff have alleged extreme brutality and human rights violations.

Camp 22 is perhaps more reminiscent of a concentration camp than a typical prison facility. Believed to have been established in 1959, most of its 50,000 inmates have either been interned for criticizing the ruling regime or for simply being related to those who have. It is believed that up to three generations of certain families are held here, in accordance with a proclamation by Kim Il-sung, North Korea's founding tyrant: 'Enemies of class, whoever they are, their seed must be eliminated through three generations.'

Evidence from satellite photos suggests that the camp covers approximately 48 by 40 kilometres (30 x 25 miles) near the village of Haengyong-ni, with prisoners dispersed widely across it, and that it is surrounded by fences under heavy guard. Reports from other North Korean camps indicate that electric fencing is probably employed. Much of our knowledge of what occurs within its confines comes from testimony delivered by defectors from North Korea, including the camp's one-time chief of management.

They have described how prisoners are expected to labour for between 12 and 15 hours a day, surviving on a meagre diet. Death from malnutrition and other diseases is common, as well as from work-related accidents and during interrogations.

Most prisoners are believed to arrive at the camp without due legal process and are forbidden contact with the outside world. Anyone caught attempting to escape is liable to be executed in front of fellow prisoners. Suicide, meanwhile, is punished by extended sentences for the dead prisoner's family.

Guards mistreat prisoners with impunity, with allegations of rape and child-killing voiced by various sources. Perhaps most shockingly of all, former camp employees have claimed that some inmates were subjected to chemical experimentation, while others were killed en masse in gas chambers. Amid such allegations, it is little surprise that Pyongyang denies the camp even exists.

Ise Grand Shrine

96

LOCATION Honshu, Japan
NEAREST POPULATION HUB
Ise
SECRECY OVERVIEW
Access restricted: the
most sacred shrine of
the Shinto religion.

Claiming some 120 million followers in Japan, Shinto is a Japanese system of beliefs and traditions that encourages devotion to spirits but has no central 'god' figure. The shrine at Ise is so sacred to Shintoism that access to the inner sanctums is strictly regulated – in fact, only the high priest or priestess can enter the shrine, and he or she must come from the Japanese Imperial family.

The city of Ise on the central Japanese island of Honshu has a population approaching 150,000 but plays host to more than 6 million pilgrims each year. It is home to a complex of more than 120 Shinto shrines connected to two main shrines about 6 kilometres (3.8 miles apart: the Imperial Shrine (Kotai Jingu), also known as the Naiku, or Inner Shrine, and the Toyouke Shrine, or Geku (Outer) Shrine. Naiku is dedicated to Amaterasu Omikami (the Sun Goddess and purported ancestor of the Japanese Imperial family) while Geku venerates Toyouke Omikami (the Goddess of Agriculture).

The Inner Shrine lies in the shadow of Mount Kamiji and Mount Shimaji, next to the Isuzu River. It sits amid a forest thick with Japanese cedars and cypress trees. According to the eighth-century *Nihon Shoki* (*Chronicles of Japan*), the shrine was built around 2,000 years ago, its location having been selected by Yamatohime-no-mikoto, the daughter of Suinin, 11th Emperor of Japan. Yamatohime-no-mikoto was said to have spent 20 years wandering in search of a suitable site from which to worship Amaterasu. The goddess is reported to have informed her that Ise 'is a secluded and pleasant land. In this land I wish to dwell.'

The shrine's traditional foundation date is usually given as 4 BC, but others have argued for some time later. It is believed that the first shrine building was erected in the seventh century. From the seventh until the 14th centuries, high priestesses (known as Saiō) were appointed from among the unmarried females of the Imperial family, the first of whom was Princess Oku. Later, during the Empire of Japan era in the 19th and 20th centuries, the role of high priest of the shrine was taken by the serving emperor. In the period after the Second World War, the honour fell to descendants of the Imperial family, both male and female.

Ise also purports to be the home of *Yata no Kagami*, a sacred mirror from the Imperial Regalia of Japan. It is one

HOLY LIGHT *Shinto priests in traditional robes prepare for the ceremony of Tsukinamisai, when prayers are made for a bountiful harvest. Toyouke Omikami, to whom the Outer Shrine is dedicated, is considered the Goddess of Agriculture.*

of three treasures of the regalia (the others being a sword and a jewel) and is said to represent wisdom. By tradition, these treasures are presented to each new Emperor at a private enthronement ceremony. They were supposedly brought to Japan by Ninigi-no-Mikoto, grandson of Amaterasu and a forefather of the Japanese Imperial dynasty.

Both the Naiku and Geku shrines are constructed from hinoki (Japanese cypress) wood and their roofs are thatched with kaya grass. The main Naiku shrine building measures some 11 metres by 5.5 metres (36 x 18 ft) and has a raised floor. Every 20 years since AD 692, the shrine has been completely rebuilt on one of two plots of land immediately adjacent to each other.

Even when a plot is in its two decades' of disuse, it remains sacred ground and hosts a small hut housing a 2-metre (6.6-ft) wooden post around which the shrine will later be rebuilt. The post is called *shin-no-mihashira*, which roughly translates as 'august column of the heart'. The cycle of reconstruction is considered to reflect Shintoism's belief in death, renewal and impermanence. The next rebuilding is scheduled to take place in 2013, and will take a full eight years to complete.

Access to the Naiku comes via the Uji Bridge that traverses the Isuzu. At either end of the bridge are spectacular *tori* (traditional Japanese) gates. The main structures of both shrines are surrounded by high fences that allow onlookers only a glimpse of their thatched roofs. A no-photography policy is strictly enforced. Pilgrims, who are expected to wash their hands and mouths with water from a ritual pool, may offer prayers at a large gate nearby but can proceed no further. That is, of course, unless you can prove your familial links to the Imperial dynasty and talk your way into the job of high priest or priestess.

97

Fukushima Dai-ichi Nuclear Power Plant

LOCATION Okuma, Fukushima Prefecture, Japan
NEAREST POPULATION HUB Fukushima
SECRECY OVERVIEW Access restricted: site of nuclear disaster in 2011.

In March 2011 a massive earthquake triggered a tsunami that swept along much of the eastern Japanese coast, and was at its highest as it struck the nuclear power plant near the city of Fukushima. Chaos reigned as the authorities struggled to assess exactly what had happened and how it might best be dealt with. The result was the second worst civilian nuclear disaster in history.

Operated by the Tokyo Electric Power Co., Fukushima Dai-ichi power station stands on a 350-hectare (860-acre) plot and consists of six light water reactors. Construction began in 1967 on a site that was originally high above the water line but which was lowered in order for the facility to be anchored on to bedrock (so increasing its resistance to earthquakes). Its reactors came into operation at intervals throughout the 1970s and by the time all six were up and running, Fukushima was one of the largest nuclear power plants in the world.

Fukushima prefecture in eastern Honshu island is largely rural, with striking terrain including spectacular green mountains. The name Fukushima, somewhat touchingly, translates as 'Lucky Isle'. Few would claim that it has lived up to its name (*dai-ichi*, incidentally, means 'Number 1'). On 11 March 2011, a powerful earthquake of magnitude 6.6 hit a short distance from the mainland. It was followed by a huge tsunami that swept across Japan's east coast, leaving 20,000 dead in its wake.

Fukushima Dai-ichi was only designed to withstand waves of up to 6 metres (20 ft), and it has been alleged that the International Atomic Energy Agency (IAEA) expressed concern over this design failing years prior to the disaster. The high waters of 11 March were estimated at 14 metres (46 ft) and found the plant tragically wanting. Fukushima's essential cooling systems were knocked out and a series of explosions followed, leading to meltdowns in reactors 1, 2 and 3, with an associated release of radiation. It was the worst nuclear accident since the Chernobyl disaster of 1986 (see page 172).

On the International Nuclear Event Scale, the Fukushima event was provisionally given the maximum score of 7 – only Chernobyl had ever previously been given this designation. The possible impact on the area around Fukushima was soon realized, and the government proclaimed a 20-kilometre (12.5-mile) no-go area around the plant, later extended to 30 kilometres (19 miles). Police roadblocks continue to enforce the exclusion zone.

NO MAN'S LAND
An overhead view of Fukushima Dai-ichi, showing both its proximity to the sea and to areas of high population density. When the people who lived here can safely return remains a matter of conjecture but the effects of the tragedy will last for many years.

DEFENCELESS
Fukushima's tsunami defences failed when faced with the vast surge of water that swept through the region in March 2011. Allegations have since emerged that the defensive wall had been identified as inadequate years earlier.

Defensive sea wall 5.7 metres (19 ft) high

Reactor 1 – partial meltdown and explosive damage

Reactor 2 – partial internal meltdown

Reactor 3 – partial meltdown and major explosive damage

Reactor 4 – spent fuel pool exposed

PACIFIC OCEAN

GeoEye

160,000 people were forced to evacuate in the immediate aftermath of the disaster. By late 2011, 80,000 remained unable to return to their previous lives, and few had any clear of indication of when they would be able to. Some areas are not expected to be habitable again for at least 20 years. Estimates of long-term casualties are hard to gauge but at least several hundred people suffered exposure to worrying levels of radiation. In addition, concerns about food originating in the area have had devastating consequences for commercial farmers. For example, peaches – one of the prefecture's most famous products – halved in price in the months following the meltdown.

By the end of 2011, Tokyo Electric Power announced that the plant was in cold shutdown, and it was declared stable on 16 December. However, it is expected to take a further ten years to remove fuel and decontaminate the surrounding area. Complete decommissioning of the damaged reactors is predicted to take several decades. What is more, workers on the site are now required to dress head-to-foot in safety gear, a precaution that slows down work and has the unfortunate side effect of causing dozens of cases of serious heatstroke.

As Japan began the struggle back to normality in the aftermath of the tsunami, both Tokyo Power and the Japanese government were subject to domestic and international recriminations for their handling of the tragedy, which severely undermined public confidence. In a bid to make up some lost ground (most of the country's 54 commercial reactors were shut down amid safety fears after the accident), Tokyo asked the IAEA to establish a constant presence at Fukushima to give an independent seal of approval to its clean-up operation.

The end result is that a once-fruitful region of the country has been left devastated and faces a long battle to reclaim its sense of normality. Areas previously blessed with rich soil are no longer suitable for agriculture, while farmers throughout the wider region are forced to sell their produce at greatly reduced prices, having been tainted by association. Perhaps most unfortunate of all, though, are the people who once lived bountiful lives in what is now the exclusion area, and who are now unsure if they can ever hope go back to what one government spokesman described as a 'forbidden zone'.

UP IN SMOKE *The scene at Fukushima ten days after a tsunami struck on 11 March 2011. The plume of smoke is emanating from the fourth of the plant's six reactors. Independent reviews found the Tokyo Electric Power Co. utterly unprepared for an emergency on this scale.*

Woomera Prohibited Area

LOCATION Woomera, Australia
NEAREST POPULATION HUB Adelaide, South Australia
SECRECY OVERVIEW Operations classified: the world's largest land-based weapons testing area.

Established in 1947, the Woomera Prohibited Area (WPA) is most famous as a huge missile testing range, but has enjoyed several different lives, including as a rocket-launch site, a spy hub and a detention centre. Covering an area larger than England, its desert location has helped keep unwanted visitors away from numerous highly classified projects.

Situated several hundred kilometres northwest of Adelaide, the Woomera Prohibited Area is home to the Royal Australian Air Force (RAAF) Woomera Test Range, and is strictly off-limits to the public. It covers 127,000 square kilometres (49,000 sq miles), down from a historic high of 270,000 square kilometres (104,000 sq miles) in 1972.

The WPA began as a joint initiative between the Australian and British governments. In the aftermath of the Second World War, the UK was keen to develop a cutting-edge rocket-testing programme, but lacked the space to do so. A collaboration with the Australian government that provided an opportunity to share knowledge and expenses suited all sides.

Woomera was chosen as it offered a huge swathe of land largely devoid of human habitation. A mixture of desert and scrubland, temperatures regularly exceed 35°C (95°F) and can go far higher. As such, the area was never conducive to mass human colonization. However, it

was ideal for weapons-testing, boasting as it does mostly cloud-free skies all year round and little electromagnetic interference. The name Woomera itself derives from an Aboriginal word for a spear-throwing device.

The Joint Project, as it was known, began missile testing in earnest in 1949. This phase included nine major atomic-bomb trials that led to the nuclear contamination of an area in excess of 3,000 square kilometres (1,150 sq miles). Section 400, as this area has been designated, remains strictly off-bounds on safety grounds. Environmentalists have claimed that clean-up attempts were flawed, and many Aboriginal people who were present in the region at the time of the tests allege that they are still suffering harmful effects.

A town, also called Woomera, was established to support life at the WPA in 1947 – at the peak of the Joint Project, it had a population of over 7,000. For much of its life, Woomera has been a closed town, accessible only to authorized

UP, UP AND AWAY
In 2005, Japan's Aerospace Exploration Agency used Woomera to test a prototype supersonic jet that might one day take the place vacated by the decommissioned Concorde. During this launch, flames burst spectacularly from a rocket booster.

KEEP OUT *A warning sign on Stuart Highway at Lake Hart, which is a live bombing and ammunition target within the WPA. Anyone straying into the area could hardly claim they were not told of the dangers.*

inhabitants. Since 1982, it has been open to the public, but remains under the control of the Australian Department of Defence. None of Woomera's properties are privately owned: they are leased from the government and anyone considered undesirable can be asked to move on.

The Joint Project came to a halt in 1980. By then the WPA was also being used for rocket testing, playing an important role in assorted classified space programmes during the 1950s and 1960s. In 1969, Australia had entered into a separate agreement with the US to construct the Nurrungar Joint Tracking Facility within the WPA. Nurrungar's three golfball-like radomes contained huge antennae dishes and were maintained under intense security, behind razor-wire fences and complete with bullet-proof security rooms.

The reason for this heightened level of protection was that Nurrungar lay at the centre of a space-based surveillance programme, and was key to providing early warning of Intercontinental Ballistic Missile attacks on the US. As such, it was considered a high-priority target for the Soviet Union, a fact that did not play well with an Australian public unwilling to invite the Cold War into its backyard. Some protesters claimed that Nurrungar was also used to pinpoint targets during the 1973 US bombing of Cambodia.

By the time Nurrungar closed in 1999, the futures of the WPA and the town of Woomera were uncertain. The resident population was down to a few hundred, where once it had been several thousand. For a while, it looked like the construction of a migrant detention centre would come to its rescue, but that too proved something of a poisoned chalice. In a four-year lifespan, the centre attracted many column-inches of negative publicity for holding up to 1,500 illegal immigrants in a prison camp-style setting. Inmates rioted on several occasions and some even sewed their lips together in protest at the conditions.

But in recent years, the WPA has rebounded and has never been busier in its role as the largest on-land missile testing site in the world. Buoyed by hundreds of millions of dollars of state investment since the turn of the century, its client list now includes governments and space agencies from around the world, providing bookings well into the 2020s. Although the Test Range remains at the core of the WPA, other parts of the territory are being opened up to potentially lucrative mining (there are thought to be significant quantities of gold, iron ore, opals and uranium).

Anyone finding themselves in the WPA ought to keep their eyes open though. As Roger Henwood, manager of the Woomera Range, noted in 2006: 'You find a whole lot of things sticking out of the ground that supposedly never got launched.'

Pine Gap Joint Defence Facility

LOCATION Central Desert, Australia
NEAREST POPULATION HUB Alice Springs, Northern Territory
SECRECY OVERVIEW Operations classified: joint US-Australian satellite station.

Originally established to keep a watchful eye on goings-on in the Soviet Union and nations throughout South East Asia, Pine Gap is a satellite station under the joint jurisdiction of the US and Australian governments. Since coming into operation, it has attracted the distrust of peace campaigners and conspiracy theorists alike, united in concern at the secretive nature of the work carried out there.

The initial development of the Pine Gap facility was mapped out in a treaty agreed between Canberra and Washington in 1966. The facility was constructed in an area traditionally peopled by the indigenous Arrernte people and began functioning around 1970, ostensibly as a weather station. The land on which it was built was owned by a cattle rancher who had been reluctant to sell until the federal government eventually enforced a compulsory purchase. By the end of the 1970s, Pine Gap had grown rapidly, to become one of the biggest satellite ground stations on the planet.

The base hosts several multi-faceted 'radomes', vast banks of computers and a large infrastructure network, but the exact nature of the work undertaken in this remote desert location has never been made explicit. In the mid-1970s Australia's Labor Prime Minister, Gough Whitlam, is said to have made mutterings about closing Pine Gap amid general disquiet about its activities.

However, Whitlam's tenure was a much troubled one, culminating in the opposition blocking his budget and effectively paralyzing his government. In 1975, the Australian Governor-General John Kerr sparked a constitutional crisis by dismissing Whitlam. Some have subsequently speculated that the actions of Kerr (an unelected official appointed directly by the British Queen) reflected the CIA's desire to remove a troublesome prime minister from office.

Though its operations remain highly classified, one of Whitlam's successors as Australian premier, Bob Hawke, made a rare government statement about Pine Gap in 1988. At that time he confirmed that intelligence gathered at Pine Gap 'contributes importantly to the verification of arms control and disarmament agreements'. The facility is widely assumed to have taken over some of the duties in relation to monitoring ballistic missile launches previously conducted by the Nurrungar operation at Woomera (see page 242). Pine Gap is also said to have played an important

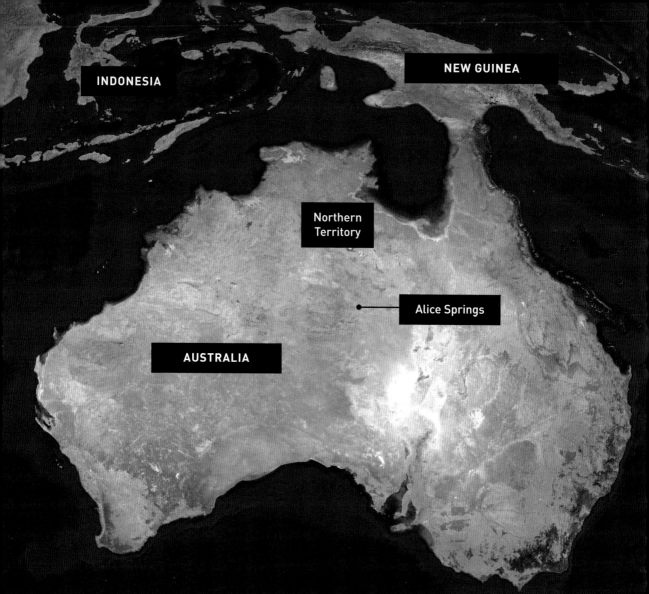

INDONESIA

NEW GUINEA

Northern Territory

Alice Springs

AUSTRALIA

MIND THE GAP *Many of Pine Gap's extensive array of giant satellite dishes are kept under the cover of radomes, which sit incongruously in the desolate expanse of Australia's Central Desert. Originally purporting to be a weather station, rumours soon abounded as to the facility's real purpose.*

support role during the US-led Afghan and Iran conflicts in the opening decade of the 21st century.

In addition, the facility is regularly cited as one of the key intelligence-gathering stations within the purported ECHELON global surveillance network (see page 111). ECHELON (if it does indeed exist as a great deal of evidence suggests) is a highly controversial 'eavesdropping' system in which public and private communications – from phone calls and text messages to faxes and emails – are routinely scanned and analyzed. The network's participating nations are said to include Australia, Canada, New Zealand, the UK and the US, although none of the relevant governments has

ever formally acknowledged the project's existence. Pine Gap is widely suspected of being the hub for Australia's part of the operation.

Today the facility employs a staff of over 800, with much of the American contingent associated with the US National Security Agency. Pine Gap's main entrance is adorned with one Australian flag and one American flag, symbolizing the apparently equal relationship that operates on the base.

For many of its opponents, though, Pine Gap epitomizes how Australia has been dragged into the political machinations of the United States. That each nation maintains parts of the complex (including, reportedly, cypher rooms) as respectively off-limits to personnel from the partner nation is another source of consternation. What, they argue, might the US be doing on Australian soil that must be kept secret from Australian officials?

Pine Gap has regularly witnessed peace protests down through the years, including one memorable occasion when a small phalanx of demonstrators cycled onto a runway, disrupting the landing of a large military aircraft. Yet despite these occasional breaches, security is intense. Signs on an approach road read ominously: 'No Through Road – Joint Defence Facility Pine Gap – Prohibited Area – Turn Around Now.'

Compared to many other nations, the skies of Australia are notably devoid of restricted airspaces, but a strict no-fly zone is enforced around Pine Gap, with access prohibited for any aircraft flying beneath 5,500 metres (18,000 ft). Anyone tempted to infiltrate Pine Gap would be wise to remember that you risk the wrath of not one but two nations' defence forces – not encouraging odds in anyone's books.

DO NOT ENTER *Lest anyone be in doubt, signs like this on the way to Pine Gap make quite clear that casual visits are not well received. The approach to Pine Gap is via Hatt Road, which is an offshoot of the Stuart Highway.*

100 Headquarters of Joint Operational Command

LOCATION Australian Capital Territory, Australia
NEAREST POPULATION HUB Canberra
SECRECY OVERVIEW Operations classified: command centre for the Australian Defence Force's global operations.

Founded in 2004, the Headquarters of Joint Operational Command (HQJOC) moved to a new purpose-built home east of the Australian capital, Canberra, in 2008. With HQJOC responsible for overseeing the international operations of Australia's Army, Navy and Air Force, it is little surprise that the organization's headquarters is one of the most secure buildings in the country.

HQJOC is a successor organization to Headquarters Australian Theatre (HQAST), which was established in 1996 to serve as a coordinating body for Australia's combined armed forces when they were on deployment. When HQJOC first came into being, it was based in a temporary facility in Potts Point, a suburb of Sydney.

However, after a major review in 2005, the organization underwent a significant restructure that included a move in 2007 to new temporary facilities in Kowen, close to the towns of Bungendore and Queanbeyan. By December 2008, HQJOC's newly constructed permanent headquarters at the same location were ready to begin operations.

Constructed by Praeco Pty Ltd at a cost of some A$360 million, the facility (officially named the General John Baker Complex) covers around 220 hectares (540 acres) and houses some 750 personnel. It is centred around a two-storey, almost windowless building surrounded by concentric steel and razor-wire security fences, one at a distance of 100 metres (330 ft) and another at 500 metres (1,650 ft). A central control room boasts a huge screen known as the 'knowledge wall'. Measuring almost 19 metres (62 ft) across, it allows commanders to monitor Australia's military activities around the world.

Access to the site is via a Ministry of Defence-owned, restricted-access road. The high-security inner zone is accessible by foot only, with visitors having to pass through several checkpoints that utilize handprint and biometric controls. Vehicles used within the inner zone are kept permanently within the perimeter fence to guard against the risk of them being tampered with. The outer zone, meanwhile, contains lower-security office buildings.

The site is permanently monitored by private security contractors, using electronic surveillance measures and a system of intruder alarms. Employees within the complex require electronic key cards to move between areas. With the central nerve centre open to only those with the highest security clearance, this is a truly modern military command centre.

CONTROL CENTRE *A view of the Joint Control Centre at the General John Baker Complex, including the fabled 'knowledge wall' that can simultaneously broadcast live images of Australian operations from across the globe. Baker's widow was present at the base's official opening in 2009.*

Index

Acknowledgements

In researching this volume I made use of both official (where available) and unofficial reports. Particularly useful sources of information were the Federation of American Scientists (www.fas.org), Global Security (www.globalsecurity.org) and the International Atomic Energy Agency (www.iaea.org).

I was able to glean much other useful information from assorted news sources and recognize a debt of gratitude to the following publications and news organizations: the BBC; *The Daily Telegraph*; *The Guardian* (which published a 2001 article by Jon Ronson from which I took Denis Healey's quote about the Bilderberg Group); *The Independent*; *National Geographic*; *The New York Times*; Reuters; *Der Spiegel*; *Time Magazine*; *The Times of India*; *The Washington Post*; and *Wired* (www.wired.com). For further information on some on the more muscular conspiracy theories, the website Above Top Secret (www.abovetopsecret.com) was never less than entertaining.

For general historical background research, the venerable annual almanac of geo-political affairs, *The Statesman's Yearbook*, proved as doughty a companion as ever. And for those whose appetite for secret places has been whetted, there is much of interest to be found in Taryn Simon's *An American Index of the Hidden and Unfamiliar* (Steidl, 2007) and at www.forbidden-places.net.

I must also heartily thank my agent, James Wills, my editor, Richard Green, and the rest of the team at Quercus, as well as Giles Sparrow and Tim Brown of Pikaia Imaging, who had the unenviable job of sourcing high quality images of places that by their nature are often not well documented.

I greatly appreciate the many friends and family members who suggested intriguing and fascinating contenders for inclusion in this volume – I only wish I had been able to include them all. And a final thanks, as ever, to Rosie.

For Will, Helena, Noah, Toby, Rowan and Zoë

Picture credits

Quercus Editions Ltd
Carmelite House
50 Victoria Embankment
London
EC4Y 0DZ

First published in 2012

A catalogue record of this book is available from the
British Library

UK and associated territories:
ISBN 978 1 78087 311 4

Printed and bound in China

10 9 8 7 6 5